1969

The Achievement of

Samuel Johnson

The engraving of Mary Palgrave Turner after the drawing by Ozias Humphrey

SAMUEL JOHNSON IN 1773

The Achievement of

SAMUEL JOHNSON

Walter Jackson Bate

New York

OXFORD UNIVERSITY PRESS

1955

PREFACE

THE PRESENT BOOK is hardly more than an expanded essay on the theme of its title. For the subject is large, and special aspects of it have been repeatedly explored for over a century. But it is large because it is hypnotic, and people cannot let it alone. No matter how much the detail about him continues to accumulate, the character and achievement of Johnson still grip the human imagination and conscience, constantly rising above the waves of our commentary, and moving us to reconsider them. Also the mere size of the subject is one excuse for this book. Largeness and variety offer protection as well as challenge. Where no one work, however detailed, can pretend to a rounded completeness anyway, briefer interpretations such as this are able to take heart, and are free to vary among themselves without fear of copying or contradicting each other. A writer is 'not wholly useless,' as Johnson said, who merely diversifies the 'surface of knowledge' and calls us back 'to a second view.' Johnson will stand repeated views as few other men can.

The emphasis in this book has been on Johnson's own writing, especially on that part of his writing which is concerned with human experience in the broadest sense. Instead of trying, however, to duplicate the existing analyses of his indi-

v

vidual works, the intention here has been to distribute the discussion according to the over-all themes of his writing and the character of his thinking as far as I understand it. Since so much of Johnson's writing is scattered through a large number of short essays, few of which could be taken up individually in a book of this size, there seemed no alternative to a general thematic treatment. Any such discussion, of course, runs the risk of seeming subjective. This risk has to be faced by any attempt to distil widely scattered material. A second aim of this book has been to relate the discussion of his writing, as different themes are taken up, to the more directly personal aspects of Johnson that have intrigued readers of every sort for several generations. Yet it was also thought helpful to devote a beginning chapter to sketching once again this immediately personal side of Johnson as it appears within the chronology of his life, especially during his first fifty years, which occupy less than a quarter of Boswell's great biography. However well known, Johnson's moving life will always endure summary; and it can never be dissociated from the writing, although the life is finally to be understood only through the writing. The concluding chapter on Johnson's criticism is only an extension of the previous chapters. Whatever substance it possesses is derived from the context of the book as a whole. Perhaps because of the present writer's own occupations and methods — to use Johnson's phrase — of 'wearing out the day,' this final chapter in particular has seemed painfully inadequate. So much that appears directly relevant has had to be put aside. The embarrassment is not so much in having to discard further points that the writer himself would like to include (especially those that would connect Johnson more with the critical thinking of the period). These can be put aside if necessary, although 'we are seldom tiresome to ourselves.' The real frustration — as everyone who has discussed Johnson knows first hand — comes in having to reject so much that we should like to quote from Johnson himself, who habitually states things in a way that makes us despair in trying to paraphrase. Perhaps the only consolation in trying to discuss the subject of Johnson's criticism in so perfunctory a manner is to remember that, however interesting it is to us as critics or as historians of criticism, it is not the whole of Johnson. As Thomas Tyers wrote after Johnson's death, he 'belonged' not to criticism or any other single field of learning but 'to the world at large.'

To try to discuss Johnson as a whole, and above all in terms of what he himself thought most interesting — the possibility of human achievement — has an advantage that makes the task very simple, but which can create problems embarrassing to any writer who tries to rephrase or interpret him. Both the advantage and the difficulty is that almost every aspect of his thought is so intimately connected with all the others. The problem comes in trying to discuss it consecutively and yet honestly. For as soon as we pick up one corner of the blanket, we suddenly find the whole of it brought directly into our arms. Still, one point has to be taken up before another. Yet at the risk of repetition, I have tried to avoid an arbitrary topical discussion that would cut the organic character of his thinking and the constant interplay of his principal concerns with his own personal struggle. At the same time I have hoped not to avoid any of the special significant problems Johnson presents, such as his political attitudes, his religious convictions (though these are touched on only tangentially), the character of his style, the psychiatric problems, and his strangely infectious humor. I had even hoped that, however brief and cavalier the present treatment of these matters might be, they would gain some further clarification — especially the disturbing psychiatric symptoms that are so often considered in an isolated way — simply by being restated in the context of his general thinking. Although the success is doubtful, I cannot feel that it would be increased by deferring this brief introduction to Johnson still longer. 'Our energies,' as Johnson said, 'are in proportion to our hopes.' Like so many others who have thought to write on Johnson, I have found that every year that passes leaves one feeling less qualified to do it.

A general work of this sort constantly draws on the labors and insights of others. On the other hand, the brevity of the book is such that few details, especially controversial ones, can be followed out and supplemented with particular documentation. To the numerous writers who have discussed Johnson my debt is therefore too pervasive to detail; to those professionally interested in the subject the debt will be obvious enough.

For permission to look over material still unpublished, I wish to thank the McGraw-Hill Book Company and the Editorial Committee of the Yale Editions of the Private Papers of James Boswell. Among members of the Committee, I wish particularly to thank Professor Frederick A. Pottle, Mr. H. W. Liebert, and Mr. Robert F. Metzdorf of Yale University. I am grateful to Professor R. W. Chapman, of the University of Oxford, for many corrections and helpful suggestions. I owe a large general debt to the work of Joseph Wood Krutch and the late Sir Walter Raleigh. In discussing the thorny subject of what we may call the pathology of Johnson, which no study of his character can honestly disregard, I am indebted to conversations over the years with friends far more versed in psychiatry than I am. No sympathetic interpretation of Johnson's character can fail to be obligated to the brilliant work of Mr. W. B. C. Watkins. I myself am especially obligated, and I also thank him for his personal encouragement and kindness. The location of the original drawing by Ozias Humphrey, if the drawing still exists, is apparently unknown. But the copy reproduced as the frontispiece is available in the engraving made and published after Humphrey's death by Mary Palgrave Turner. I wish to thank Professor Geoffrey Tillotson, of the University of London, for helping me ascertain this. My largest and most personal debt is to the many colleagues and friends, at Harvard and elsewhere, who for a decade and a half have encouraged me in my impetuous attempts to understand Johnson. To Professors George Sherburn, Douglas Bush, and Harry Levin, my debt is particularly heavy and long-standing. I also thank Professor Levin for looking over portions of the book that gave me persistent difficulty in my attempt to condense. It was he, moreover, who introduced me, many years ago, to the work of Sainte-Beuve; and he will note some of my attempts, however halting, to profit from that experience now. Nor have I forgotten the salutary injunction of Sainte-Beuve that, in our thinking about a great writer, we should also try to imagine what he would think of us and of the spirit in which we approach him.

There is a final debt, difficult to particularize but perhaps apparent in every chapter, to the late Alfred North Whitehead. To go back to the living and concrete nature of experience was the first principle of his thinking. As with Johnson himself, the high level of generality that resulted was one that cleansed the mind of routine labels, and spread open a perspective at once larger and at the same time more directly personal. This gave encouragement, and on the highest authority, to the timid sense we all have that — however numerous the details or however massive the formal analyses that exist and can exist — the principal need, as we try to consider the details, is to retain at all times an awakened sense of 'the concrete achievement of a thing in its actuality.' Another of Whitehead's principles has been in the mind of the writer since this small introduction to Johnson was first planned —

PREFACE

the premise that 'moral education is impossible apart from
the habitual vision of greatness.'

W.J.B.

Cambridge, Massachusetts
August 1955

CONTENTS

xi

THE ACHIEVEMENT OF
SAMUEL JOHNSON

I

A LIFE OF ALLEGORY

'WHAT IS NEAREST US,' said Johnson, 'touches us most.' His own life captures interest for many reasons. For one thing it is the subject of the most readable of biographies, and of a large number of other vivid accounts by people who knew him. But whatever the first fascination may be, Johnson's life continues to hold attention because it is so close to general human experience in a wide variety of ways. This may help to explain why the personal incidents and circumstances of it have taken on the strange, magnetic attraction they possess for so many different individuals. For since the publication of Boswell's *Life of Johnson* (1791), every scrap of evidence relating to Johnson's life has continued to be examined and many more details have been added. This sort of scrutiny has been given very few men indeed. As a result, most of Johnson's life is more fully as well as more widely known than that of any other writer.

Johnson was born in the small cathedral town of Lichfield on 18 September 1709, the first of two sons of a bookseller and his wife who were both well past their youth. Michael Johnson, the father, a large, melancholy man, was fifty-two at the time, and his wife, Sarah, was forty. This had its effect. For the long pent-up expectation of the parents was concentrated on

3

the boy, who showed unusual precocity; and, with a pride that made him acutely self-conscious, they could not prevent themselves from placing him on exhibit before neighbors and visitors. Johnson grew, he said, to loathe his father's caresses; for he knew that they were to be followed by a request to show his accomplishments. When neighbors dropped in, he sometimes ran and climbed a nearby tree so that he might not be found. 'That is the great misery of late marriages,' he once told Mrs. Thrale, 'the unhappy produce of them becomes the plaything of dotage: an old man's child leads much such a life as a little boy's dog, teased with awkward fondness, and forced . . . to sit up and beg . . . to divert a company, who at last go away complaining of their disagreeable entertainment.' Years later, when an acquaintance wanted his two children to recite Gray's *Elegy,* one after the other, in order to see which repeated it better, Johnson could not refrain from suggesting: 'let the dears both speak it at once; more noise will by that means be made, and the noise will be sooner over.'[1]

Almost from birth until Johnson was six, his left arm was kept open and running with an 'issue' that is difficult now to identify but was obviously a trying experience for any child. Much worse, as a baby he contracted from a wet-nurse the disease known as scrofula, a tubercular infection of the lymph glands. This not only disfigured his face, but badly affected his sight for the rest of his life; for it spread to the optic nerves, and glasses proved of no help. Johnson never forgot when, as a child, he heard an aunt state that 'she would not have picked such a poor creature up in the street.' Poverty as well as illness sharpened the quick, irritable pride that Johnson later fought against in himself. He disliked speaking of his family and his early years, wrote Mrs. Thrale; 'one has,' he said, '*so* little pleasure in reciting the anecdotes of beggary.' If a man talks much of his misfortunes, as he said on another occasion, there is something in them not wholly disagreeable; but when there is pure misery, the desire is not to mention but to forget it. Not until fifty years after its occurrence did anyone extract from him a story of an incident that had 'ever since lain heavily' on his conscience. On a visit to Lichfield, late in life, he was absent the greater part of the day. Pressed to say where he had been, he reluctantly explained. Michael Johnson had tried to supplement his little book business by using a stall at Uttoxeter on market days. Confined to bed with illness, he asked his son to attend the stall. But 'my pride,' said Johnson, 'prevented me, and I gave my father a refusal.' Now, on a rainy day precisely fifty years later, Johnson — with the violent bending over backwards that was at times typical of him — had forced himself to perform, in a way still harder for his pride, what he had refused his helpless father. For he had taken a postchaise to Uttoxeter, 'and going into the market at the time of high business, uncovered my head, and stood with it bare an hour before the stall which my father had formerly used, exposed to the sneers of the standers-by and the inclemency of the weather.' [2]

Johnson attended nearby schools, and he read voraciously among the books in his father's shop. He quickly began to master various languages, especially Latin; and, in addition to the classics, he dipped extensively into modern philosophy and literature before going to college. His reading was impulsive rather than systematic; he was far from being a boyish pedant. He was often flogged at school, and he rarely finished a book he started. But he read rapidly, with extraordinary retentiveness: he could repeat by memory a page he had lightly skimmed if it had aroused his interest. The vivid imagination which Johnson later strove to control in himself is as apparent as his intellectual curiosity in this boyhood reading; for what he read ranged from metaphysics to escapist romances. Bishop Percy, later the famous editor of the *Reliques of Ancient English Poetry* (1765), stated that Johnson 'when a boy . . . was immoderately fond of reading romances of chivalry. . . . I have heard him attribute to these extravagant fictions that unsettled turn of mind which prevented his ever fixing in any profession.' At the age of nineteen he entered Pembroke College, Oxford, where he remained for a little more than a year. Here he astonished his tutor the first day by quoting the obscure Roman grammarian, Macrobius. He read Greek intensively, though he was otherwise irregular in his study. Boswell was rightly puzzled that Johnson was financially able to go to Oxford in the first place, and assumed it was because he had a position as a servitor or companion to a young man of means from Shropshire. But it now seems likely that a small legacy received by Johnson's mother was used to defray his minimal expenses.[3] Within a short time, his clothes, already shabby, became rags; and he ceased attending lectures because his shoes were so bad that his feet could be seen through them. He became wretchedly sensitive. When a kind-hearted member of the college left a pair of shoes by his door, Johnson, in lacerated and youthful pride, threw them out of the window. His friend, Dr. Adams, a tutor at Oxford, stated many years later that Johnson, while he was attending the university, was 'caressed and loved by all about him, was a gay and frolicsome fellow, and passed there the happiest time of his life.' But Johnson explained it differently: 'I was mad and violent. It was bitterness which they mistook for pride. I was miserably poor, and I thought to fight my way by my literature and my wit; so I disregarded all power and all authority.'

It is not known whether Johnson left Oxford in December 1729 because of the complete lack of funds or because of mental distress.[4] Despite his immense physical strength, he was still frequently ill. Also, the scrofula that had spread to his nervous system when he was a boy now began to show after-effects in the form of various nervous ailments. He knew that he appeared strange and impulsive to others; and his melancholy temperament—the natural product of a vivid imagination in unhappy circumstances — became accentuated. Certainly the challenge and excitement of Oxford, the contrast of the people and general atmosphere with his boyhood surroundings, and his bitter realization that he would hardly find the money to stay helped to bring on the 'vile melancholy' which he thought he had inherited from his father, and which he once impulsively said had 'made me mad all my life, at least not sober.' But it is equally certain that, when he returned to Lichfield, he found that his father, who had been unable from the beginning to make his little business profitable, was in more severe straits than ever; and Johnson plainly had to support himself.

2

It is not clear what Johnson did for support after his return from Oxford. What we know of the next two years largely concerns the appalling state of mind in which he now found himself. One of the ironies of literary history is that its most compelling and authoritative symbol of common sense — of the strong, imaginative grasp of concrete reality — should have begun his adult life, at the age of twenty, in a state of such intense anxiety and bewildered despair that, at least from his own point of view, it seemed the onset of actual insanity. A torturing irritability, obsessional neuroses of the most acute kind — producing an embarrassing eccentricity of manner of which he himself was only too conscious — a deep-felt and pervasive frustration of all hopes, and what would now appear to be the effects of a strong aggressiveness partly turned in against himself: the conflict and combined effect of these, joined with the self-condemnation of Johnson's own high and exacting moral sense, could at this time so neutralize and disengage his mind that he would stare in languor at the town-clock without being able to tell the hour. On other occasions, his condition plainly produced a despair so wild that, in later life, he could hardly be brought to refer to it. He would only say, 'I did not then know how to manage it.' But we can infer more of both its character and intensity from what we know of its recurrence some thirty-five years later, in the 1760's: in the period when he became acquainted with the Thrales, and when they found him on his knees, with a rector, Dr. Delap, 'beseeching God to continue to him the use of his understanding,' and later — for Dr. Delap quickly left — speaking so 'wildly' in self-condemnation that Mr. Thrale 'involuntarily lifted up one hand to shut his mouth.'[5] Moreover, Johnson's physical health from the time that he returned to Lichfield was such, as he later said, that it 'seldom afforded me a single day of ease'; and he once admitted to Sir John Hawkins that he 'knew not what it was to be totally free from pain.'

Few examples are more moving, and offer more encouragement to human nature, than that of Johnson, with almost all the odds against him, temperamentally and otherwise, strenuously trying to surmount them during the next twenty years and slowly succeeding. For the odds he faced — at least such liabilities of temperament as his turbulent imagination, his panic anxieties and aggressive pride, his almost pathological tendency to indolence, his fitful and impatient hunger for novelty and escape — were not very distinct in kind from the temptations and compulsions faced by many others. Instead, they differed in degree and intensity. 'His soul,' as Mrs. Thrale said, 'was not different from that of another person, but . . . greater.' Indeed, it is this sameness in kind, but greatness in degree, that finally characterizes Johnson's thought, giving it universality, deepening its genuineness, strengthening and warming its authority.

Frightened at what seemed to be happening to him, he threw himself into violent exertions. He would frequently force himself to walk to Birmingham and back, a distance of thirty-two miles. Such pathetic devices were to become characteristic. Often, in trying to control his own state of mind, he would assert that most of man's mental and physical ills were within his own power to govern; that they resulted from idleness, luxury, or boredom; that 'labouring men who work hard, and live sparingly,' are rarely inclined to such ailments. Johnson's constant emphasis on the therapeutic value of *activity* of both body and mind gains an added poignance from such efforts and resolutions. 'Ease' — he was later to say in one of the essays written for the *Rambler* — is a *'neutral* state,' which, 'if it is not rising into pleasure, will be falling towards pain'; 'Nature abhors a vacuum'; 'imagination never takes such firm possession of the mind, as when it is found empty and unoccupied'; almost any sport or recreation is desirable, and labor itself 'may be styled its own reward,' when it is considered 'how much happiness is gained, and how much misery escaped, by frequent and violent agitation of the body.' [6] In what survives of the private jottings that have been called the *Prayers and Meditations,* the first entry — dated October 1729, two months before he left Oxford — significantly reads (in Latin): 'I bid farewell to Sloth, being resolved not to listen to her syren strains.' Such resolutions were to continue throughout his whole life:

Sept. 7, 1738: 'O Lord, enable me . . . to redeem the time which I have spent in Sloth . . .' Easter Eve, 1757: 'Almighty God . . . look down with mercy upon me depraved with vain imaginations . . . *Enable me to shake off sloth,* and to redeem the time mispent in idleness and sin by a diligent application of the days yet remaining . . .' Easter Day, 1759: 'Enable me to shake off idleness and sloth . . .' Easter Eve, 1761: *'I have resolved . . . till I am afraid to resolve again.'* April

9

21, 1764: 'My indolence, since my last reception of the Sacrament, has sunk into grosser sluggishness . . . My purpose is from this time To reject or expel sensual images, and idle thoughts. To provide some useful amusement for leisure time. To avoid Idleness. To rise early.'

On his birthday the following autumn (18 September), he determines again 'to rise early. *Not later than six if I can.*' The next Easter, writing at three a.m. — and the late hour is characteristic — Johnson, now fifty-six, resolves 'to rise at *eight* every morning . . . I purpose to rise at eight *because though I shall not yet rise early it will be much earlier than I now rise,* for I often lye till two.' Four years later:

Jan. 1, 1769, after midnight: 'I am not yet in a state to form many resolutions; I purpose and hope to rise early in the morning, at eight, and *by degrees* at six.' June 1, 1770: 'Every man naturally persuades himself that he can keep his resolutions, nor is he convinced of his imbecillity but by length of time and frequency of experiment.' July 22, 1773: 'My Nights are now such as give me no quiet rest, *whether I have not lived resolving till the possibility of performance is past, I know not. God help me, I will yet try.*' Good Friday, 1775: 'When I look back upon resolutions of improvement and amendments, which have year after year been made and broken . . . why do I yet try to resolve again? *I try because Reformation is necessary and despair is criminal.* . . . As my life has from my earliest years been wasted in a morning bed, my purpose is from Easter day to rise early, not later than eight.'

From many others, one final moving entry may be cited. The date is 2 January 1781, less than four years before he died: 'I

will not despair. Help me, help me, O my God.' And the familiar list of resolutions again occurs, beginning with 'To rise at
eight or sooner' and ending with 'To avoid Idleness.'

The impulsive devices to which Johnson had recourse at the
age of twenty — especially the desperate walks to Birmingham and back — anticipate the sudden outbursts of will and
energy that later characterize his unusual feats of mind. For
much of Johnson's work, despite the consistently rounded and
considered judgment it reveals, was written rapidly with the
printer's boy waiting at the door. Sunk in a state of despair so
acute that he feared it would turn to 'madness,' Johnson, after
leaving Oxford, also turned to a Lichfield physician, Dr. Swinfen, writing in Latin as full a statement of his case as he could.
Swinfen, struck by the brilliance and pathos of the document,
showed it to others. Though Swinfen's motives were kindly,
Johnson was rightly offended at this breach of professional
trust, and nothing further developed between the two. But
the writing of this document was to prove even more symboli-
cally typical of Johnson — at least Johnson at his best — than
the impetuous attempts to clutch at any activity that might,
as he said, 'fix' his mind and attention. For the struggle to rise
above what threatened to overwhelm him by trying to isolate
and describe it, hold it at arm's length, — to pluck its teeth,
so to speak, by seeing it intellectually for what it was, and at
the same time to avoid self-absorption and subjective rationalization — is, in a sense, the real story of Johnson's personal
achievement.

3

Shortly after his father's death, in December 1731, Johnson,
now twenty-two, at last found a position as usher, or assistant
instructor, in a school at Market-Bosworth, Leicestershire.
Lacking other means of transportation, he walked from Lich-

field. The school, shut off from the surrounding country by impassable, muddy roads, was of a meagre bleakness and brutality difficult now to realize. The Dotheboy's Hall sort of school pictured in the novels of Dickens a century later helps to suggest what it was like. Here, where Johnson also served as a domestic chaplain and a general handyman, the drudgery and persistent harshness were such that he remembered the place all his life with 'the strongest aversion, and even a degree of horror.' Considering Johnson's state of mind for the previous two years, and the general hopes with which almost any young man would begin teaching, the situation must have seemed almost intolerable. He tried unsuccessfully for a position at another school, and then went to Birmingham, staying for a while with a former school friend, Edmund Hector. In time, he was able to sell some essays to the local newspaper. Here he also wrote his first book, a translation from the French version of Father Lobo's *Voyage to Abyssinia*. There is something a little grotesque in both the subject and the way in which it was translated. Johnson, despite his need, characteristically deferred doing it. Mr. Hector, knowing that an argument based on charity would be effective, persuaded him that the printer and his family were in want; and Johnson, lying in bed with the book, rapidly dictated the translation, which Hector took down and carried to the printer.

In 1735, Johnson, now twenty-six, married Mrs. Henry Porter, a large, florid widow twenty years older than himself. The marriage puzzled the relatives of each. Johnson's friends, later on, never quite understood it, nor what they thought was an excessive fondness for her memory after her death. Certainly, during the years in London, 'Tetty' seems to have endeared herself to few people besides her husband. Garrick thought her 'a little painted poppet; full of affectation and rural airs of elegance.' Johnson's old friend, Dr. John Taylor, stated that she became 'the plague of Johnson's life, was abominably drunken and despicable every way.' There are other accounts of her drinking in later years, including Mr. Levet's graphic description of her — 'drunk and reading romances in her bed, where she killed herself by taking opium.' [7] Despite Boswell, there seems to have been some point to the belief of Sir John Hawkins that 'there was something crazy in the behaviour of them both; profound respect on his part, and the airs of an antiquated beauty on hers.' At least it is now clear that Boswell romanticized the marriage; that a year after 'Tetty' died in 1752, Johnson was thinking of a second marriage — though to whom is not known; [8] and that dearly as Johnson loved company, and liked to entertain after his wife's death, he encouraged few people to visit them during her life. But Johnson's attraction to her, at least at the beginning, is not hard to explain. He had probably long felt a frustration arising from his own scarred and at times shocking appearance. He had thus far had few opportunities of meeting other women who could offer much standard of comparison, at least few who would be favorably inclined to himself, and his near-sightedness did not, perhaps, lead him to be too critical of 'Tetty's' personal beauty. Also the long unhappiness and lack of intimacy unquestionably heightened the warm quickness and gratitude with which he always responded to any kindness or interest; and that Johnson's gratitude, once felt, was permanent helps to explain the continuing forbearance and affection he showed her. At all events, with the help of the little money his wife brought, Johnson tried to start a small school near Lichfield. The school failed completely. Only a few pupils showed up, among them David Garrick, later the famous actor, and his brother. The following year, reduced again to poverty, Johnson left his wife for the time being at Lichfield, and, with two pence half-penny in his pocket and accompanied by Garrick, journeyed to London in the hope of finding employment.

The next fifteen years were among the unhappiest of any writer's life. Johnson trudged the streets, lived on the poorest food, and became intimately acquainted with the large, floating body of the London poor. With Richard Savage, a colorful but minor writer, who claimed to be the deserted illegitimate son of the Countess of Macclesfield, Johnson sometimes walked the London streets all night because neither had enough to pay for lodging, even in a 'night cellar.' Much of the atmosphere of Grub Street lingers in the moving *Life of Savage* (1744), which Johnson wrote after his friend's death. Meanwhile, Johnson was working spasmodically for Edward Cave, the publisher of the *Gentleman's Magazine.*

The inspired hack-work Johnson did for Cave and other publishers is almost unparalleled in range and variety. The writings were 'so numerous, so varied and scattered,' and so frequently published under the names of other persons, that Johnson himself could not make a complete list. There are lives of men eminent in literature, science, and naval warfare; essays, prefaces, and reviews that reveal knowledge of agriculture, trade, medicine, chemistry, classical scholarship, metaphysics, politics, and even Chinese architecture. As a sheer feat of imagination, the most impressive of his hack-work was the reporting of the debates of the House of Commons for the *Gentleman's Magazine,* although he was never in the gallery of the House except once. The proceedings of the Commons were not at this time recorded or allowed to be reported. Abridged accounts, however, were occasionally published when the House was in recess. In time, the *Gentleman's Magazine* began publishing what were assumed to be rather full reports. For two years (1741–3) Johnson was their sole author, with hardly any information given him except the subject of the debate, the names of the speakers, the order in which they appeared, and an indication of the arguments used. Yet these debates, 'the mere coinage of his own imagination,' were written with astonishing speed — three printed columns in an hour, according to John Nichols, and 'faster than most persons could have transcribed that quantity.' Many years later, the reports were still generally accepted as true. It was like Johnson to stop writing them as soon as he discovered that they were being regarded as genuine; for he would 'not be accessory to the propagation of falsehood.' A few days before he died, he said, according to Nichols, that 'the Parliamentary Debates were the only part of his writings which then gave him any compunction: but that at the time he wrote them, he had no conception he was imposing upon the world.' [9]

There is a strange, almost unreal quality about the twenty years of Johnson's life after he left Oxford. It is crossed by such fantastic contrasts that it is difficult to visualize this period as a whole and feel it progressively unfold. Instead, it tends to pass before the mind in a series of incongruous but sharply etched pictures, variously touching, heroic, and grotesque. There are the wretched school at Market-Bosworth, surrounded by the wet, muddy roads of the spring of 1732, and then the pathetic school Johnson himself tried to start, with the pupils peeping through the bedroom keyhole, according to Garrick, to watch Johnson's 'awkward fondness' for his new wife. There are the vivid scenes of his knocking down the bookseller, Thomas Osborne, with a huge folio because Osborne had impudently forgotten the respect due a writer; and of the night-long walks through London with Richard Savage. And yet there is the fact that Johnson not only acquired an extraordinary knowledge of human life at all levels but, despite the comparative lack of access to books, he was able to enlarge still more the range of learning that led Adam Smith — a rather grudging critic — to believe that 'Johnson knew more books than any man alive.' We should remember that Johnson was one of the great Latinists of modern times; that despite the John Bullish interpretations of him in the nineteenth century, he was

15

widely read, as we now know, in almost every department of French literature. There are also the stories of the odd, compulsive gestures. The artist, William Hogarth, for example, first noticed him at the home of Samuel Richardson — standing at a window, 'shaking his head and rolling himself about in a strange ridiculous manner' — and concluded he was an 'ideot, whom his relations had put under the care of Mr. Richardson.' And yet, to Hogarth's surprise, 'this figure stalked forwards to where he and Mr. Richardson were sitting, and all at once took up the argument . . . [with] such a power of eloquence, that Hogarth looked at him with astonishment, and actually imagined that this ideot had been at the moment inspired.' [10]

Edmund Burke was later convinced that, if Johnson had entered Parliament early enough, he 'certainly would have been the greatest speaker that ever was there.' And not least among the almost grotesque incongruities of these years is the unforgettable picture of Johnson dining at the home of the publisher of the *Gentleman's Magazine*, eating behind a screen because his clothes were too shabby, and yet for two years writing Parliamentary debates that included speeches supposed to be by England's foremost statesman. One of Pitt's great speeches, as printed in the *Gentleman's Magazine*, was particularly admired. Years later, the classical scholar, Philip Francis, who had spent eight years in the study of Demosthenes, praised Pitt's performance as surpassing in brilliance and power anything that Demosthenes himself had composed. Arthur Murphy, the playwright, relates that others of the company remembered the debate, and joined in citing particular passages for praise, but that Johnson, who was also present, remained silent while the others were speaking. He had himself written the speech, rapidly and with little care, in a garret in Exeter Street.[11]

4

While still teaching school, Johnson in free moments had begun and finished three acts of a tragedy, *Irene*, which he completed after reaching London. Curious as a museum-piece
largely because Johnson wrote it, this stiff, formal tragedy,
the scene of which is laid in Turkey, does not appear more impossible to act than many other plays of the same type that had
been performed during the previous fifty years. After more
than ten years, Johnson's now famous pupil, David Garrick,
kindly performed it at Drury Lane, and managed to keep it
going for nine nights. Still later, coming on friends reading it
aloud, Johnson, after listening awhile, left the room in embarrassment. Pressed to say why, he could only answer, 'I thought
it had been better.' Though the play has had apologists, it is
far from presenting the qualities Johnson himself looked for in
the poetic drama. The circumstances under which it was written should also be remembered. By the time he was committed to the subject, and had more than half completed the
play, his acquaintance with the theater had been confined to
what he learned from the touring players who visited Lichfield. For over a generation, stiff, Oriental tragedies seemed to
be bringing a return to authors, and it was quite natural, as
Mr. Krutch points out, that the young schoolmaster in the provincial town of Lichfield should have taken such a model.

More successful was the poem *London*, an imitation of the
third satire of the Latin poet, Juvenal, published in 1738,
three years after Johnson left Lichfield. As a mature critic, years
later, he was often to judge harshly the imitations that eighteenth-century poets were fond of writing; and he would not
have considered his own an exception. But the vivid impact that
the crowded world of London made on the young provincial
rustic gives a personal genuineness to the stately heroic coup-

lets as the poem dwells on the crime, the political corruption, and the squalor of the London metropolis, and as it works toward the climactic theme, *'slow rises worth, by poverty depressed.'* Johnson's second major poem, *The Vanity of Human Wishes*, a loose imitation of the tenth satire of Juvenal, was published in 1749. On the basis of the vigorous moral strength and elevation of this poem, T. S. Eliot has eloquently urged Johnson's claim to being a major poet, although it is doubtful whether Johnson would ever have regarded himself thus. But it is certainly true that this sweeping survey of the vanity and hopelessness of man's ambitions and desires is treated with a courageous manliness and a rational stoicism joined with a strong religious fervor; and the pathos remains, indeed increases, through repeated rereading. Even at the height of the romantic period — when the tightly intellectual poetry that we find in this poem was not much in favor — it's 'deep and pathetic morality,' according to Sir Walter Scott, 'has often extracted tears from those whose eyes wander dry over pages profoundly sentimental.' Certainly English poetry, from the middle of the seventeenth century down to the present, contains nothing else quite like the style of *The Vanity of Human Wishes*, in which complexity of thought is gripped and compressed into a strangely powerful, abbreviated generality.

Whether we merely paraphrase the poem, or take the cumulative effect of recurring images and metaphors as a guide, its general subject is the enormous clutter of fitful desires and rival ambitions, of fears, projections, envy, and self-expectation that human feelings create in their confused impulse to assert themselves and find satisfaction. To this is added the unwelcome discovery, which we naturally try to resist, that even to attain our wishes brings languor or indifference afterward, while at the same time we are inspiring envy and hostility in others, and moving into the decay that seems so rapid and remorseless to a conscious being. Working through the ample, shared sense of this is a second theme: the desire of the human heart to free itself from this suffocation; 'Where then shall Hope and Fear their *objects* find?' Certainly the desiring, restless heart of man creates most of its own demands and fears, shunning '*fancied* ills' or chasing '*airy* good,' fixing its hopes obsessionally upon some one object, while projecting its fears, just as obsessionally, upon rivals, who will tumble into misfortune, unhappiness, or death as rapidly as ourselves. But the fact remains that man is a living, desiring creature, and that 'hope and fear' are inevitable reactions. Is 'helpless man' automatically condemned, therefore, by the evils that his own blind, warring impulses create, or can the desiring heart be refined and given healthful direction?

Images of cloudiness and mist alternate with those of clutter, crowds, and swelling; and each at times gives way to images of rising and sinking. So, at the start, man is seen as a traveler, condemned to 'tread the dreary paths without a guide,' surrounded by mist. In this 'clouded maze,' he chases 'treach'rous phantoms in the mist' or starts with fear at the 'rustling brake.' But a second train of images — in which 'anxious toil' is associated with '*crowded* life' — suggests both the confused wants and rivalries we ourselves start to feel, and also the nudging pressure of others in the same condition, until the busy energy and preoccupations of this swarm of hope and fear, desire and hate, '*O'erspread with snares* the clouded maze of fate.' The 'teeming,' spawning welter of our wishes, during our brief moment of life, intermeshes and conflicts with those of others, who also '*Crowd* Preferment's gate.' And the poem, with a kind of heavy breathing, and as if in some 'clouded' atmospheric swelling and sinking, begins to suggest the rise and fall of human destiny, from small, familiar examples —

> the *sinking* statesman's door
> Pours in the *morning worshipper* no more;

For *growing* names the weekly scribbler lies,
To *growing* wealth the dedicator flies. . . .

and from the voter at election-time, primed with ale and the froth of propaganda, 'full' and pregnant with momentary eagerness to assert himself, on up to the swelling 'full-blown dignity' of a Cardinal Wolsey, so 'near the steeps of fate,' who raises 'On weak foundations . . . th' enormous weight.' And the heaped up waste of war adds its own pile of destruction, as when, surrounded by the tossing jumble of bodies, 'Th' encumbered oar' of the fighting ship moves through the bloodstained 'billows and a floating host.' Caught in this cloudy and crowded Babel, the heart is seen as 'burning' — as catching, in its hunger for fulfilled assertion, the 'fever of renown,' and '*burning* to be great.' And we find suggested, in these massive, abstract couplets, the parched thirst for wealth and possession, from all the more obvious examples down to the young scholar who 'quits his ease for fame,' and, toiling in the library and failing to 'pause a while from letters, to be wise,' finds that throughout his 'torpid veins' a 'fever of renown /*Spreads from the strong contagion* of the gown,' as though he had put on a veritable 'Shirt of Nessus.'

The range of the poem, as it moves through the subject of human experience and frustration, is humanized by Johnson's characteristic inability to be content simply to document or satirize a thing and then stop. This wide coverage is only one element in the chemistry of the situation. Almost from the beginning of *The Vanity of Human Wishes,* it is brought into focus by relating it to the reactions of the human heart. It is seen as both the accumulated, swarming product of the human heart, and also as the environment, in which the individual, as soon as he appears, suddenly finds himself, and to which he instinctively starts to contribute. So, at the outset, '*wav'ring* man' is unwittingly '*betray'd* by vent'rous pride,' by the desire to assert and contribute his mite, into strewing the 'snares' before his own and others' paths. The premise — perhaps the principal premise of the poem, and one which Johnson's later writing unfolds more completely — is the 'treachery of the human heart,' which leads man to betray his own interests as he snatches, in his 'clouded maze,' at what he hopes will at last bring satisfaction. Remaining still with the somber images of the poem: we have, running as a thread throughout the work, the 'supplicating,' the pliable or bending capacity of the human mind — its yielding ability to bow before the wind, seek preferment, mask itself hypocritically, and — through the same ability — to give itself over to something really better, and through this to attain what freedom is possible. We have Johnson's own version, in short — translated to the London of the 1740's — of the classical vision that knowledge or experience are formative and that they can operate upon human desires (however blind and warring desire may be otherwise), and, in doing so, both develop and free them. Thus, at the start, we have the pliable, desiring, 'suppliant' voice, so eager to worm its way, or to attain possessions, power, or superiority over others, so yielding, as it succumbs to pet projects and obsessive desires, that finally whole 'nations sink, by darling schemes oppress'd, /When Vengeance listens to the fool's request.' In politics, as in all other walks of life, 'Unnumber'd *suppliants* crowd Preferment's gate.' After Wolsey's fall, 'his *suppliants* scorn him,' and his followers look for the rising star; and after his fall, the warlike Swedish king, Charles XII, still left with his desires, becomes a 'needy suppliant.' But the pliable, often destructive, potentially improvable heart is all that we have to work with in any tension upward. And the climax of *The Vanity of Human Wishes,* as it turns to man rolling in torment, or in 'ignorance sedate,' in foolish and carefree oblivion, 'down the torrent of his fate,' points up the theme of the 'suppliant' yearning of 'helpless man,' and puts it in on another level, where it becomes the hunger of sincerity:

> Still raise for good the *supplicating* voice,
> But leave to Heav'n the measure and the choice.
> Safe in His pow'r, whose eyes discern afar
> The secret ambush of a specious pray'r. . . .
> Pour forth thy fervours for a healthful mind . . .

Characteristically, this powerful, condensed poem was written with extraordinary speed — a hundred lines of it in one day — and, with this as with other poems, Johnson ran his finger down the margin as he wrote to note the number of lines written and the number he had yet to do. Boswell rightly states that Johnson's mind was so fertile in imagery and metaphor that he 'might have been perpetually a poet.' Yet the amount of verse he wrote was not large; and there is reason to believe that it is not typical of what he could have done if he wished. It is also paradoxical that most of it dates from the years when he was urgently occupied in doing other things. Later, when there was ample opportunity, he wrote little. Nor is it a matter of the poetic vein drying up. Such romantic criteria do not apply. The range and power of Johnson's use of imagery, in his prose, increased as the years passed. As for versification, he could extemporize verse until the end. If we proceed not on the basis of legend but on written evidence only, there is no record of any poet who has ever excelled him in the speed of extemporaneous versifying. Also, we know that he composed long sections of poems in idle moments, and carried them in his head, but was too 'indolent' to write them down. But it is not too difficult to explain both the comparative meagerness and the abstract quality of Johnson's poetic output, despite his extraordinary talent and broad critical interest. For the compulsive, almost self-protective drive to distil experience into the most condensed generalization possible — a compul-

sion that seemed to take hold of him with a giant's hand —
was especially sharpened when he sat down to write formal
poetry. And the result of such a compulsion was not a poetry
that would itself exhibit a dynamic evolving of general truth
from concrete detail, actively reproducing experience, and
appealing simultaneously to different levels of the mind. Instead, the result is a powerful abbreviating of all detail into
a final maxim or generalization. No one could have realized
this more acutely than Johnson himself.

5

The work of these years which was to establish his reputation was far different in character from the poems. The great
English Dictionary, which Johnson began to compile at the
age of thirty-eight, is more than the first modern English dictionary. In fact, all later English dictionaries of any importance
may be described as a development or rewriting of Johnson's.
And yet these two monumental volumes were not the lifelong
work of a professional student of lexicography. Instead, they
were the constantly interrupted creation of one man, impatient and strongly emotional by nature, working irregularly
throughout seven years. Considering the short time consumed,
and the range of his interests and talents, this pioneer achievement, like certain others of history, appears as a kind of by-
product of what he himself considered to be genius — 'a mind
of large, *general* powers.'

In estimating this work, it is helpful to bear in mind what it
means to compile a large dictionary even at the present time.
The methods of compiling are now fairly well established, and
need only to be followed. Previous dictionaries are available
to be copied, expanded, or refined. Even so, scholars are as-
sembled in large numbers; elaborate filing systems are used;
and secretarial labor is plentiful. These circumstances sharply

contrast with the upper room in Gough Square, Fleet Street, where, despite a comparative lack of books, Johnson wrote the incisive definitions not merely of 40,000 words but of the different senses in which these words are used, and illustrated them with approximately 114,000 quotations, drawn from the entire range of English writing, in every field of learning, from the mid-sixteenth to the mid-eighteenth centuries. The project had been decided on by June 1746, when the contract with the booksellers was signed. A year later, seeking some sort of patronage to help him, he published the *Plan of an English Dictionary*, dedicated at the request of one of the publishers to Lord Chesterfield, whose response was negligible. Here Johnson outlines the procedure that he was later to follow. Previous dictionaries were more in the nature of word-lists; the most important of them — that of Nathaniel Bailey (1721) — was mainly concerned to give the origins of words. Only one, by Benjamin Martin, consistently tried to make distinctions between the various senses in which a word is used; and this, which appeared in 1749, was influenced by Johnson's own plan of two years before.

Johnson's aim was to provide far more than a word-list with etymologies and explanations for different terms. Instead, it was to offer comprehensive definitions of the different shades of meaning in the use of a word, and to establish by examples a flexible standard of propriety and good usage. Here we can sense the general eighteenth-century ideal — in the study of history, social customs, psychology, or art — of discovering what has proved to be most generally durable or characteristic, and then profiting by using it as a standard or working basis. Johnson's *Dictionary* illustrates the same effort to stabilize language which also, in a different way, encouraged the eighteenth-century use of a formal poetic diction. The effort becomes more understandable when we remember the marked changes that took place in the language during the two centuries between Chaucer and the death of Shakespeare, and the fear that, if the process continued, the great writers from Shakespeare to the beginning of the eighteenth century would in time cease to be generally read. The standard Johnson hoped to establish was elastic, and was kept so by his own empirical, and to some extent historical, practice. Also behind the happy decision to determine and illustrate meanings by selected quotations, was the hope, said Johnson, to offer a 'kind of intellectual history.' The great bulk of the definitions are unrivaled. Because a few puckish ones — and a very few slips — are still cited, they are sometimes assumed to be typical. They tell as little about what one finds in the *Dictionary* as a list of Shakespeare's puns would indicate the range and character of his plays. Of the enormous number of quotations, many were adopted by Webster (1828) and later by the great ten-volume *New English Dictionary* (1888–1928). It is significant that the latter — compiled with the help of thirteen hundred scholars — was originally planned to be issued simply as a supplement that could be used with Johnson. When the plan was enlarged, and it was decided to depart from Johnson by including all English words ever known to have been used, whether obsolete or not, the title *New* was suggested partly because of the desire to dissociate it from Johnson. In a sense, it is the only really 'new' English dictionary since Johnson. From another point of view, it may also be regarded as the final edition, the completing on a thoroughgoing scale of Johnson's work.

Johnson's way of proceeding, according to Bishop Percy, was first to make a 'diligent perusal of all such English writers as were most correct in their language.' Under each sentence he decided to quote, he drew a line in pencil, indicating in the margin the first letter of the word which the quotation illustrated. The books were 'what he had in his own collection,' says Hawkins, 'a copious but a miserably ragged one,' or what he could borrow. These in turn were handed to six copyists, who

25

transcribed them on single slips of paper, and arranged them under the appropriate words. When this part of the work was completed, Johnson sat down, inserted etymologies (which, considering the state of etymology at the time, were inevitably the least effective part of the work), determined the spelling and pronunciation, and wrote the definitions.[12] The only direct aid offered him by another scholar was a list of twenty etymologies sent him by the Bishop of Rochester. He also received help on current slang and gambling terms from one of the copyists. The illustrative quotations proved far too bulky. Many had to be cut; while still others were added — often from Johnson's own memory — to illustrate any further diversities of meaning that now suggested themselves. He had originally hoped to complete the work in three years; and when his friend Dr. Adams reminded him that the French Academy of forty members had taken forty years for their dictionary, Johnson had whimsically replied: 'forty times forty is sixteen hundred. As three to sixteen hundred, so is the proportion of an Englishman to a Frenchman.' But Johnson had not counted on his own fits of indolence. There was other writing that drew on his energy, and in 1752, three years after the remark to Dr. Adams, his wife died. Alone, grief-stricken, and poor, he pushed on for another three years with a task that demanded, he said, no 'higher quality than that of bearing burdens with dull patience, and beating the track of the alphabet with sluggish resolution.' Lord Chesterfield, to whom Johnson had originally been persuaded to address his *Plan*, now became interested as the work neared completion, and wrote two papers for *The World*, commending the forthcoming *Dictionary*. Johnson's famous letter in reply has become a miniature classic:

'Seven years, my Lord, have now past, since I waited in your outward rooms, or was repulsed from your door . . . Is not a Patron, my Lord, one who looks with unconcern on a man struggling for life in the water, and, when he has reached ground, encumbers him with help? The notice which you have been pleased to take of my labours, had it been early, had been kind; but it has been delayed till I am indifferent, and cannot enjoy it; till I am solitary, and cannot impart it; till I am known, and do not want it.'

Chesterfield was much struck with the letter. According to the publisher, Robert Dodsley, he said 'this man has great powers,' pointing out to Dodsley 'the severest passages, and observed how well they were expressed.' Only in the noble conclusion to the Preface to the *Dictionary* is there an indication of the personal history that lay behind it:

. . . though no book was ever spared out of tenderness to the authour . . . yet it may gratify curiosity to inform it, that the *English Dictionary* was written with little assistance of the learned, and without any patronage of the great; not in the soft obscurities of retirement, or under the shelter of academic bowers, but amidst inconvenience and distraction, in sickness and in sorrow . . . I may surely be content without the praise of perfection which, if I could obtain, in this gloom of solitude, what would it avail me? I have protracted my work till most of those whom I wished to please have sunk into the grave, and success and miscarriage are empty sounds; I therefore dismiss it with frigid tranquillity, having little to fear or hope from censure or from praise.

There is a curious parallel with Noah Webster that highlights the achievement of this work. The contrasts suggest the difference in circumstances under which Johnson's and other dictionaries were composed — a difference in this case between seven agitated years and a life 'insensibly' passed away in the quiet devotion to scholarship. At the same time the parallel indicates the compelling hold that the example of Johnson has kept on the imagination of all later men who have done similar work. For in concluding his own prefatory 'Advertisement' seventy-three years later, Webster unwittingly echoes the last sentence of the Preface of his great predecessor: 'In my endeavors,' said Webster, 'a long life has passed insensibly away; and, in now submitting it to the scrutiny of the world, I am feelingly reminded how near these labors have brought me to that period, when I shall be beyond the range of *censure or applause*.'

6

Though Johnson never complained, but thought the booksellers generous in taking the risk, most of the £1575 they advanced him for the *Dictionary* seem to have been used merely for expenses. If it brought comparatively little money, however, the work permanently established his reputation. He was already becoming known as a man of letters because of the essays published in periodical form as the *Rambler* (March 1750 to March 1752), and written while still in the midst of compiling the *Dictionary*. For although these essays, appearing twice a week, had a small circulation at first, they reached a distinguished audience; and, printed in volume form, they later came to be widely read. They were written with Johnson's usual haste. It is eminently typical that one of the best discussions in English of the temptations of idleness and procrastination (No. 134) should have been 'hastily composed,' according to Mrs. Thrale, 'in Sir Joshua Reynolds's parlour, while the boy waited to carry it to the press.' Also, as Johnson said in the last issue, 'He that condemns himself to compose on a stated day, will often bring to his task an attention dissipated . . . an imagination overwhelmed, a mind distracted with anxieties,

a body languishing with disease.' Yet the *Rambler* contains
some of the ripest proverbial wisdom in the language. Boswell
does not much exaggerate in saying that 'in no writings whatever can be found more bark and steel [quinine and iron] for
the mind.'

During the nineteenth century, the essays of the *Rambler*
were often contrasted unfavorably with those of Addison's
Spectator. To critics that merely glanced at them, they seemed
elephantine, ponderous, and too serious when compared with
the mild gaiety of Addison and Steele. The *Rambler* certainly
lacks the light and carefree touch with which Addison, writing in financial ease and unemotional complacency, gratified
the fashionable tea-table morality of his day. And though the
wisdom of the *Rambler* is such that the immature mind has
the greatest need of it, the appeal of these essays has always
seemed to have been in direct proportion to the maturity and
range of the reader's experience. The style of the *Rambler*, unlike that of Johnson's poetry, contains some of the fertile and
vivid imagery that characterizes his talk and his later prose.
Even so — and despite the speed with which he wrote them —
the composing of moral essays still seemed sufficiently formal
and responsible an obligation to keep taut Johnson's compulsive tendency toward condensed generality. One result is
the frequent use of the abstract nouns and general terms that
seemed 'heavy' to nineteenth-century devotees of the familiar
essay. But the frequency is exaggerated; what there is of it
was partly a by-product of the work on the *Dictionary*; and it
decreased rapidly in his later writing.

The habit of concentrating experience into manageable generalization appears more effectively in the constant centripetal
pull toward maxim or aphorism that Johnson was never to lose
but to develop more strongly in his later work. Nor is this
quality found solely in isolated sentences or precepts, as it so
often is in Bacon. It is a quality that characterizes the organic

development of each essay. But one can pluck single sentences or phrases from their context; and, though they lose much of their effect, they still read like isolated maxims: 'The natural flights of the human mind are not from pleasure to pleasure, but from hope to hope.' 'The general remedy of those, who are uneasy without knowing the cause, is change of place.' 'The vanity of being known to be trusted with a secret is generally one of the chief motives to disclose it; for . . . most men seem rather inclined to confess the want of virtue than of importance.' 'Men seldom give pleasure, where they are not pleased themselves.' 'Discord generally operates in little things; it is inflamed . . . by contrariety of taste, oftener than of principles.' 'We are more pained by ignorance than delighted by instruction.' 'Many need no other provocation to enmity than that they find themselves excelled.' 'Among other pleasing errors of young minds, is the opinion of their own importance. He that has not yet remarked, how little attention his contemporaries can spare from their own affairs, conceives all eyes turned upon himself, and imagines everyone that approaches him to be an enemy or a follower, an admirer or a spy.' [13]

The years from 1750 to 1759, from Johnson's forty-second through his fiftieth year — half of them still devoted to the *Dictionary* — mark the emergence of Johnson in his full stature as a moralist directly concerned with the practical problems of human experience. The *Rambler* is followed by essays contributed to the *Adventurer* (1753-4); by Johnson's weekly periodical, the *Idler* (1758-60); and by the short philosophical novel, *Rasselas* (1759), written in the evenings of one week to defray the expenses of his mother's funeral. In all of these works there are the same weight and density of meaning, the same constant and energetic lifting toward generality. They are also united in theme: they may be described as the expansion or prose explication of Johnson's poem, *The Vanity of Human Wishes* (1749).

William James, after reading the poems, *From Old Fields*,

by the brilliant and warm-hearted geologist, Nathaniel Shaler,
spoke of 'a great epic wind of sadness blowing all through it.'
Exactly this impression arises from the series of majestic prose
threnodies that begin with the *Rambler* and conclude with
Rasselas. But just as *The Vanity of Human Wishes* had ended
not in complete pessimism but in urging the need for a fuller
awareness and more enduring courage, the prose of the decade
that follows *The Vanity of Human Wishes* enlarges upon this
need and concretely illustrates it. For the 'epic wind of sadness,' even the powerful general observations that reverberate
throughout this prose like muffled drum rolls, are not themselves the principal content or aim of this writing. They are
both a background and also a by-product. They emerge or-
ganically through the incisive treatment of specific problems
and failings, and finally encompass it. But the treatment itself
is always practical in its grasp of particular fact, unsleeping in
its vivid, almost satiric clairvoyance and humor, and yet sympathetic in its largeness and understanding. There is the constant
'looking before and after' that Hamlet prized as the preroga-
tive of the human mind: 'Whatever withdraws us from the
power of our senses,' as Johnson said, 'whatever makes the
past, the distant, or the future predominate over the present,
advances us in the dignity of thinking beings.' At the same
time, Johnson's continual concreteness, his empirical grasp
of the immediate problem or occasion, is probably unparalleled in the history of moral thought. The 'looking before and
after' is in this case the opposite of a neglect of the present: it
is an active rising from and through the present, and then a
return back to it with an enlarged and nuanced sense of its
dimensions and meaning.

7

A recurring theme of Johnson's is the need to exploit habit
rather than be made its victim. More often than not he has

in mind the strong clutch of indolence, the prolonged apathy into which he himself, at least, could fall and become 'dissolved.' The word is his own; and it is a strong one, still carrying the full force of the chemical metaphor. Hence he clung to the realization that activity begets activity; and that motion once begun can be more easily transferred, or changed in direction, than started from nothing. Certainly the enforced activity of working on the *Dictionary*, which was published in 1755, helps to explain the five volumes of moral writing that appeared in the ten years after 1750. Far from cramping his imagination, it acted as a spur; and the momentum of the habit of application continued for another five years. For in sheer bulk of output this decade is the most productive of Johnson's life. At the very time when he was most pressed with other work, he continued to do incidental writing even surpassing the hack-work of the 1740's in variety. There are such diverse lives as those of Sir Thomas Browne and Frederick the Great; there are prefaces to works ranging from the *Introduction to the Italian Language* (1755), by his friend Guiseppi Baretti, to Rolt's *Dictionary of Trade and Commerce* (1756) and Payne's *Introduction to the Game of Draughts* (1756); and there are numerous reviews of works ranging from one on Sir Isaac Newton's proofs of God to 'Home's Experiments on Bleaching.'

At least one of Johnson's anonymous works deserves a certain immortality. It is so altogether typical, both in its charity of purpose and in its unpredictable talent. There had been for many years a standing prize, offered by Parliament, for improved methods of determining longitude at sea. An elderly Welsh physician, Zachariah Williams, who had pursued navigation in his free hours, came to London, hoping to be favorably considered for the prize. His work had partly rested on a study of the variations of the magnetic needle of the compass in different parts of the world. Heartbroken at his failure, the helpless and aged Williams aroused the ready sympathy of Johnson, who was already assisting Williams' blind daughter. Williams was plainly ill and had not long to live. Busy as Johnson was — the *Dictionary* was just completed, and he was also engaged in other work — he quickly studied the subject of navigation, and, in order to restore the self-respect of the dying Williams, expanded his ideas, wrote them up for him as *An Account of an Attempt to Ascertain the Longitude at Sea* (1755), and deposited a copy in the Bodleian Library at Oxford.

The contrasts of this decade verge as closely to the grotesque as those of the previous fifteen years. They are also as poignant. For it seems eminently typical that in the year he wrote the preface to Rolt's *Dictionary of Trade and Commerce* (1756) — a year after he had published his own *Dictionary* and charitably made his fitful study of navigation to help the pathetic Williams — the first great Shakespearean critic issued the *Proposals* for his famous edition of Shakespeare.

Meanwhile, Johnson's circumstances and habits of life were in some respects beginning to settle into the pattern made familiar by Boswell, and by the accounts of others who knew him in later life. 'He nursed whole nests of people in his house,' said Mrs. Thrale, 'where the lame, the blind, the sick and the sorrowful found a sure retreat from all the evils whence his little income could secure them.' Not long after his wife's death in 1752, the large, rather bare house in Gough Square began to take on something of the appearance that his later dwellings were to have — an informal home for the destitute and the infirm. In addition to his colored servant, Francis Barber, and his wife, Johnson's household in the 1750's included Mr. Robert Levet and Anna Williams. Levet was, as Boswell says, 'an obscure practiser in physick amongst the lower people,' without formal training in medicine. But having worked as an apothecary, he gradually developed a wide practice among the London poor, daily walking long distances to minister to them for little or no fee. Mrs. Williams — to give her the title bestowed in the eighteenth century on unmarried women who were no longer young — had earlier come to London hoping to be cured of a cataract in both eyes. She had been kindly treated by the neighboring Johnson and his wife, and, after being brought to his house in order to have an operation performed more easily than in her little lodging, simply stayed on for the rest of her life.

Among the later additions, perhaps the most important was Mrs. Desmoulins. This impoverished widow, who assumed charge of the kitchen, was the daughter of the Lichfield physician, Dr. Swinfen, to whom Johnson had turned in the desperate years after he left Oxford, and who had so hurt Johnson by showing to others the Latin statement Johnson had written of his own case. The quarters, at least in later years, seem to have been rather close. There is an amusing understatement in Boswell's remark that, after returning to London, he found Johnson 'sitting with Mrs. Williams, and was informed that the room formerly allotted to me was now appropriated to a charitable purpose: Mrs. Desmoulins, and I think her daughter, and a Miss Carmichael, being all lodged in it.' As time went on, little love seems to have been lost among Johnson's pensioners. 'Williams,' he wrote to Mrs. Thrale, 'hates everybody; Levett hates Desmoulins, and does not love Williams; Desmoulins hates them both; Poll loves none of them.' The constant quarreling seems to have worn on Johnson. He tried to treat them with complete equality, and gave them, if they needed it, a settled allowance for pocket-money. But the rancor was so constant — particularly after the advent of Mrs. Desmoulins and the shadowy Poll Carmichael — that his only relief, at times, was to plunge into the fray and encourage it. The young Fanny Burney, some years later, was naturally fascinated with the situation. Her lively record of a conversation between Johnson and Mrs. Thrale concludes:

Mrs. T. 'But pray, sir, who is the Poll you talk of? She that you used to abet in her quarrels with Mrs. Williams, and call out, *At her again, Poll! Never flinch, Poll!*' Dr. J. 'Why, I took to Poll very well at first, but she won't do upon a nearer examination.' Mrs. T. 'How came she among you, sir?' Dr. J. 'Why, I don't rightly remember, but we could spare her very well from us . . . I had some hopes of her at first; but when I talked to her . . . I could make nothing of her; she was wiggle waggle, and I could never persuade her to be categorical.' [14]

Given the necessary charitable inclinations, the presence in Johnson's house of what Macaulay called his 'menagerie' was less of a trial than it would have been in more recent times. Eighteenth-century London was still very much of a man's world; and men were accustomed to entertain each other as much in taverns and clubs as in their own homes. Johnson's fondness for tavern life became lasting after his wife's death. The wide circle of his friends had already begun to include men either distinguished or soon to be so. One of the most valuable friends at this time — in some respects the closest friend he was ever to have — was the serene and generous painter, Joshua — later Sir Joshua — Reynolds. Others included David Garrick, now almost at the height of his fame; the versatile and still impoverished Oliver Goldsmith; and a young gentleman, Bennet Langton, who deliberately sought out Johnson after reading the *Rambler,* and, expecting to find a 'decorous philosopher,' was surprised to see descending

from his bed-chamber, about noon . . . as newly risen, a huge uncouth figure, with a little dark wig which scarcely covered his head, and his clothes hanging loose about him. But his conversation was so rich, so animated, and so forcible . . . [that Langton] conceived for him that veneration and attachment which he ever preserved.[15]

Public recognition was also coming. In 1762, the government awarded him an annual pension of £300 for life. Nor was it given him, of course, as any political inducement. Johnson's strong, even sentimental, Toryism needed no encouragement. The later political tracts that he wrote for the Tory party — tracts that he tossed off as rapidly as the Parliamentary Debates he had once written for the *Gentleman's Magazine* — were in no way affected by the grant. Pensions far larger were common until long after Johnson's time, and he himself had to be assured by Lord Bute that 'It is not given for anything you are to do, but for what you have done.' Without it, Johnson's life would certainly have been difficult. In 1765, Trinity College, Dublin, awarded him the honorary degree of Doctor of Laws, as did Oxford a decade later. Because eighteenth-century society was fond of using the title, the memoirs of Johnson's later life have permanently associated it with his name, although Johnson hardly ever used the title, as Boswell says, 'but called himself *Mr.* Johnson,' and, according to Sir John Hawkins, actually disliked being addressed by it. The growing recognition was plainly gratifying. But the transition from the unhappy hack-writer, who had once trudged the streets all night for lack of money to pay for lodging, to the life that Boswell pictures so fully, was not simple. It was crossed with pain and despair.

8

An almost ominous subsiding of effort seems to have followed the outburst of energy during the 1750's. 'The advance of the human mind,' Johnson had written in an issue of the *Rambler*, 'toward any laudable pursuit, may be compared to the progress of a body driven by a blow': the initial force may be strong, but it is 'perpetually decreasing,' and weariness and negligence begin to prevail by 'silent encroachments.' [16] The proposals for the edition of Shakespeare had aroused a fairly wide interest; subscriptions for it were received. But the years were passing with little or nothing being done. Johnson had not even kept a list of the subscribers. After an attack by the satirist, Charles Churchill (1762), reflecting on Johnson's honesty in taking subscriptions and then apparently forgetting the whole matter, Reynolds and other friends, more concerned for his reputation than he was, at last maneuvered him into performing the work. Fitfully Johnson roused himself, and the work finally appeared (1765) through what Boswell, in retrospect, justly called a 'Caesarian operation.' A year afterward, Boswell, who was just getting to know Johnson — he had first met him in 1763 — and was not yet acquainted with all the circumstances, joined with Goldsmith in pressing him to write more. To Goldsmith's remark, 'We have a claim upon you,' there is the testy — and quite justified — reply: 'I am not obliged to do any more. No man is *obliged* to do as much as he *can* do.' After Johnson rationalizes in a way that sits uneasily on his own conscience, Boswell pushes the matter: ' "But I wonder, Sir, you have not more pleasure in writing." JOHNSON. "Sir, you *may* wonder." '

But the *Prayers and Meditations* that survive from the records he burned shortly before his death reveal the strength of the paralysis into which he thought he was falling, and the strong sense of guilt at not being able to attain '*superiority over my habits.*' The growing sense of powerlessness begins to be crossed with moving suggestions of the anxious despair and confusion of thirty years before:

Easter Eve, 1761: 'Since the Communion of last Easter I have led a life so dissipated and useless, and *my terrours and perplexities have so much increased,* that I am under great depression . . . I have resolved . . . till I am afraid to resolve again.' April 21, 1764: '*A kind*

37

of strange oblivion has overspread me, so that I know
not what has become of the last year, and perceive that
incidents and intelligence pass over me without leaving
any impression. . . . *Yet I will not despair.'* Sept. 18,
1764: 'I have done nothing, the need of doing therefore
is pressing, since the time of doing is short.' Easter Day,
1765: *'about 3 in the morning':* 'Since the last Easter . . .
my time has been unprofitably spent, and seems as a
dream that has left nothing behind. *My memory grows*
confused, and I know not how the days pass over me.'
Oct., 1765: 'If I can hear the sermon, to attend it, unless
attention be more troublesome than useful.' March 28,
1766: 'I was twice at church, *and went through the*
prayers without perturbation.' March 29, 1766: 'O God!
. . . *Grant that I may be no longer distracted with*
doubts, and harassed with vain terrors.'

Also, there are darker indications than the long walks he
had forced himself to take to Birmingham and back. Not least
among them is the item listed in the catalogue at the sale of
Mrs. Thrale's library (1823) after her death: a padlock, with
the ominous note attached — *'Johnson's padlock, committed*
to my care in 1768.' The insane, in the eighteenth century,
were, of course, commonly chained. And, when an account of
Johnson written after his death mentioned his fear of insanity,
Mrs. Thrale wrote in her diary: 'they will leave *nothing untold*
that I laboured so long to keep secret; & I . . . retained no
Proofs of it — or hardly any'; and there is also her provocative
note, 'the Fetters & Padlocks will tell Posterity the truth.' [17]
Johnson's 'supreme enjoyment,' said Boswell, 'was the *exercise*
of his reason.' And it now seems clear that the dreadful fear
of insanity — of the inability to surmount the turbulent waves
of guilt and anxiety, and the magnetic pull of his despairing,
morbid imagination — had risen to such a degree that he feared

lest it might at any moment be beyond control. It also seems
likely that this vivid and intolerable fear had led him — in a
final burst of desperation or hopeless exhaustion — to buy the
fetters and padlock, which were later surrendered to Mrs.
Thrale. Yet now he was more secret than before. Even his old
friend, Dr. Adams, could say no more than that he found Johnson, in the spring of 1764, 'in a deplorable state, sighing, groan-
ing, talking to himself, and restlessly walking from room to
room,' and that Johnson went so far as to say that he 'would
consent to have a limb amputated to recover my spirits.' To
his friend, the physician, Dr. Thomas Lawrence, he was more
open. Of this, however, we know only that Lawrence was
caught up and moved enough to say that if Johnson 'would
come and beat him once a week he would bear it; but to hear
his complaints was more than man could support.' It was at
this time that the wealthy brewer, Henry Thrale, and his wife
came to know Johnson. Partly because of their generosity and
kindness, partly because they were not old friends whose opinion he was afraid would change, and partly through accident
— notably the time when they happened to find him on his
knees, with the clergyman, Dr. Delap, 'beseeching God to continue to him the use of his understanding' — it was they, more
than anyone else, who knew 'the horrible condition of his
mind.' It was to Mrs. Thrale that he at length entrusted
'a secret far dearer to him than his Life' — in all probability the
belief that he had been actually insane for a while. 'Well does
he contradict,' wrote Mrs. Thrale, 'the Maxim of Rochefoucault,
that no Man is a Hero to his Valet de Chambre. — Johnson is
more a Hero to me than any one — and I have been more to
him for Intimacy, than ever was any Man's Valet de Chambre.' [18] Certainly the kind understanding shown him by the
Thrales was to soothe, as he said, 'twenty years of a life radically
wretched,' and it was at their home at Streatham that he slowly
recovered health.

The contrasts that always characterized Johnson's life — contrasts that seem more extreme than can be found in any other great writer — now, in his fifties, reach their apex. In his daily life, for example, there is the habitual charity despite his poverty before he received his pension. There are the scenes of Johnson, in 1755, finishing the *Dictionary*, about to be arrested for debt and securing a hurried loan from Samuel Richardson, the novelist. At the same time there are the pictures of the quarreling 'menagerie' he supported at Gough Square; of Johnson learning navigation in order to write the little book on it for the dying Zachariah Williams; and of Johnson emptying his pockets to beggars — to enable them to live 'to beg *on*,' if for no other reason — and slipping pennies in the pockets of the little boys who slept in doorways so that they could buy breakfast. There is the constant and capacious sympathy, even at the height of his own mental and physical distress. One thinks of the unhappy Lear on the storm-swept heath, still remembering the shivering and suffering Fool:

> Poor fool and knave, I have one part in my heart
> That's sorry yet for thee.

But these are the periphery, characteristically peculiar to Johnson as an individual. They begin to rise in importance to the degree that they are seen as a deeply human aspect of the great theme of Johnson's own work: that human fulfillment — the developing and completing of human nature — arises from awareness, from going beyond the slavery of our own subjective cage, however powerful the impulses, habits, and stock responses that control us, into a rounded, charitable, and vital grasp of persisting forms and principles. While still in the midst of personal struggle, the famous edition of Shakespeare was made, which, with its incisive notes, 'threw more light' on Shakespeare, as Edmund Malone said, 'than all his predecessors had done.' And the pioneer *Preface* — one of the most decisive documents in the entire history of criticism — is still one of the best general discussions of Shakespeare. In fact, it remains, as Adam Smith said, 'the most *manly* piece of criticism ever published in any country.' When the circumstances under which it was written are considered, the achievement of this work can only become a matter of conjecture for the moralist or the historian of human genius. For this triumph of sanity, of rounded understanding, was attained against an ominous background of personal experience. After the magnificent general opening occurs the famous paragraph which makes the transition to the basic premise on which the *Preface* is to build. In it we may sense the pull of 'novelty' — of the 'romances of chivalry' he had read as a boy — and of the 'irregular' agitation of his own unruly emotions. We may feel the weight of the 'satiety of life' of which he speaks, the irritable and nervous 'quest' for novelty which it incites, and Johnson's own weary but constant realization that the vividness of 'sudden wonder' that he craved is only too 'soon exhausted.' And so hard-won is the weight of experience that the muscular laying aside of all that 'novelty' signifies, in favor of the 'repose,' the 'stability' and ordering of experience through objective perception, is all the more final and genuine. 'Nothing,' he begins, 'can please many, and please long, but just representations of general nature' — of the broad, enduring aspects of external reality: 'The *irregular* combinations of *fanciful* invention' — the taking apart and fanciful recombining of aspects of life in a way that has no counterpart in reality —

> may delight a-while, by that *novelty* of which the *common satiety of life* sends us all in quest; but the pleasures of sudden wonder are *soon exhausted,* and *the mind can only repose on the stability of truth.*[19]

41

9

It is Johnson from the age of about fifty-five, in 1764, to his death twenty years later, of whom Boswell could say, near the beginning of his biography, that his 'character . . . nay his figure and manner, are, I believe, more generally known than those of almost any man.' This is also the Johnson who passed into legend during the century after his death. For perhaps the most engaging group of memoirs in literary history have Johnson in his later years as their subject. Of them, those of Mrs. Thrale, Fanny Burney, and especially Boswell, together contain records of direct conversation richer and more complete than those for any man before the twentieth century. Boswell's great *Life* has the additional attraction of providing, as does no other biography or memoir, a panorama of the social and intellectual life of its age. Aside from the range of topics discussed, some of the most remarkable men of the period appear directly, like characters in a drama. For the company in which Johnson appears includes such men as Edmund Burke, Sir Joshua Reynolds, Oliver Goldsmith and David Garrick; and, to a less degree, Adam Smith and Edward Gibbon. The famous Club founded in 1764, originally composed of nine members, had expanded to thirty-five after Johnson's death. It is doubtful whether any similar group has had so distinguished a membership.

But if Johnson's character and manner at the time of his death were 'more generally known than those of almost any man,' the principal reason is Johnson himself. It is not a series of happy accidents that the accounts of Johnson's conversation during these years are unrivaled in their vitality and completeness. He said even 'the most common things,' as Thomas Tyers wrote, 'in the *newest* manner.' Johnson's habitual power of phrase, and the ready range of his knowledge, stimulated

the desire of Boswell and others to record what he said. To this
was joined the strong personal appeal he made to so many different people, even those unacquainted with the struggles of
his earlier life. Boswell's unrivaled art has only recently begun
to be understood. Still, the ultimate greatness of Boswell's *Life*,
as Mr. Tinker has said, is really Johnson, who is 'not merely
the subject, but in the last analysis the author too.' Yet the very
vividness with which Johnson's conversation is recorded proved
so attractive that, during the nineteenth century, it drew attention from his work to his life, and to his life principally in
his later years. Hence the common picture of him enthroned in
a tavern or at the home of the Thrales. Also the recorded remarks of Johnson naturally tend to be the sort that would be
remembered and written down. The enormous charity of Johnson is stressed by Boswell and others, and examples of it appear repeatedly. But Johnson's wit and occasionally abrupt
remarks were naturally more quotable. Particularly when edged
with exasperation, they have lingered picturesquely in the
minds of Boswell's readers; and one finds a widespread assumption that his talk was always thus. When, after an argument, a rather dense acquaintance stated, 'I do not *understand*
that,' Johnson replied, 'I have furnished you with an argument,
I am not obliged to furnish you with an *understanding*.' And
there are the even more irritable replies in Mrs. Thrale's *Anecdotes*. Abominating, as he did, loose talk about the ease of
being content and happy in a world of misery, he became
heated when a friend pushed the matter by suddenly stating
that 'his wife's sister was *really* happy, and called upon the
lady to confirm his assertion.' When she did so 'somewhat
roundly,' and with a pert superiority, Johnson exploded:

> 'If your sister-in-law is really the contented being she
> professes herself . . . her life gives the lie to every re-
> search of humanity; for she is happy without health,

without beauty, without money, and without under-standing.' [When Mrs. Thrale later] expressed some-thing of the horrour I felt, 'The same stupidity (said he) which prompted her to extol a felicity she never felt, hindered her from feeling what shocks you . . . I tell you, the woman is ugly, and sickly, and foolish, and poor; and would it not make a man *hang* himself to hear such a creature say, it was happy.' [20]

Often painfully ill, and, particularly in his last years, forcing himself out into company in a healthy attempt to get his mind on other subjects than himself, the temptation to make such testy remarks was naturally strong. Though Boswell and others remind us of the physical and mental pain Johnson was often suffering, this context is easily forgotten. Instead, the remarks start out from the page and are then coalesced with others of a similar sort. When further joined with the various oddi-ties of manner mentioned by Boswell, Mrs. Thrale, Miss Rey-nolds, and others, they could produce, especially for the nine-teenth century, a caricature of fascinating grotesqueness. Macaulay's famous essay is the classic example: 'The old philosopher is still among us, in the brown coat with the metal buttons and the shirt which ought to be at wash, blinking, puffing, rolling his head, drumming with his fingers, tearing his meat like a tiger, and swallowing his tea in oceans.'

By its very success and vividness, then, Boswell's portrait of Johnson has often tempted readers to substitute it for John-son himself. The hardy persistence of the nineteenth-century legend of Johnson illustrates the danger of building wholly on Boswell, particularly if this fires one to do some additional decoration. Still, Boswell's *Life* is not only the most fascinat-ing but, for the later years, the most truthful of biographies. Without a doubt, he was able, in reworking his notes, to achieve the authentic tone of Johnson. There is the same ready imagery that we find in his written prose: 'Learning among the Scotch is like bread in a besieged town: every man gets a little, but no man gets a full meal.' 'A woman's preaching is like a dog standing on its hind legs. It is not done well, but we are surprised to find it done at all.' There is the same common-sense seizing of essentials, the same habitual and sharp distinctions, in even the smallest matters. Speaking of Mrs. Elizabeth Montagu's *Essay on Shakespeare,* Reynolds states, ' "I think that essay does her honour": JOHNSON. "Yes, Sir; it does *her* honour, but it would do nobody else honour. I have, indeed, not read it all. But when I take up the end of a web, and find it packthread, I do not expect, by looking further, to find it embroidery." ' Later: ' "Mrs. Montagu has dropt me. Now, Sir, there are people whom one should very well like to *drop,* but would not wish to be *dropped by*." ' Thomas Newton's *Dissertations on the Prophecies,* said Dr. Adams, ' "is his great work": JOHNSON. "Why, Sir, it is *Tom's* great work; but how far it is great, or how much of it is *Tom's* are other questions." ' And there are the engaging, quite unexpected touches, heightened by Johnson's own amused self-awareness of his temptation to 'talk for victory.' Doubtless expecting an elaborate defense, Boswell once asked: 'can you trace the cause of your antipathy to the Scotch?' But the reply was simply, ' "*I can not, Sir*": BOSWELL. "Old Mr. Sheridan says, it is because they sold out Charles the First." JOHNSON. "Then, Sir, *old Mr. Sheridan has found out a very good reason*." '

To recount the last twenty years of Johnson's life is indeed to quote from Boswell. The uniqueness of a work often appears in the extent to which it resists summary. The quality of Johnson's talk, as of his writing, is lost by summary: it can only be quoted. And so impressive and copious are the recorded conversations of these years that any narration of this period of his life — or even an attempt to analyze it topically — inevitably gives up and relapses into an anthology of selected quotations. The appeal of Johnson's talk is to be found in the union of strength, quickness, and range. The desperate clutch upward from the dark welter of his own subjective feelings gives urgency and impetus to his expressions. But to stop here is to stumble into the fallacy of interpreting genius by compensation. For the need to order experience does not by itself explain the final order achieved. Simultaneously accompanying it is the uncanny readiness of mind, whatever the occasion: in the brilliant defense Johnson dictated for the escaped Negro pleading his liberty in the Scottish courts; or in the eighteen-line birthday poem extemporized at Mrs. Thrale's request — in which the lines all rhyme with 'five,' and the rhyme-words are arranged alphabetically. It appears even in mere grumbling: — Boswell asks whether Bishop Burnet did not give ' "a good Life of Rochester." JOHNSON. "We have a good *Death:* there is not much *Life*" '; 'BOSWELL. "Is not the Giant's Causeway worth seeing?" JOHNSON. "Worth seeing, yes; but not worth *going* to see" '; ' "I mentioned there was not half a guinea's worth of pleasure in seeing [the new amusement-center, the 'Pantheon']. JOHNSON. "But, Sir, there is half a guinea's worth of inferiority to other people in *not* having seen it." ' As for range, he could repeat *verbatim*, as we have noted, whole pages he had lightly skimmed, from the entire body of known literature at the time, and yet arouse admiration by his discussion of mechanics before the Society of Arts and Manufacturers. The inventor, Richard Arkwright, thought him 'the only person who, on a first view, understood the principle and powers of his most complicated piece of machinery' — the spinning-jenny.[21] 'Last night,' Boswell records in the *Tour to the Hebrides,* Johnson 'gave us an account of the whole process of tanning, and of the nature of milk and the various operations upon it, as making whey, etc.'; and then Boswell tells that, before the company, he successfully tried out Johnson on the intricacies of what he thought would be as

'far out of the way of a philosopher and poet' as he could think
of at the moment — 'the trade of a butcher.' Earlier, there were
the talks with the officers at Fort George on granulating gun-
powder — where Johnson later felt he had spoken too 'osten-
tatiously.' 'He this morning gave us all the operation of coin-
ing, and at night . . . the operation of brewing spirits.' Mrs.
Thrale tells of his talk with her daughter's dancing-master
about dancing, 'which the man protested, at the close of the
discourse, the Doctor knew more of than himself.' As he grew
older, he became more consciously deliberate in his effort to
avoid the easy gossip and routine anecdotes that serve as the
mainstay of most conversation: to avoid 'stagnation' by the
constant incursion of 'new images' and 'new topics.' And on
one of the rare occasions when he spoke favorably of any
quality in himself, he admitted to Boswell:

> 'I value myself upon this, that there is *nothing of the
> old man in my conversation.* I am now sixty-eight, and
> I have no more of it than at twenty-eight . . . Mrs.
> Thrale's mother said of me what flattered me much. A
> clergyman was complaining of want of society in the
> country . . . and said, "They talk of *runts;*" (that is,
> young cows). "Sir, (said Mrs. Salusbury) Mr. Johnson
> would learn to talk of runts." . . . He added, 'I think
> myself a very polite man.' [22]

Certainly the years from 1766 to about 1781, when he was
seventy-two, brought Johnson more happiness than he had
ever had. From Monday night through Friday he commonly
stayed with the Thrales at Streatham, and spent the week-
ends, as Mrs. Thrale said, with 'his numerous family in Fleet-
street . . . treating them with the same, or perhaps more cere-
monious civility, than he would have done by as many people
of fashion . . .' There were the frequent trips to Lichfield, and
the visits with Dr. Adams at Oxford and Dr. Taylor at Ash-

bourne. At sixty-four, he took the exacting, at times even dangerous, tour with Boswell through Scotland and the Hebrides (1773), recounted in his *Journey to the Western Islands* (1775) and Boswell's *Tour to the Hebrides* (1785). With the Thrales he traveled both to North Wales (1774) and France (1775). During the thirteen years after 1765, when the edition of Shakespeare appeared, he wrote very little. Except for the prefaces, dedications, and other contributions he made for friends and others who needed help, there are only the *Journey to the Western Islands* and the political pamphlets — *The False Alarm* (1770), the *Falkland's Islands* pamphlet (1771), *The Patriot* (1774), and *Taxation no Tyranny* (1775) — which he wrote with a fraction of his mind and in no time at all. But there is little of the lacerating sense of guilt about indolence, and the fright at month-long states of helpless languor that he felt before and after his work on Shakespeare. We may think of the precept he keeps quoting from Robert Burton's *Anatomy of Melancholy:* 'Be not solitary, be not idle.' If, so far as writing is concerned, he was idle, he was certainly not solitary. One of the most frequently recurring words in Johnson's work is the verb 'fill.' It appears in many psychological contexts: '*filling* the time' alternating with '*wearing out* the day'; '*filling* the imagination'; '*filling* the mind.' To some extent, these years were now 'filled'; and though they seem long, because of the timeless figure of Johnson that emerges from the recorded conversations, they were only a decade and a half. It is, indeed, a relief approaching comic catharsis to find him so satisfied, at least temporarily, that he can lapse from self-struggle into a moment of complacency. This may explain the diverting appeal of an incident recorded by Miss Reynolds. It is so altogether unusual and unexpected. For Johnson's harshness with his friends came from uneasiness: the 'loud explosions,' as Boswell said, were 'guns of distress'; and afterward he was far from pleased with himself. On this occasion he spoke so roughly to

Mrs. Thrale that, after the ladies withdrew, one of them expressed indignation. But Mrs. Thrale said no more than

> 'Oh! Dear good man!' . . . [the other] Lady took the first opportunity of communicating it to him, repeating her own animadversion . . . He seem'd much *delighted* with this intelligence, and sometime after, as he was lying back in his Chair, seeming to be half asleep, but more evidently musing on this pleasing incident, he repeated in a loud whisper, *'Oh! Dear good man!'* [23]

More frequent, however, was the sudden and impulsive sense of shame, sometimes appearing as an irritable admission when he was pressed — 'I am sorry for it. I'll make it up to you *twenty different ways,* as you please' — but at other times as genuine contriteness. A remark often quoted is the reply to the rather foolish question of Mrs. Thrale's nephew, 'Would you advise me to marry?' — 'I would advise no man to marry, Sir . . . who is not likely to propagate understanding.' But the sequel is rarely cited. Johnson, who had left the room, suddenly returned, said Mrs. Thrale, 'and drawing his chair among us, with altered looks and a softened voice . . . insensibly led the conversation to the subject of marriage,' and talked so effectively 'that no one ever recollected the offense, except to rejoice in its consequences.' [24]

10

Indeed, the history of Johnson's later years may be partly described as a self-enforced, often pathetic, attempt to cultivate habitual good nature and overcome the strong aggressiveness his bitter life and sensitive pride made inevitable. He once despondently admitted to Mr. Thrale that he had never even 'sought to please till past thirty years old, considering the matter as hopeless.' Long after most people's characters have set like plaster, Johnson continued to try to remake his own. His constant belief that one can be a 'free agent,' that it is never impossible to gain 'superiority over habits' and remold one's character, underlies his insistent assertion that 'All good humour and complaisance is *acquired*.' Indeed, in his eagerness to maintain this, he was sometimes led to violate the ideal of the 'art of pleasing' he had in mind. When a clergyman, at the house of Sir Joshua Reynolds, said that 'after forty-five a man did not improve,' 'I *differ* with you,' interrupted Johnson, roused to unusual antagonism: 'A man *may* improve, and' — he unfairly added — 'you *yourself* have great room for improvement.' The 'nice people,' said Mrs. Thrale, who could only dine at a certain time, who 'cannot bear to be waked at an unusual hour, or miss a stated meal,' 'found no mercy' from Johnson: '*He* had no such prejudices . . . "Delicacy does not surely consist (says he) in *impossibility to be pleased*."' And there is the almost comic outburst in the *Tour to the Hebrides* for the cause of 'good humour.' In order to avoid liquor, Johnson had long taken to lemonade. When Boswell proposed carrying lemons so that lemonade would be sure to be available, Johnson became angry. 'I do not wish to be thought that *feeble man who cannot do without anything*. Sir, it is very bad manners to carry provisions to any man's house, as if he could not entertain you.' [25] Repeatedly, said Reynolds, he was 'the first to seek after a reconciliation.' His aggressive habit of 'talking for victory' on any side of a question also lay uneasily on his conscience. So habitually did he regard conversation as a contest that he once let slip the remark, when he was quite ill, that he was glad Edmund Burke was not present — he 'calls forth all my powers. Were I to see Burke now, it would kill me.' Increasingly, Johnson tried not to interrupt others; he even felt he could say he was unusually 'attentive when others are speaking.' The habit, which all his friends noted, of never beginning a conversation, but waiting till others spoke — even if it meant, as at Dr. Burney's famous evening party, sitting all evening without saying a word — is obviously a result of this deliberate attempt not to obtrude himself on the company. Indeed, all the stock characteristics associated with the legendary Johnson can easily be matched by resolutions and efforts to overcome them. The compulsive tics, the touching of posts, the St. Vitus' dance, have their counterpart in his often-expressed dislike of gesticulation and his resolutions, in the *Prayers and Meditations*, *'to avoid all Singularity.'* The often playful pushing of his Tory prejudices is matched by the disarming admissions that he did not really much care. Like all his attempts to operate by principle, there is a certain desperation in the effort to cultivate 'good nature' and 'the state of being pleased.' It reminds one a little of the stories of the feats of physical strength that he performed even when old and ill: Johnson climbing high trees, or plunging into the stream and swimming when the current was said to be dangerous; his riding to hounds 'fifty miles on end sometimes,' as Mrs. Thrale said, and then violently jumping over a cabriolet stool when Mr. Thrale had done the same thing to show he was not tired.[26]

The attempt to turn outward, to attain 'good humour' — a 'state of *being* pleased' — was, in a sense, Johnson's most difficult task in his later years. There are always so many more reasons, as he said, for rejecting than embracing; and few lives could have been more justified in ending in such an habitually negative state. Against this temptation is to be put his clairvoyant realization, even in his darkest years, that such an end is destructive of everything; that outgoing concern and vital, receptive emotion must be preserved at all costs. 'He loved the poor,' said Mrs. Thrale,

as I never yet saw any one else do, with an earnest desire to make them happy. — What signifies, says some one, giving halfpence to common beggars? they only lay it out in gin or tobacco. *'And why should they be denied such sweeteners of their existence* (says Johnson)? it is

51

surely very savage to refuse them every possible avenue to pleasure, reckoned too coarse for our own acceptance. *Life is a pill which none of us can bear to swallow without gilding . . .'* [27]

And this same compassion he learned to extend to others in very different circumstances, though few men would have had more excuse for not doing so. Even when he was pressed by the most bitter poverty, his essays in the *Rambler* were weighted with a close and feeling knowledge of the acid of the boredom, self-dissatisfaction, and pain that can eat into any condition of life, however wealthy. Again, no one valued active and thoughtful conversation more than Johnson. No one, indeed, has more exemplified it. Yet when Boswell complained that at a sumptuous dinner there was 'not one sentence of conversation worthy of being remembered,' and asked, 'Why then meet at table?' Johnson could say, 'Why, to eat and drink together, *to promote kindness,*' and then add — with sympathy, but no approval — that 'perhaps this is better done when there is no solid conversation; for when there is, people differ in opinion, and get into bad humour, or some of the company, who are not capable of such conversation, are left out, and feel themselves uneasy.' Again, as a young man eager for intelligent talk, he could disparage anyone who would 'shuffle cards and rattle dice from noon to midnight without tracing any new idea in his mind.' But he was now 'sorry I have not learnt to play at cards': in its own way, it somewhat *'generates kindness* and consolidates society.' So with all other things except positive evils like envy and malice. 'A man,' as he said during the Scottish tour, 'grows better-humoured as he grows older, by *experience.* He learns to think himself of no consequence and little things of little importance; and so he becomes more patient, and better pleased.' Two days before his death, he asserted that he was 'ready now to call a man *a good man,* upon easier terms than I was formerly.' Often this growing charity was to wrestle against some of his strongest inclinations. We may think, for example, of his struggle all his life against the temptation to drink, of his complete abstinence from it for years at a time, of his natural attempts to buttress his resolution by attacks on drinking, and of his frequent, self-defensive outbursts — 'I will argue with you no more,' as he roared to Reynolds when they were debating the advantages of drink: 'you are too far gone.' But when Mrs. Williams, as he thought, spoke too lightly of drink, and said, 'I wonder what pleasure men can take in making *beasts* of themselves,' Johnson, whose pity could now extend to what he could least commend, retorted, '*I* wonder, Madam, that you have not penetration enough to see the strong inducement of this excess; for he who makes a *beast* of himself gets rid of the *pain of being a man.*' [28]

The result of this enlarging and deepening of sympathy, this readiness to share, is to strengthen the moral premises that underlie Johnson's great writing on life and literature. In a different way, it may also be seen, with quick personal application, in his own daily life. One aspect is the engaging delight in comedy that fifty-five years of mental misery and physical pain could never destroy. There is Miss Reynolds' charming story of Johnson's race with the young lady in Devonshire who boasted she could outrun any of the company. 'Madam,' he cried out, 'you cannot outrun *me*':

> The lady at first had the advantage; but Dr. Johnson happening to have slippers on much too small for his feet, kick'd them off up into the air, and ran . . . leaving the lady far behind him, and . . . returned, leading her by the hand, with looks of high exultation and delight.[29]

This is the Johnson — never sufficiently stressed — who gleefully climbed a high tree when an elderly gentleman pointed to it and boasted he had often climbed it as a boy and 'thought nothing of it': the Johnson who rolled exuberantly down a long hill; who, in a gloomy place in Scotland, said Boswell, playfully 'diverted himself with trying to frighten me,' and later put on a Scottish 'war-bonnet,' and strutted about the room; and who, one morning, said Boswell,

> called me to his bedside . . . and to my astonishment he *took off* Lady Macdonald leaning forward with a hand on each cheek and her mouth open — quite insipidity on a monument . . . To see a beauty represented by Mr. Johnson was excessively high. I told him it was a masterpiece and that he *must have studied it much*. '*Ay*,' said he.[30]

A week before this, he had visited a Scottish minister, Alexander Grant. Grant never forgot the occasion. Years afterward he was to tell others of the incident, which occurred on a solemn Scottish Sunday. Johnson spoke of the trip of his friend, Sir Joseph Banks, to Australia, where Banks discovered 'an extraordinary animal called the *kangaroo*.' The appearance and habits of the animal were so singular that, 'in order to render his description more vivid,' Johnson rose from his chair and

> volunteered an imitation of the animal. The company stared . . . nothing could be more ludicrous than the appearance of a tall, heavy, grave-looking man, like Dr. Johnson, standing up to mimic the shape and motions of a kangaroo. He stood erect, *put out his hands like feelers*, and, gathering up the tails of his huge brown coat so as to resemble the pouch of the animal, *made two or three vigorous bounds across the room!* [31]

11

In 1778, Johnson, now approaching seventy, began writing the *Lives of the English Poets* (1779–1781). A group of forty booksellers joined together to publish a large collection of the *Works of the English Poets* spanning the century from about

1660 to 1760, excluding whatever poets were still alive. The publishers appointed a committee to ask Johnson to write what finally amounted to fifty-two biographical prefaces, one for each poet, indicating that he could name his own terms. Johnson agreed, gave much more than was expected, and took virtually nothing. For it is understatement to say that most of the *Lives* turned out to be far from mere biographical prefaces. As for money, Johnson asked for £200. He might easily, as Edmund Malone believed, have asked for £1500. After Johnson's death, Arthur Murphy received £300 for his comparatively short *Essay on the Life and Genius of Samuel Johnson.* Years before, after Johnson had finished the *Dictionary,* Sir John Hawkins, speaking of the forthcoming edition of Shakespeare, said, 'Now you have finished your *Dictionary,* I suppose you will labour your present work *con amore.*' Johnson answered, 'No, Sir, nothing excites a man to write but necessity.' Certainly, Johnson always needed some external incentive to write. Simply because it had been a task for so long, the whole process of writing had become inevitably associated with need and effort; and in such cases, as he himself said, 'an habitual dislike' gradually steals over one's approach to an occupation. On the other hand, Boswell is probably justified in believing that he gave 'less attention to profit from his labours than any man to whom literature has been a profession.' The *Prayers and Meditations* record the completion of the *Lives of the Poets* in March 1781 — written 'in my usual way, dilatorily and hastily, unwilling to work, and working with vigour and haste.' But the haste mattered less now than ever before. Drawing on his own copious memory, often dealing with writers at whom he had hardly glanced for many years, these volumes are not only a landmark in the history of criticism. They are also the finest example of one of the great English prose-styles.

Characteristically, Johnson took no initiative in his last great work. He had no particular 'theory' of literary biography in mind. He simply wrote the requested prefaces in so superior a way that, in the process of doing so, he 'gave to the British nation,' as the editor of the 1825 edition said, 'a new style of biography' — of biography, that is, extensively filled with specifically literary criticism of the man's works and general attainment. Seventy years were to pass before another critic, Sainte-Beuve, could focus on so many individual writers in so penetrating a way. And if Sainte-Beuve brings to bear on the personal character of his subjects the more subtle psychological knowledge of his own day, he does not equal Johnson in his critical grasp of particular works of literature or of specific problems of form and style. Least of all did Johnson plan or edit the *Works of the English Poets;* and he was later to protest to the publishers that the edition should be 'very impudently called mine.' One of the quaint ironies of literary history is the frequent impression during the nineteenth century that the period of the poets represented was determined by Johnson himself, and that their achievement represents his *beau ideal* of what poetry should be. The irony is heightened by the fact that this impression was especially current among critics or historians who possessed at most a fraction of Johnson's *verbatim* knowledge of English poetry before the period covered by the *Lives.* From one point of view, the entire *Lives of the Poets* may be called a conscientious study of English poetry after what Johnson himself called its 'golden age.' The sympathy and consideration he brings to bear is a tribute to his own ability to think by principle. Johnson's strong attraction to the works of the 'giants before the flood,' and to the 'larger *genres*' (especially the tragic drama and the epic), and his sense of the subsiding power of imagery and 'strength of thought' in poetry after 1660, all furnished strong temptations to follow a theory of 'decline' — a theory by no means uncommon in eighteenth-century England. But to surrender to such a temptation was to fold one's hands before historical determinism, and deny what Johnson most prized as a moral premise: the ability of man to remain a 'free agent' and to determine within limits his own destiny. There is consequently the effort to see this period sympathetically for what it is. The situation is analogous to what we should hope to find in any fair critical treatment of the past century and a half. To few critics of the present day — to still fewer two centuries hence — is our own era likely to appear as one of the supreme triumphs of poetic genius. Yet any honest survey of its achievement must not only include the large vision, the constant remembrance of other achievements, the lack of narrow partisanship which Johnson possessed. It must also retain the same active interest in whatever recent or contemporary genius can produce.

12

Now begins the period to which sympathetic students of Johnson's life have always found themselves, as they grow older, recurring with a certain awe. 'There are few things not purely evil,' as Johnson wrote in the last issue of the *Idler,* 'of which we can say, without some emotion of uneasiness, *this is the last.* . . . The secret horror of the last is *inseparable from a thinking being,* whose life is limited, and to whom death is dreadful.' Nor is there anything morbid in this solemn fascination with the final three and a half years of Johnson's life. The appeal resides in the indomitable courage with which Johnson, during this long death-agony, faced the literal tearing from him of the few 'sweeteners of existence' that he had so precariously acquired. The happy life at the taverns and at Streatham, even the quarreling inmates of his house are gone. In their place are the scenes of the dying and lonely Johnson: of Johnson back in 1779 weeping at the grave of Garrick, and bidding farewell to Streatham in 1782, the year after Thrale's

57

death; Johnson alone in the house in London, wracked with four fatal diseases, sitting up in pain all night and coughing, and fighting energetically to turn outward to new interests. The last few years were the final or acid test of his ability — against a temperament almost impossibly obdurate — to transmute objective and moral awareness into concrete and daily life.

Beneath the note in the *Prayers and Meditations* that mentions the finish of the *Lives of the Poets* is a restrained account of the death of Henry Thrale, in April 1781, and of Johnson looking 'for the last time upon the face that for fifteen years had never been turned upon me but with respect or benignity.' Within another year and a half, the comfort and gaiety of Streatham were lost to him; the place was closed down. Moreover, Mrs. Thrale — who had been much younger than her husband — became interested in an Italian musician, Gabriel Piozzi, and later married him. Johnson's own bleak dwelling, to which he now had to return, was meanwhile emptying. Mr. Levet died not long after Mr. Thrale. Mrs. Williams was gravely ill. Johnson's letters — he had typically always disliked writing them — refer only briefly to the 'cheerless solitude' in which he now found himself. Suddenly, in June 1783, he awoke early in the morning to find that he had a paralytic stroke. He wrote to a neighbor:

Dear Sir,

It has pleased GOD, this morning, to deprive me of the powers of speech; and as I do not know but that it may be his further good pleasure to deprive me soon of my senses, I request you will on the receipt of this note, come to me, and act for me, as the exigencies of my case may require.

I am,
Sincerely yours,
SAM. JOHNSON.

Two days later, he wrote to Mrs. Thrale, describing the stroke: 'I was alarmed, and prayed to GOD, that however he might afflict my body, he would spare my understanding. This prayer, that I might try the integrity of my faculties, I made in Latin verse. The lines were not very good, but *I knew them not to be very good.*'[32] His powers of speech returned. But his heart was meanwhile failing, and produced a dropsy so extreme that the water began to invade his lungs — ten quarts being drained from his body at one time. Other ailments quickly followed, and then Mrs. Williams suddenly died. If he could admit to Bennet Langton that he now lived in a 'habitation vacant and desolate,' he could also, in the same letter, state that 'Disease produces much *selfishness*. A man in pain is *looking after* ease . . .' Quite naturally, Johnson's lifelong, almost pathological fear of death now became constant. A vivid sense of guilt alternated with horror at possible annihilation. For many years, said Arthur Murphy, Johnson — in those fits of absence of mind to which he was liable — might be heard muttering to himself the speech from *Measure for Measure:*

> Ay, but to die and go we know not where;
> *To lie in cold obstruction and to rot . . .*[33]

But the result is nothing like the virtual collapse of twenty years before, with its almost hopeless fear of madness. The startling insertions in the *Prayers and Meditations* keep recurring in one's thought of Johnson now: 'I try because reformation is necessary and *despair is criminal . . . I will not despair.* Help me, help me, O my God.' To recount these last years in detail is to see a courage rising in direct proportion as the need becomes higher. The courage is, indeed, one of protest — 'I will be *conquered*,' as he said to Dr. Burney, 'I will not capitulate' — and it is crossed with frantic snatches at hope. But in general this last struggle of an heroic life against extinction may be described as an exemplification of the great statement of William the Silent, in the black days of Holland: 'It

59

is not necessary to hope in order to undertake, or to succeed in order to persevere.'

With a final effort of will, Johnson tried, even in his last two months, to 'find *new topicks of merriment,* or *new incitements to curiosity.*' 'Life,' he wrote now, 'is very short and very uncertain; let us spend it as well as we can.' 'The first talk of the sick,' he reminded himself, 'is commonly of *themselves.*' And his own talk was very different. Partly because he was so often alone, he now read more persistently than he had since the age of eighteen. In order to supplement the Literary Club, he also started its pitiable shadow, the little 'Essex-Head Club.' Though he was so ill that he had to rest four times between the inn and his lodgings, Fanny Burney, in the same week, could say that he was 'in most excellent good humour and spirits,' though she had little notion of the upsurge of will behind this active and outgoing Johnson. In his farewell to Boswell, he sprung away from the carriage 'with a kind of pathetic briskness.' Boswell, shortly afterward, wrote complaining of melancholy. Johnson's reply is typical. For he quotes a remark of Sir William Temple he had read long ago, now recurring to him when harassed by a solitude, fear, and perhaps physical pain beyond Boswell's own experience: *'Be well,'* he wrote, *'when you are not ill, and pleased when you are not angry.'* [34]

As he lay dying the last week, and the heart-disease that finally killed him had produced a dropsy that spread from his breast to his feet, he turned on the surgeon who refused to make further incisions: 'Deeper, deeper, *I want length of life,* and you are afraid of giving me pain, which I do not value.' He grasped a pair of scissors, and after the physicians were gone, awkwardly stabbed himself in three places, hoping to drain the accumulated water, but succeeded only in letting unneccessary blood. In one of the most moving passages in the *Life of Johnson,* Boswell compares Johnson's mind to a gladiator in the Coliseum meeting the beasts as they emerge from the center of the arena, and driving them back to their dens. It is a fitting comparison. Among Johnson's last words are those recorded by Sir John Hawkins: '*Iam Moriturus*' — 'I who am now about to die.' Uttered almost in delirium, they seem to echo the ancient salutation of the Roman gladiators to Caesar.

After his death on 13 December 1784, two acquaintances dropped by — Seward and Hoole — who were never to forget 'the *most awful sight* of Dr. Johnson *laid out on his bed, without life!*' [35] The finish of the lifelong achievement of Johnson struck home in the same way to almost everyone acquainted with him. Especially to those who knew of Johnson walking the muddy roads to Birmingham and the school at Market-Bosworth, leaving Lichfield with the tragedy of *Irene* in his pocket, tossing off the Parliamentary Debates in a garret, and trudging the streets of London all night; who knew at least a little of what underlay the *Dictionary*, the moral essays, and the *Preface to Shakespeare* — who had seen something of the Johnson that rolled down the hills, imitated the kangaroo, and sat in the bed with the handkerchief atop his head, exclaiming 'O brave we!' — the complete evaporation of this enormous capacity for life seemed hardly credible. The reaction of one of them is typical: 'He has made a chasm, which not only nothing can fill up, but which *nothing has a tendency to fill up.* — Johnson is dead. — Let us go to the next best: — *There is nobody;* — no man can be said to put you in mind of Johnson.' [36]

There is a suggestive distinction of William James between the 'once-born,' who are naturally serene and harmoniously integrated, and the 'second-born,' who attain fulfillment only precariously, after prolonged self-struggle and despair. The life of Johnson, of course, is almost a prototype or *exemplum* of the latter. But the universality of its force is to be found in the fact that all human attainment is, to some extent, 'second-born.'

The moral of its struggle is the freedom of the human spirit, however adverse the circumstances, to evolve its own destiny. It is this as much as anything else that increasingly leads us to think of Johnson almost as an allegorical figure, like Valiant-for-truth in *The Pilgrim's Progress*. But fortunately Johnson was also one of the supreme writers of English prose; and both the struggle and the final achievement are written in large and graphic outline throughout his own work. To Johnson as to few others we may apply Keats's remark about Shakespeare — that he 'led a life of Allegory: his works are the comments on it.'

II

The Hunger of Imagination

In *Rasselas*, the little group, which has been traveling about in search of a fuller understanding of human nature and destiny, is taken by the philosopher, Imlac, to see the pyramids. Neither Rasselas nor his sister is excited by the prospect of the visit. They state, rather pretentiously, that their 'business is with *man*' — with human manners and customs — not with 'piles of stones' or 'fragments of temples.' Imlac replies that in order to know anything we must also know the products and traces it leaves behind: to understand men, we must see what they did 'that we may learn what reason has dictated or passion incited, and find what are the most powerful motives of action. To judge rightly of the present, we must oppose it to the past; for all judgment is comparative . . .' The travelers enter the Great Pyramid, and descend to the tomb. As they sit to rest awhile before returning, Imlac, in an altogether Johnsonian way, starts to speculate why the pyramid was ever built in the first place, and why a king, 'whose power is unlimited, and whose treasures surmount all real and imaginary wants,' should be compelled to 'amuse the tediousness of declining life, by seeing thousands labouring without end.' Secrecy for a tomb or treasure could have easily been secured by less costly and more effective means:

It seems to have been erected only in compliance with
that *hunger of imagination which preys incessantly upon
life* . . . Those who have already all that they can enjoy, must enlarge their desires. He that has built for use,
till use is supplied, must begin to build for vanity . . .
*I consider this mighty structure as a monument of the
insufficiency of human enjoyments.*[1]

The 'hunger of imagination,' or what he elsewhere calls the
'hunger of mind,' puts in a strong metaphor a perception almost constantly present in Johnson's writing: that 'few of the
hours of life are filled up with objects *adequate to the mind
of man*,' since the mind of man can conceive so much more than
the present can ever supply. We are therefore 'forced to have
recourse, every moment, to the past and future for *supplemental* satisfactions.'[2] The recognition appears in the phrasing of almost every page, sometimes with comic impatience and
more usually with charity: riches fail to '*fill up* the vacuities
of life'; '*fill* the day with petty business'; the recourses of people at summer resorts to 'rid themselves of the day'; '*filling the
vacuities* of his mind with the news of the day'; literary quarreling gratifies the malignity of readers or 'relieves the vacan-
cies of life' for them. 'The *vacuity* of life,' said Mrs. Thrale,
'had at some early period of his life struck so forcibly' on
Johnson's mind that it appeared in every context, even in casual
talk; and she cites some instances. For example, a rake noted for
gaming and sensuality was mentioned: 'Why, life must be
filled up (says Johnson), and the man who is not capable of
intellectual pleasures must content himself with such as his
senses can afford.' Another is mentioned as a hoarder: 'Why,
a fellow must do something; and what so easy to a narrow mind
as hoarding halfpence till they turn into sixpences.'[3]

'The truth is,' said Imlac, 'that no mind is much employed
upon the present: recollection and anticipation fill up almost

all our moments.' Our emotions, he goes on, take some form of love, hate, fear, or hope. In all of these, we find ourselves glancing back to what occurred five minutes, five days, or five years ago. Or we flit ahead into the future in the same way. In fact, as Johnson says elsewhere, we can hardly think at all except in terms of the past and future. For 'the present is in perpetual motion, leaves us as soon as it arrives,' and is hardly felt for what it is until we note 'the effects which it leaves behind. The greatest part of our ideas arises, therefore, from the view *before* or *behind* us'; and we are happy or miserable as we are affected by what we believe has happened or is to come.[4] The context of Imlac's remark that 'recollection and anticipation fill up almost all our moments' is the defense of the study of history that he makes before the group visits the pyramids. To employ the mind by studying the different forms that men's motives and desires have taken is itself a way of satisfying the restless appetite of 'looking before and after'; and it is a method that is valuable and self-enlightening. The ironic corollary is that the Great Pyramid itself, which the group then visits, is still another result of the constant need to find 'supplemental satisfaction,' but a result that takes a very different form. When fed with objective knowledge the 'hunger of imagination' may be turned to profit and lead to growth. But if this awareness is lacking, as is generally the case, the imagination will seek to fill itself in some other way, or will uneasily begin to prey upon itself. In doing so, it can only too often transform man's state into one 'in which many of his faculties can serve only for his torment.'

2

If we take into consideration the sheer amount of time spent in 'recollection and anticipation,' the appetite for novelty as a means of 'disburdening the day' or inciting new interest is perhaps man's most constant and pervasive desire. The term 'novelty,' as Johnson uses it, suggests the whole seductive vista of everything we desire, do not actually need, and do not have at the moment. It includes the desire for possessions, of course, whether we want more of the same or something different. Considering the lack of vivid enjoyment we feel once we possess them, novelty also provides much of the attraction we feel in our hunger for reputation or fame, for learning, for possessing the love of others, our desire for seeing a task completed, or even — once it is finished — to have it brought back in order to keep ourselves occupied. With that leap of the imagination which is 'always breaking away from the present,' the novelty desired may even be the wish that we ourselves should be able to feel differently, just as emotional or passionate people envy the calm and serene, or as those who feel they cannot love envy those they think able to love. Even Rasselas, in the Happy Valley, where all desires are gratified, envies an existence where active and unsatisfied desires would stimulate him to some sort of activity. Infants, as we know, cry more frequently from mere boredom than from pain. When they toss away their toys in spite or weariness, they cry to have them back — not because the toys are really prized, but because to have them again will be different from the present moment when they are lacking. Nor do we live down the desire for novelty and difference as we grow older, though it may take subtler forms and use a more elaborate vocabulary. The sheer capacity to desire is so much greater than any possible satisfactions that can be wrung from attaining what we want that satiety, as we all know abstractly, provides no joy or durable contentment. Nor does satiety, as a general state at least, last very long. 'We desire, we pursue, we obtain, we are satiated; we desire something else, and begin a new pursuit.' [5]

Even when we cling to familiar memories of the past in an imaginary hope for security, we are often indirectly responding to the tug of novelty. The nostalgia for lost childhood in Words-worth's *Ode on Intimations of Immortality* ('Whither is fled the visionary gleam? Where is it now, the glory and the dream?'), the garden and the lost pool of sunlight in Eliot's *Burnt Norton,* bring back the haunting memory of circumstances in our past that were once graphic and fresh. They look back to a time when, as Johnson said, the 'diversity of nature *pours* ideas in,' when neither search nor labor is necessary to gratify the imagination, and 'we have nothing more to do than to open our eyes.' The contrast with Wordsworth's *Immortality Ode* is singularly pointed: what is now going on about Wordsworth ('The young lambs bound . . . The cataracts blow their trumpets from the steep') lacks the visionary splendor it once had. Johnson, a half century before, states that 'we all remember a time when nature . . . gave delight which can now be found no longer, when the noise of a torrent, the rustle of a wood . . . or the play of lambs, *had power to fill the attention,* and suspend all perception of the course of time.'[6]

Few classical moralists are closer to Freud than Johnson, or have so uncanny a sense of what repression can mean. Yet in the nostalgic pull backward to one's childhood, whether with Wordsworth's sense of vision or simply Proust's absorption in early impressions, the attraction, from Johnson's point of view, is not simply to security in the ordinary sense. What we really want is a security that includes more than mere safety; we want to recapture a keener, fresher fullness of impression than we now feel. However tamed or circumscribed they may now be beneath the proscenium arch of memory and familiarity, the luster of what was once an eager newness still floods these recollected scenes. The situation is comparable to the occasional envy of the single by the married, who sometimes describe 'the happiness of their earlier years,' and, at least secretly, 'blame the rashness of their own choice.' But they forget that the days they wish to call back 'are the days not only of celibacy but of *youth,* the days of *novelty* and . . . of hope.' Sheer novelty, in fact, explains much of the vivid impact that sexual love makes on us in youth; and the memory of this creates the nostalgia in later years for those infatuations that could once *fill* the attention,' and stirs the vicarious interests of those 'who employ themselves in promoting matrimony, and . . . without any discoverable impulse of malice or benevolence, without any reason, but that they *want objects of attention* and topics of conversation, are incessantly busy in procuring wives and husbands.' [7] Yet, in this remembered vividness, we forget that there were fears as well as hopes, and that not everything that 'fills the attention' through freshness or novelty does so in an agreeable way. The pleasures that we recall may actually have been outweighed by disadvantages we now forget. We should remember how rarely we look back with painful longing on any past circumstances that closely parallel our present state. But when once the past has become irretrieveable, and the portcullis closed, the liabilities and disadvantages of former conditions more easily lapse from memory; and recollected novelties and attractions blend without hindrance into a simpler and denser unit of pleasure than had ever really existed.

3

Nothing is so typical of the dynamic character of Johnson's thinking as the way in which he follows the human craving for 'novelty' and immediately recognizes it despite its agile, Proteus-like ability to take any form. He is always getting directly to the activity of 'looking before and after.' The procedure contrasts with the optical illusions of naïve naturalism, which lead us to interpret or at least label instincts or desires in terms merely of the particular objects on which they happen to fix. It is, in fact, this clear-eyed ability to brush aside the clutter of labels, and to seize on the actual process of desiring itself, that enables Johnson's moral thought to avoid the ego-centric determinism of Thomas Hobbes and of moralists or psychologists who have repeated or refined on Hobbes for the past three centuries. Johnson does not, like Shaftesbury, Rous-seau, or other romantics, simply deny Hobbes's arguments that man is basically selfish. Instead, he takes them for granted. Where Johnson differs from Hobbes is in supplementing these arguments with other considerations which Hobbes overlooks or disregards. He does this especially by recurring always to the nature of desire itself, as an activity inherent in a living creature 'whose motions are gradual.' Those only, said Cole-ridge, 'can acquire the *philosophic imagination* . . . who within themselves can interpret and understand the symbol, that the wings of the air-sylph are forming within the skin of the caterpillar. . . . They know and feel that the *potential* works in them, even as the *actual* works on them.'[8] Exactly this sense of process is immanent throughout all of Johnson's writing on human nature. By reaching down to the active function of desire itself, Johnson's thought touches a greater generality than that of Hobbes. Indeed, from this standpoint, the naturalism of Hobbes and his modern descendants is just another side of the coin to the romantic temptation to glorify the particular objects of desire. In either case, what we have is a confusion of a process with a static concept: a confusion of the instinct — of the desiring mechanism, so to speak — with particular images or objects on which desire happens to fasten. Both of them mirror — one in a poetic, the other in an analytic way — the common tendency of the imagination to simplify its own wants and then to mistake the objects to which it happens to turn for actual *ends* — as ends that are somehow able, because of nature or one's own personal character, to serve as permanent sources of satisfaction once we get them. Precisely this mistake — a variety of Whitehead's 'fallacy of misplaced concreteness' — is, as Johnson conceives it, the source of most of the chronic dissatisfaction we feel when, once our basic physical needs are met, 'we begin to form wants in consequence of our wishes.'

The insight is that of Ecclesiastes: 'All the rivers flow into the sea; yet the sea is not full . . . the eye is not satisfied with seeing, nor the ear filled with hearing.' Of course, general wishes have to localize themselves into definite wants. Human existence could hardly continue otherwise. Also the objects of what we desire may vary in value. Some may satisfy a greater range of human needs, and some may offer a more enduring satisfaction. The protest, in Johnson's case, is only against the quick answer, against the flat, two-dimensional interpretation, whether in philosophy, in the criticism of literature, or in daily ambitions. Increasingly, as we look back on the great series of reflections on human nature that begin with the *Rambler* and continue through *Rasselas,* one of their prevailing themes appears to be the paradox of the human imagination itself. It is the paradox that the human imagination is potentially boundless in what it desires, and yet will fix itself hypnotically on a single aim or object. For what Swift called the 'converting imagination,' or the 'mechanical operation of the spirit,' has a frightening way of over-simplifying or restricting its field of interest for the moment. Hence its slap-dash tendency, as Swift says, 'to reduce all Things into *Types,*' to pluck out of context, interpret according to one aim, engross itself in only one object or aspect, and conveniently remove other elements or else twist them around to this immediate concern. But the paradox appears less extreme when we recall that the tendency to over-simplify — at least as far as our hopes for happiness are concerned — is only one more by-product of the fact that the 'capacity of the imagination' is so 'much larger than actual enjoyment.' Finding the present moment inadequate, the imagination bounds ahead to something else that contrasts with it.

Naturally, the future, not yet being experienced, is 'pliant and ductile,' and will be imperceptibly molded by our wishes. The past, too, once it is safely removed, becomes 'ductile' in our memories. For the 'hope of happiness . . . is so strongly impressed, that the longest experience is not able to efface it. Of the present state, whatever it be, we *feel* . . . the misery; yet, *when the same state is again at a distance,* imagination paints it as desirable.' [9]

4

'The general remedy,' said Johnson, 'of those, who are uneasy without knowing the cause, is *change of place*,' or of condition generally: 'they are willing to imagine that their pain is the consequence of some *local* inconvenience, and endeavour to fly from it . . .' [10] To the extent that it snatches at whatever seems to contrast with the present, hope, like nostalgia for the past, also simplifies outlines and blots out the probable context. Hence, in our 'anticipation of change' to other conditions and different possessions, too often 'the change itself is nothing; when we have made it, the next wish is to change again.' The hard-driven merchant, chained down by a lifetime of routine, will naturally have periods when he looks forward to retirement from 'the fatigues of business, and the confinement of a shop'; it may even become an obsession; and then we find, when the looked-for retirement is attained, that he relieves the 'vacuity' of life in his country retreat by watching carriages from his window, and eagerly hoping he will be interrupted. Johnson himself, in his own reactions, certainly provides examples. The difference is that he cannot refrain from thinking about them. So, after writing the long series of the *Rambler,* the occasion of the next to the last issue suggests its own subject, in which he notes — and he was still at work on the *Dictionary* — that 'When once our labour has begun, the comfort that enables us to endure it is the prospect of its end.' Pleasing intervals may occur, as he goes on to say, during which we day-dream about the work in its completed form. But these intervals are short-lived. The mind is pitched to getting the thing done, and to being able to look back on the finished work as a whole. Yet like Gibbon, who had so long looked forward to the 'freedom' he would possess when he completed the *Decline and Fall of the Roman Empire,* we find the experience of this freedom does not fill the imagination with the vivid pleasure we expected; and the liberty quickly proves empty, until some further desire charges this vacant freedom with uneasiness and stimulates us to start something new. One thinks of Johnson, himself, while he was writing, impatiently running his finger down the margin to see how many verses were completed and how many were yet to be written, and at the same time seeing exactly what he was doing.

'Every man recounts the inconveniences of his own station, and thinks those of any other less, because he has not felt them. Thus the married praise the ease and freedom of a single state, and the single fly to marriage from the weariness of solitude. . . . *Whoever feels great pain, naturally hopes for ease from change of posture . . .'* [11] Indeed, Johnson seems to become most light-hearted and amusing in the *Rambler* and *Idler* sketches when he is discussing either marriage, the pursuit of wealth, or the hopes we place in retirement to country retreats. The expectations we feel, in all three cases, also serve for Johnson as recurring symbols of the way in which the imagination, in common and daily life, is always simplifying the endless desires of the heart into specific wants, and then finding them insufficient. To interpret the sprightly essays on marriage, or the debates about it in *Rasselas,* as an expression or rationalization of Johnson's own disillusionment about 'Tetty' only suggests the limitations and projections of the interpreter. It is on a par with interpreting the great *Preface to Shakespeare,* with its massive plea for sanity of outlook, as a compensatory recoiling from Johnson's own distress of mind in the 1760's. Moreover, Johnson's point of view is generally that 'Marriage has many pains, but celibacy has few pleasures'; that much of the pain simply results from that tendency by which 'every animal *revenges his pain upon those who happen to be near'; and* that 'we see the same discontent at every other part of life which we cannot change.' Again, it is plain that marriage is far from being really miserable, if for no other reason than that we find 'such numbers, whom the death of their partners has set free from it, entering it again.' In fact, he himself, after the death of 'Tetty,' was apparently thinking of marrying again, even though, on hearing of another's remarriage, he referred to it as 'the triumph of hope over experience.'

Indeed, whatever is subjective in Johnson's own experience he generally uses in an opposite way from rationalization. That is not to say that he automatically swings away from it through simple compensation. Instead, the immediately personal in Johnson remains openly and honestly present, serving as a bond, as a basis for charitable sympathy with the illusion he is dispelling. And if we at times find him cutting through the illusion with phrasing that seems too vigorous, we also find him equally able to turn against the next level — against psychological compensation in practically every temptation to it that he experienced (and his range of susceptibility was large) — and then qualifying the compensation itself with equal vigor. We know how strongly Johnson clung to religious orthodoxy, for example (and there may be an element of compensation here, in reaction from his own disturbing doubts), and that he had misgivings about the work of the brilliant Samuel Clarke. But when the Reverend Hector Maclean said that 'Clarke was very wicked for going so much into the Arian system,' 'I will not say he was *wicked*,' answered Johnson; 'he *might be mis-*

taken.' And when Maclean blandly asserted that 'worthy men since, in England, have confuted him to all intents and purposes,' Johnson burst out, 'I know not *who* has confuted him *to all intents and purposes.*' [12]

5

When we recall Johnson's poverty during the years before he wrote the *Rambler,* his enlightened treatment there of the hunger for wealth or possessions provides an especially graphic example of the balance and purity of his thinking — of his ability to resist not merely the temptation to rationalize the bitterness of poverty but also the temptation to compensate for it by a sour-grapes attitude toward wealth. True enough, he later admitted that 'When I was running about this town a very poor fellow, I was a great arguer for the advantages of poverty; but I was, at the same time, very sorry to be poor.' Yet the spectrum of his thinking in the *Rambler* ranges from 'that *false estimation* of the value of wealth, which poverty, long continued, always produces,' to the balancing reminder of how few desires 'can be formed which riches do not *assist* to gratify.' [13] Even the 'art of pleasing,' of being sympathetically receptive to others, is made very difficult by poverty; for 'by what means can the man please whose *attention is engrossed* by his distresses?' Moreover, defensive pride, even if it does not turn into truculence or freeze into awkward reserve, may still incite too aggressive and eager a desire to excel and 'attract notice.' Here indeed Johnson was speaking from his own experience. He admitted to Mrs. Thrale that he was thinking of himself when he wrote the story of the poor scholar in *Idler,* No. 75, who tried to fight his way by his learning and wit, and who found that wherever 'he had remarkably excelled, he was seldom invited a second time.'

These essays persuade because nothing that can attract the human imagination or bias judgment is ever lightly or easily dismissed. In fact, any such quick dismissals of the desire for wealth are themselves anticipated and exposed as simply another variety of over-simplification. Once a man attains wealth, and finds himself in a state of 'imagination operating on luxury,' where other desires begin to spawn 'in numberless directions,' he who wishes 'to become a philosopher at a cheap rate' can only too easily gratify himself by speaking lightly of poverty 'when he does not feel it, and by boasting his contempt of riches when he has already more than he enjoys.' Years later, when the wealthy Mrs. Thrale 'dwelt with peculiar pleasure' on David Garrick's line, 'I'd smile with the simple, and feed with the poor,' he at once interrupted: 'Nay, my dear Lady, this will never do. Poor David! Smile with the simple! What folly is that! *And who would feed with the poor that can help it?* No, no; let me smile with the wise, and feed with the rich.' [14] But if Johnson undercuts cant in this he is not satirizing it. Instead there is charity in seeing it as being itself one more instance of man's 'dream of happiness in *novelty*' — of happiness from different circumstances. Again, almost everyone values 'esteem and influence,' and 'whoever has found the art of securing them without the help of money, ought, in reality, to be accounted rich, since he has all that riches can purchase to a wise man.' Even the monk, though he is living an ascetic life, is not entitled to brush aside too quickly the powerful desire of the human heart for possessions, which convinces us that, 'Whatever is the *remote or ultimate* design, the *immediate* care is to be rich,' with no 'disagreement but about the use.' For if the monk resides in a monastery, he ought to remember that 'he converses only with men whose condition is the same with his own.' He should recall that 'the munificence of the founder' saves him from that destitution which is an 'impediment to virtue' simply because it does not allow 'the mind to *admit any other care.*' Temptations to 'envy and competition' are kept down: he is not exposed to the same range of 'pains and insults' as others; and if 'he wanders abroad, the sanctity of his character amply compensates all other distinctions.' Nor, lastly, are we to forget that many who neglect opportunities to amass wealth do so not because 'they value riches *less,* but that they dread labour or danger more than others.' Practically none would refuse 'to be rich, when to be rich was in his power.'[15] Hence the confidence inspired by Johnson as he illuminates the 'fallacies of imagination' that attach themselves to the image of wealth or possessions. We simplify reality when we dispose of the powerful appeal of wealth after we ourselves have attained it and found it inadequate. We do so when we cannot attain wealth, and therefore, by compensation, dismiss it as unimportant. We do so, thirdly, when the imagination narrows itself by confusing one means — the possession of wealth — with the end, and creates an image of possessions without which happiness is deemed impossible. Especially in the light of the other realizations, we can accept this final perception as something more than an abstract moral cliché.

Thus Johnson describes the hope of an entire family, waiting for the death of three wealthy, elderly aunts, and governing every action in this expectation. When snubbed or outshone by their neighbors, the family has always the solace of the future before them. They dream of putting their neighbors in their place, and chalk up 'every act of civility and rudeness.' As the years pass, the nerves of the father of the family become more edgy, and he occasionally barks out that no creature has 'so many lives as a cat and an old maid.' Finally, when one of the aunts recovers from a severe illness, the father begins to pine away and dies. The family continues in the *'shackles of expectation,'* meeting together

> only to contrive how our approaching fortune should be enjoyed; for in this our conversation always ended, on whatever subject it began. *We had none of the*

76

*collateral interests which diversify the life of others
with joys and hopes,* but had turned our whole attention on one event, which we could neither hasten nor
retard.

Finally, the two eldest aunts die, but leave their fortunes to
their younger sister. She, in turn, plunges the remaining family
into dismay by contemplating marriage now in her old age.
In time this panic subsides. The nephew consoles himself
with the undeniable truth that 'all are mortal,' without making
the obvious application back to himself; for he is fast moving
into middle age. When the remaining aunt dies at ninety-three,
he now finds himself *'accustomed to give the future full
power over my mind,* and to start away from the scene before
me to some *expected* enjoyment.' [16]
Yet the almost savage irony of this brief satiric sketch is at
once crossed by the large sadness through which Johnson's
range of perception is always passing. For the 'shackles of expectation' have, as the aging nephew finds, now chained and
reduced his own mind to 'an *inveterate disease of wishing* . . . unable to think on anything but *wants.*' Elsewhere,
with more pity, Johnson can stress that 'Of riches, as of everything else, *the hope is more than the enjoyment* . . . no sooner
do we sit down to enjoy our acquisitions, than we find them
insufficient to fill up the vacuities of life.' [17] Hence the blind
attempt, when we do have money, to 'fill our houses with useless ornaments, only to shew that we can buy them,' and to
show not only others but principally ourselves; — or else we
congratulate ourselves upon now dismissing the belief that
money is a good, and turn instead to other ends. Turning to
other ends is desirable, even though the self-congratulation
and lapse of sympathy are to be avoided.
Our motives, as Johnson continually reminds us, can rarely
be completely pure. But they are not for that reason to be

left unused. The value is to be judged by the *final* degree of purity. This is one of the ways in which Johnson goes beyond Swift, who so frequently darkens his interpretation by recurring to original motives. If 'poverty long continued' leads to a 'false estimation' of the importance of wealth, then one of the advantages of wealth is certainly that it can help free us, though it does not do so automatically, from stumbling into this false estimate. If Johnson's treatment of the hope of riches is viewed as a self-protective method of reminding himself and of keeping his own mind clear, the fact remains that we can tell ourselves what is true and desirable while we are also telling others, particularly if we are emphasizing not one but two or more different aspects of a matter. Indeed, we may question whether what we are telling others will have the desired persuasiveness unless we are also telling ourselves. With what we know too well, as with what we already possess too abundantly, the difficulty of attaining it and the pressures that once underlay our desire for it may be forgotten. In his moral writing as in his criticism of literature, Johnson never writes in the closet or the study as one who has lived through an experience and forgotten the details but as one who is again reliving it.

6

Macaulay is largely responsible for the strange notion that, because Johnson praised the variety of London life as compared with that of a village or a hermitage, he therefore disliked traveling; that, in fact, he dismissed travel 'with the fierce and boisterous contempt of ignorance.' Macaulay seems to have forgotten Johnson's financial condition; his constant reading of books of travel; his pathetic hope that he could make a trip to Iceland; the arduous trip over the Scottish mountain-paths that he made with Boswell; the visits that he restlessly made to Lichfield, Oxford, and Ashbourne; his snatching at the opportunity to go to France with the Thrales; his final resurgence of hope while dying — which he dared not speak out, for he was dependent on another's bounty — that he might at last go to Italy.

If he had money, he once wrote to Mrs. Thrale, the very first use to which he would put it would be to travel extensively through the Orient. 'He loved indeed the very act of travelling,' said Mrs. Thrale, and was 'an admirable companion on the road, as he piqued himself upon feeling no inconvenience, and on despising no accommodations.' There are also the various remarks about the height of felicity consisting of riding rapidly in a postchaise. In fact, any inconvenience seemed so trifling compared with the enormous advantages and interest of travel that he regarded the complaints of others about 'the rain, the sun, or the dust,' about 'long confinement in a carriage' or meagerness of comfort at inns, as 'proofs of an empty head, and a *tongue desirous to talk without materials of conversation.* "A mill that goes without grist (said he) is as good a companion as such creatures." ' And when a visitor at the Thrales' who had traveled through Bohemia seemed uninterested in taking part in any sort of conversation, 'Surely,' said Johnson afterward, 'the man who has seen Prague might tell us something new and something strange, and not sit silent for want of matter to put his lips in motion.' [18]

Hence the shallowness of viewing his discussions of the restless desire for travel or for rural retreat as a rationalization of his own physical near-sightedness, his deafness, or his insensibility to those 'natural' objects to which the nineteenth century automatically assumed that the eighteenth century was oblivious, as though the neo-classic ideal of bliss were to sit at the court of George II or in the midst of Fleet Street. Instead, the impulsive hopes of travel, or of flying to rural retreats, are only one more instance, in daily life, of both the insatiability and self-defeating simplicity of the human heart. *Rambler,* No. 6, comes as close to satire as Johnson generally permitted himself. Its theme is the much advertised assertion of the poet, Abraham Cowley, that, since fame had brought him everything but rest, he now intended to sail overseas to a plantation, and *'foresake this world forever,* with all the vanities and vexations of it, and to bury myself there in some obscure retreat.' He could easily have buried himself, says Johnson, within his own country: 'There is pride enough in the human heart to prevent much desire of acquaintance with a man, by whom we are sure to be neglected . . . Even those to whom he has formerly been known, will very patiently support his absence when they have tried a little to live without him.' But Cowley, when he was interrupted or fatigued in his present state, 'conceived it impossible to be far enough from [what he thought] the cause of his uneasiness,' and picturing by contrast an idyllic state of leisure and retreat, he

determined to enjoy them for the future without interruption . . . He forgot, in the vehemence of desire, that solitude and quiet owe their pleasures to those miseries, which he was so studious to obviate . . . that *day and night, labour and rest, hurry and retirement, endear each other* . . . we desire, we pursue, we obtain, we are satiated; we desire something else, and begin a new pursuit.

If he had proceeded in his project . . . it may be doubted, whether his distance from the *vanities* of life, would have enabled him to keep away the *vexations. It is common for a man, who feels pain, to fancy that he could bear it better in any other part.* Cowley, having known the troubles and perplexities of a particular condition, readily persuaded himself that nothing worse was to be found, and that every alteration would bring some improvement; *he never suspected that the cause of his unhappiness was within* . . .

'He that travels in theory,' as Johnson says elsewhere, 'has no inconvenience: he has shade and sunshine at his disposal.' In its recoil from one's present state, the imagination selects only those advantages which seem most attractive, and then unites them into an impossible expectation that is 'indulged till the day of departure arrives.' A few miles then teach the traveler the 'fallacies of imagination': the road is dusty, and the horses slow; he 'longs for the time of dinner, that he may eat and rest,' and finds the inn crowded; while the people he has looked forward to visiting turn out to be cool, occupied with their affairs, or burdened with private sorrow. If 'Pleasure is very seldom found where it is sought' — where it is imagined and then deliberately searched for — it is because we seldom

> find either men or places such as we *expect* them. He that has pictured a prospect upon his fancy, will receive little pleasure from his eyes; he that has anticipated the conversation of a wit, will wonder to what prejudice he owes his reputation. *Yet it is necessary to hope, though hope should always be deluded; for hope itself is happiness, and its frustrations, however frequent, are less dreadful than its extinction.*[19]

The recurring theme of the 'vanity of human wishes,' then, from the poem through the great prose of the following decade, is not merely that we give ourselves unnecessary pain by desiring what is unattainable, and thus become inevitably frustrated. Least of all is it some vague, pessimistic assertion that all wishes are vain. The theme is rather that, in the very activity or process of wishing, there are inherent liabilities that are able to undercut the wish itself — the liabilities that the 'capacity of the imagination' is always so 'much larger than actual enjoyment,' and that nevertheless it tends to simplify, to fix on a specific object, if only by contrast, and to dwell 'attentively upon it, till it has wholly engrossed the imagination, and permits us not to conceive any happiness but its attainment, or any misery but its loss.' [20] But 'since life is uncertain, nothing which has life as its basis can boast much stability.'

Even if the external objects we want proved to be stable, yet we ourselves, in our ability to enjoy them, would not be. The sense of process, and the awareness of what lies beyond the horizon of the moment, is indigenous and continual in Johnson, habitually modifying fears as well as hopes; even casual conversational remarks reveal it. Not long after meeting Johnson, Boswell planned a dinner for several guests; a quarrel with his landlord left him without a house; and he was worried about the impression this would give. Johnson's immediate response is typical: 'Consider . . . how insignificant this will appear a twelvemonth hence.' Or again, in Boswell's *Tour to the Hebrides,* when Johnson was sixty-four, some young women were discussing among themselves how ugly he was. One of them took a bet to go over, sit on Johnson's knees, and kiss him. Even in this little incident, Johnson's amused awareness of the situation and his unsleeping, almost Shakespearean realization of the transitoriness of things come at once into focus, in a healthful and comic sanity of statement, entirely characteristic of him when once uttered, and yet completely unpredictable: *'Do it again,'* he said, *'and let us see who will tire first.'* [21]

7

If Johnson comes closest to comedy when he is dealing with the disappointments of what we expect in ordinary experience — expectations of happiness from riches, marriage or single life, travel or country retreats — it is because, for most of us, these disappointments have been tamed by familiarity. We are all so used to them that we feel we have such expectations — or could have them — fairly well under control. As such, they remain comparatively innocent. Of course, the frustrations that result, like any other disappointment, can arouse in us a hidden tendency to revenge ourselves on those with whom we spend our lives or whom we imagine to possess what we lack. Generally, however, we learn to take them for granted, and try to proceed to other matters, if not in our actual lives at least in what we think is reputable to discuss.

But Johnson's vigorous grip on the principal weakness of human nature has subtlety as well as range. He reaches vertically, so to speak, as well as horizontally. With shrewd perception, he discloses the motives, hopes, and frustrations that reach to the philosopher's desk, seeing them not as special reactions, cut off from more familiar desires and fears, but as refinements of them. The underlying sense of community contrasts refreshingly with the usual belief of the sophisticated that they have escaped or lived through the temptations of the unsophisticated. For while they verbally dispose of the hunger for riches, and of the more obvious desires for change of scene and condition — or even, as academic moralists, pin such desires down and describe them — we know very well that exactly these compulsions and others like them are at work within themselves.

The needless demands and the delight in machinery for its own sake that clutter up the pursuit of learning and trivialize it are seen as the product of the same simplicity and 'fallacy of the imagination,' the same confusing of the means with the end, that leads the miser to concentrate on his coins.[22] Usually Johnson cites the way in which scholars dig intently and single-mindedly in what he calls the 'secondary' fields of learning, glorify what they are doing as an end in itself, make a vested interest of it, and self-defensively fight others who seek greater generality. Now, the writer of the *English Dictionary* can hardly be charged with dismissing detailed scholarship lightly. In fact, those who do dismiss it, as Johnson implies, are rarely invigorated by any impelling concern for human values. Johnson's protest is not against labor that requires only 'sluggish resolution' but against a flatness of mind that confuses this with the end. Even more, the protest is against the habit — by which everyone seeks to 'conceal his own unimportance from himself' — of identifying ourselves too exclusively with what we are doing. For we bog down, in our habitual feeling and judgments, into a self-protective and therefore intolerant defense, which is really more of a defense of ourselves than of what we are doing. Since man's powers are limited, 'he must use *means* for the attainment of his ends.' [23] But the immediate end, when attained, is — and should be — found to be 'only one of the means to some remoter end. *The natural flights of the human mind are not from pleasure to pleasure, but from hope to hope.'* [24] Unless we feel what we are doing is important, we should neglect it — and neglect it, in all probability, not for something better but for something worse. The weakness is that, in learning as in other human activities, we institutionalize, and then seal and arm this fortress instead of keeping it open by trying constantly to generalize, to extend our vision, and to see what 'can be put to use' for daily human needs. Too often the aim is merely to keep or 'advance reputation' within a specialized groove. At the very least there is the temptation to use knowledge rather to '*diversify conversation* than to *regulate life.'* Johnson could say this while maintaining that curiosity is, 'in great and generous minds, the first passion and the last; and perhaps always predominates in proportion to the strength of the contemplative faculties.' [25]

One of the *Ramblers* (No. 61) describes a rustic who, after returning from London to his native village, took care to crowd his talk with 'names of streets, squares, and buildings' with which he knew his hearers to be 'unacquainted,' and 'when any of his phrases were unintelligible, he could not suppress the joy of confessed superiority.' In the eighteenth century, polite conversation was more frequently sprinkled with historical allusions to antiquity than the more compartmentalized talk of today. The Punic Wars became a stock symbol to Johnson of talk that 'carried one away from common life' without really extending 'ideas':

> He never (as he expressed it) desired to hear of the *Punic war* while he lived: such conversation was *lost time* (he said) . . . I asked him once [Mrs. Thrale goes on] concerning the conversation powers of a gentleman [Charles James Fox] . . . 'He talked to me at club one day . . . concerning Cataline's conspiracy — so I withdrew my attention and thought about *Tom Thumb*.' [26]

The use of knowledge for the sake of learned allusions — knowledge to impress others, 'advance reputation,' or make the day less 'vacuous' for oneself — is so obvious an example of devoting the mind to 'employments that *engross*, but do not improve it' that few people fail to recognize it. Less innocent, perhaps, is the openly analytic thinking about human values — in life, literature, or anything else — continued solely for its own sake apart from the end that gives it relevance and dignity. This has its own obvious and comic side, of course. While the moralist is analyzing the emptiness of ambition, we can only too often find him swelling 'with the applause he has gained by proving that applause is of no value' [27] (we may contrast Johnson's honest reminder that 'the applause of a single human being is of great consequence'). But the real danger is that it subtly encourages ourselves and others to believe that analysis for its own sake is the proper aim and indication of intelligence. The potential hypocrisy is greater if only because such analysis seems intellectually more respectable. It satisfies the imagination more quickly that something is being done which is immediately relevant to human values. Johnson's own greatest pleasure, as Mrs. Thrale said, was in 'metaphysical reasoning.' The delight in an incisive analytic thinking that could 'fill the mind,' even when pursued for its own sake, had a powerful attraction for him, as his literary criticism especially shows. But there is always the swing back to remember that, in technical analysis or incisive ingenuity when pursued apart from the broad concern of actual human development, there is just as much pedantry, just as much a sidetracking of effort into means, as in collecting and redistributing brute knowledge. It is the light verbalizing — however sharply analytic — about human ends and conduct that Imlac has in mind when he cautions Rasselas that the philosophers lecturing on ethics 'discourse like angels, but they live like men.' And when Rasselas himself visits a learned society, he finds that, however the members differ in other ways, 'every one was pleased to hear the genius or knowledge of another depreciated.' [28]

8

Even when our motives are as pure as human nature is able to attain, an inevitable simplification follows the process of *idealizing* — the process of plucking out from experience an ideal, a pattern, or a form. For we then find that details do not precisely fit it. 'He that has abilities to conceive perfection, will not easily be content without it'; and since perfection cannot be reached, he may neglect the chance of doing anything in the hope of impossible excellence.[29] Not that we are for

86

this reason to throw over ideals, or become embittered like Swift. Rather, it follows that we should nuance and inform our ideals with practical judgment, and watch lest we narrow charity and even our own experience by prematurely recoiling from what fails to fit exactly into our ideals. Yet almost any ideal, however objectively based, is bound to be somewhat smoothed out and simplified by the human imagination. It will be at best an abbreviation of reality. Hence, as Johnson notes, the disappointment or irritability of so many scholars, critics, or philosophers, when they are faced with all the concrete problems and exceptions which they have previously hoped to settle or iron out by clean-shaped theory. Hence also their love of system and definition, and the tendency of some of them to eulogize the past; for all the accomplishments of a lengthy past are blended together in their imagination with such density as to make the smaller unit of the present seem, by contrast, hopelessly sterile. The habit of idealizing, although no development is possible without it, can still create states of expectation and anxiety that are a mixed blessing; and the problem becomes acute when it turns on ourselves, creating a self-expectation that intimidates our inventive originality. This, as Johnson recognizes, is a real problem in literature as it becomes more self-conscious. Also, in what we talk or write about, we become afraid to deal with what is most important, as he says, because we feel we can add so little to it, and show ourselves to advantage. We start worrying about frills, occupy ourselves with minor qualifications or embellishments, and, either as a pose or a form of despair, become the victims of our ideal of 'elegance refined into impatience.' But Johnson also touches on other examples, from the stagefright of lecturing to self-consciousness in social gatherings. Bishop Sanderson, anxiously preparing his lectures, 'hesitated so much, and rejected so often,' that when the time came to deliver them he had to present not what was best but what he had at hand. Again, the lecturer who imagines an audience of admirers

> panting with expectation, and hushed with attention, easily terrifies himself with the dread of disappointing them, and strains . . . [to] show his reputation was not gained by chance. He considers that what he shall say or do will never be forgotten; that renown or infamy is suspended on every syllable; and that nothing ought to fall from him which will not bear the test of time. Under such solicitude, who can wonder that the mind is overwhelmed . . . ? Those who are *oppressed by their own reputation,* will, perhaps, not be comforted by hearing that their cares are unnecessary. . . . While we see multitudes passing before us . . . we should remember, that we are likewise lost in the same throng; that the eye which happens to glance on us is turned in a moment on him that follows . . .[30]

'Nothing is more hopeless,' said Johnson, 'than a *scheme of merriment.*' He seems to have found irresistibly amusing the way in which we form a precarious image of ourselves — or the image we imagine others to have of ourselves — and the paralysis we then feel because of our dread of disappointing it. There is the story of the wit who is invited by a friend to dinner and told how many people will be present who have heard of his reputation.[31] Instead of quickening his eagerness, the mere thought of the high expectation with which the company awaits him fills him with anxiety. Lying sleepless all night, he plans out to himself 'the conversation of the coming day,' recollects 'all my topics of raillery,' makes up 'answers to imaginary repartees,' and then shows up at dinner the next day, completely exhausted and 'sunk under the weight of expectation.' Forgetting that mirth cannot operate in a vacuum but needs 'objects,' and that most people are gay or serious by infection, the company is hushed with expectation. Dinner gives only a temporary relief. There is no real context within which his wit can get a start, especially any context like that he had imagined the night before. A few desperate efforts produce 'neither applause nor opposition.' The contagious atmosphere of expectation became so general that, if others uttered remarks 'with timidity and hesitation, there was none ready to make any reply. All our faculties were frozen, and *every minute took away our capacity of pleasing, and disposition to be pleased.*' The effect of self-consciousness, as Johnson returns to this fascinating subject, is seen to apply to all aspects of social and intellectual life arranged by 'preconcerted invitation.' To know that a thing is expected can often stimulate us, particularly in carrying out physical or mechanical actions, where an obvious or clear-cut course of action is indicated. But it can also chill invention, unless we already possess a confidence firmly grounded in experience and habit. The imagination, instead of flowing out to meet new and unexpected objects, recoils into taut or frozen self-defense. And this pause of spirits is then all the more difficult to overcome except through awkward and self-conscious jerks of effort. Johnson mentions how fortunate we are to have set conventions for beginning and ending letters. There would be an appalling loss of time if we had to decide, in every case, the most appropriate method of beginning and closing every letter. He contrasts with this the unfortunate situation of the writer, paralyzed before the blank page, searching for a beginning that will at once ensnare attention, or suggest, with impressive impact, the sum total of all he feels he can later unfold. Again, Johnson pictures a group of wits, invited together for an evening, 'with admirers prepared to laugh and applaud.' But they 'gaze awhile on each other, ashamed to be silent, and *afraid to speak.*' They become discontented both with themselves and each other, and later 'retire to vent their indignation in safer places, where they are heard with attention; their *importance is restored,*' and they 'recover their good humour.' [32]

9

On matters about which we really care, we are not usually convinced until we have seen for ourselves. The relevance of Johnson is not simply that he touches directly on so much that we care about. It is especially to be found in the way his thought proceeds, which is like that of experience itself. For his thinking goes first through everything that will not work, minimizing nothing, sharing in the attraction felt by the human heart, and even expressing that appeal memorably. And only gradually, as one thing after another gives way, do we find left a citadel of unshaken results that have withstood the test. Too often the abstract systems of the philosopher, as Sir Philip Sidney said, teach only those who are 'already taught,' appearing thin, irrelevant, or even visionary to others; while the dramatist can concretely show what happens to human beings under certain conditions, leading us to identify ourselves with them and to take in their experience as our own.

Johnson's own procedure, in other words, is ultimately dramatic, evoking personal sympathies and tapping the reader's own experience. The real actors are not, it is true, individual characters. Even in *Rasselas* the particular characters are only incidental. Instead, the motives and persuasions within this drama are always being gathered up into the great generalizations that rise from its pages. Like characters in dialogue, they give dramatic expression and even dignity to widely different motives and hopes; or, like brief asides or longer soliloquies, they serve as pauses in which human actions break out into reflection or self-knowledge. That the final outline of the action does not emerge easily or mechanically, that it is not cut to order, is a tribute to its genuineness. Like the close of *Rasselas* — a 'Conclusion in which Nothing is Concluded' — the results cannot be put into a rigid, air-tight formula, if only because every new experience will always be somewhat different. The drama, in short, is that of life itself, which is rarely neat in the answers it provides, and in which honest doubts and perplexities still persist. But when conviction does follow, it is the massive conviction that our own experience gives.

III

The Treachery of the Human Heart and the Stratagems of Defense

The majestic opening of *The Vanity of Human Wishes* pictures 'wav'ring man, *betray'd* by vent'rous pride,' lost on paths, dreary and monotonous as well as puzzling, where he 'shuns fancied ills, or chases airy good.' It then moves on to suggest the massive scale of the intense, blindly destructive hopes, ambitions, and enmities that 'helpless man' begins almost unintentionally to project, noting

> How nations sink, by darling schemes oppress'd,
> When Vengeance listens to the fool's request.
> Fate wings with ev'ry wish th' afflictive dart . . .
> With fatal heat impetuous courage glows,
> With fatal sweetness elocution flows . . .

And so the poem develops panoramically, sweeping vertically up and down history, and horizontally through every condition of life, to its climax: 'Pour forth thy fervours for a healthful mind.'

The same generality and sweep pervade the prose writings as they touch on the self-destructive reactions that are native to the human mind, preventing it from being a happy and 'free agent,' and creating traps that close on ourselves as well as others. This clairvoyance could disturb more than reassure. We all know that man only too often turns his short life into a state where 'many of his faculties can serve only for his torment' or the torment of others. But we do not like to dwell on the extent of it. It is too hard a thing to digest; it leaves us feeling rather hopeless; and where 'there is no hope,' as Johnson said, 'there can be no endeavour.' But the moving question of *The Vanity of Human Wishes* continues to reverberate throughout the later prose works;

> *Must helpless man,* in ignorance sedate,
> Roll darkling down the torrent of his fate?

Behind the question is the confidence that the sprawling complexity of man's unwitting self-betrayal can be seen for what it is, and that in some way it can be 'managed' or replaced by something else. In Johnson, the pressing sense of the caged and bewildered struggle of the human heart for freedom prevents him from turning to any quick answer or cheap panacea. His practical humanism grows step by step from a clear-eyed exploration of the nature of this cage and this bewilderment.

In the work of Freud, the principal problem is not, of course, sex, but repression. Johnson's own sense of the working of the human imagination probably provides us with the closest anticipation of Freud to be found in psychology or moral writing before the twentieth century. With the professional compartmentalizing of knowledge during the last century, psychologists, even when they are concerned with the history of their subject, quite understandably do not consult literary works — except for Shakespeare and recent novels — unless their titles suggest that they are immediately relevant to psychology. But Johnson is an exception. The frequency with which he is quoted is a tribute to his clear-sightedness and power of phrase. On the other hand, the remarks generally used are little more than aphorisms in the vein of Hobbes, La Rochefoucauld, and Swift. In fact, their ancestry goes back at least two thousand years to the Greek cynics and sophists. Thus one psychiatrist speaks of the Freudian character of Johnson's thought, and then cites such statements as: 'Children are always cruel . . . Pity is *acquired* and improved by the cultivation of reason'; 'Abundant charity is an atonement of imaginary sins'; 'Nothing is more common than to call our own condition the condition of life.' [1] We could easily multiply the list. For example: 'There is a kind of *anxious cleanliness* . . . characteristic of a slattern; it is the superfluous scrupulosity of *guilt*, dreading discovery, and shunning suspicion.' [2] But that part of Johnson — and it should be stressed that it is only a part — that really anticipates the psychoanalysis of the twentieth century is not to be found in simple thrusts that cut through a sentimental and complacent idealism about human nature. It is to be found in Johnson's studied and sympathetic sense of the way in which the human imagination, when it is blocked in its search for satisfaction, doubles back into repression, creating a 'secret discontent,' or skips out diagonally into some form of projection. The result, of course, is not a series of formal analyses. The essays of the *Rambler*, *Idler*, and *Adventurer* are brief and informal reflections on a wide variety of topics. The insights they contain are to be interpreted by the frequency of themes and the pattern into which they fall as Johnson touches on problems only superficially different.

He had 'studied medicine diligently in all its branches,' said Mrs. Thrale, 'but had given particular attention to the *diseases of the imagination*, which he watched in himself with a *solicitude destructive of his own peace*, and intolerable to those he trusted.' [3] We know something about the range of what Johnson studied — particularly that remarkable book, George Cheyne's *English Malady* (1733). What is most significant in Cheyne is his recognition of the value of counter-activity, of using the dynamic and vital capacity of the human being, instead of suppressing or throttling it. Johnson, who had so fitfully thrown himself into activities that he thought might cleanse or at least 'regulate' his mind, when he had been left stranded from Oxford, could appreciate the insight and develop it outward into a more generalized and more sensitive understanding of the need to exploit and re-direct human energies.

2

The starting-point, in short, is the commonplace we all seem to forget in practice: that the mind is an *activity,* and that if it is not used in one way it will seek satisfaction or at least outlet in other ways. Joined with this is Johnson's sense that growth of 'the healthful mind' consists in establishing active links of sympathy and understanding with what is outside. Conversely, the 'treachery of the human heart' is what isolates the individual. We are using the phrase out of context. It occurs in a discussion of literary criticism, and the opportunity criticism can give us to 'gratify our own pride or envy *under the appearance* of contending' [4] for some standard of excellence that has been violated. But our use of it for more general purposes is justified. It expresses exactly the unwitting betrayal by man of his own ultimate interests which is the theme of *The Vanity of Human Wishes.* The 'treachery' arises from the fact that the natural human desire for security, importance, or re-assurance can so easily become snarled by panic or chronic discontent that our attention is then switched to ourselves. The heart then concentrates solely on what relieves or confirms its own personal ambitions or fears; it begins instinctively to regard others as rivals to be feared or means to be used, and to wall itself still more firmly behind barriers through

95

which only a warped perception of reality filters. The whole range of misunderstandings, rivalries, and resentments that divide human beings from each other is viewed, in short, as the product of imagination acting upon what we now call 'anxiety,' or the chronic, crippling preoccupation with our own problems and fears. Johnson himself uses the word, as when he states that 'anxiety' tends to increase itself. By keeping a man 'always in alarms,' and looking at all costs for safety, it leads him 'to judge of everything in a manner that least favours his own quiet, *fills him with perpetual stratagems of counteraction,*' [5] and, by wearing him out 'in schemes to obviate evils which never threatened him,' causes him to contribute unwittingly to the very situations he fears.

As Johnson discloses them, the recourses most of us take in the face of chronic anxiety may be called — to use current terms — regression, fixation, and the various forms of hostility. But they rarely remain unmingled. Thus the consuming need to simplify life into one all-engrossing ambition or hard-and-fast interpretation — the single-minded fixation on wealth, position, the obsession of being persecuted, or the clinging to a fixed system that will brook no departure in morality, in literary criticism, or anything else — is also shot through with hostility. Certainly most fixations, from secret societies to vested professional interests, from nationalism to militant moral or intellectual systems, are exclusive rather than inclusive. They are a means of keeping others out, of asserting one's own self-hood. Finally, the fixed projections that extend to others what our own inner fears or demands suggest tend more frequently to be hostile than benevolent.

It is reassuring to see Johnson avoid the usual liabilities of a static terminology and at once penetrate to the insights that have been only gradually rediscovered by psychology, during the last half-century, in its long, patient siege of human nature. His ability to do so rounds out and justifies confidence

in other aspects of his thought. Too often, moralists, educators, and poets who preach the vision of man's development
are not inclined to look deeply into the darker, more complex
side of human life. They pick up their trousers or skirts and
tip-toe past it. On the other hand, the sharp-eyed exploration
of human motives — especially in the richly analytic psychology that began at the time of Thomas Hobbes, and has
flowered during the past fifty years — has not always, in its
clinical preoccupations, been kept supple by the large flexible
knowledge that only the history of the arts and sciences —
only the informed and immediate sense of human greatness,
in all its variety — can give us. What we really want, of course,
is the union of hope with complete practicality — the union
of the vision of ideals, which have haunted the mind of man
in its most awake moments, with the clear knowledge of the
pitfalls that embarrass or betray this vision.

3

There is a simple-minded innocence in General Paoli's idle
talk of a South-Sea paradise where there would not be the
same 'causes of dissension' that divide husband and wife in
a 'civilized state,' though Johnson cannot refrain from punc-
turing it: 'they would have dissensions enough, though of
another kind. One would wish to go a hunting in this wood,
the other in that'; [6] and he goes on to imply that if their bicker-
ing were not long enough drawn-out to lead to a deep-rooted
rancor, it is only because the husband could quickly dispose
of the wife in a way in which he could not in a civilized state;
or, at the very least, they would simply part company. There
is innocence in Cowley's desire for rural retreat; in the author,
outwardly nonchalant, who walks about expectantly on the
day he is published in the hope of catching stray comments
about his work; and, to a less degree, the desire for riches has

a certain innocence. On the whole, 'There are few ways in which a man can be more innocently employed than in getting money.' Unless his rapacity has obviously injured others, and has involved gross injustices, it will be generally found that he has only 'disburdened the day' in an activity that is ultimately unrewarding. What he has accumulated will in time be spent or dissipated by others. So, too, with the works of scholars or writers, whose original motives may be far from disinterested, or whose attention seems locked to the means rather than the end. For their exclusive concentration on 'secondary' pursuits of learning may disclose what will benefit others if not themselves. Also, original motives can be purified or enlarged simply by being exposed enough to other values. Finally, a man's self-respect is never to be cheaply swept aside. Few efforts of any sort, Johnson always recognizes, would ever be carried out if we inquired too scrupulously into every possible motive or incentive. The cumulative process of Johnson's thought is thus diagonally upward. For he zig-zags back and forth from one positive and lucid perception to another, correcting or modifying one assertion, rooted though it is in human experience, by sympathetically tapping another view of experience equally genuine and giving it an assertion just as vigorous. But in this large sweep of sympathy there is a partial pause, a cooler and more careful probing of the 'hunger of imagination' as it ricochets or bounds aside into other emotions.

For frustration is rarely simple and final. It can quickly grow fresh horns and claws. In Freudian terms, it commonly transforms itself from suppression — from mere blocking of the end desired or imagined — into *repression*, into a pressing back of the imagination, and the tunneling of desire into new and unexpected veins. The imagination of even the old man in *Rasselas*, for whom everything has 'lost its novelty,' and who believes that 'Nothing is now of much importance beyond myself,' is not at rest. In no one, without the most dangerous risks, can the hate and fear created by constant frustration be turned solely against himself for very long. The mad astronomer, also in *Rasselas,* who has ended believing that he regulates the weather, is only one picturesque outcome of the need for every man to 'conceal his own unimportance from himself.'

But there are subtler methods of concealing our own unimportance which take other forms of projection. The projection may show itself in that constant and uneasy suspicion by which — unless we have been extraordinarily victimized by others — we really betray our own inclinations or guilt.[7] Another familiar reaction is found in the sort of person who, consciously or unknown to himself, tries to inflict 'on others what he had formerly endured himself,' as if to gain some assurance, as Johnson said, that his own suffering and trials have not been wasted. More insidious, because less obvious, are those who seek to enforce on other people moral or legal obligations that they themselves have broken or secretly resent having to follow. They begin to 'extenuate their own guilt' or resentment by making 'vague and general charges upon others,' or by circulating more particular suspicions in the hope that their own attention as well as that of others will 'be employed on any rather than themselves.' But the imagination can take still more 'artful subterfuges.' An individual can ease his guilt by magnifying or dwelling on faults or habits that seem different from his own: 'He then triumphs in his comparative purity, and *sets himself at ease.*'[8] Even here Johnson notes how commonly the quality we censure in another is the counterpart to an 'opposite fault' in ourselves, as if we hoped to transform our own lack into a virtue.

Yet in the hue and cry on others the principal relief is not so much that it distracts public attention from what we fear in ourselves as that it distracts our own. Repeatedly

Johnson supplements his probing of human malice by recalling that it is 'not so much the desire of men . . . to deceive the world as themselves.' [9] But exactly this charity of understanding points up the greater seriousness of what is implied. For self-deception can lock itself up — at least from one's own scrutiny — into a closed cell of apparent virtue, and become water-tight to outside influence or correction. Few human beings, at least consciously, and however uncertain they may be underneath, place any but a favorable interpretation on their own motives. 'It is natural to *mean well*, when only abstracted *ideas* of virtue are proposed to the mind.' We can constantly see the temptation in others — if not ourselves — to substitute 'single acts for habits.' [10] From the reproaches of others or of our own conscience, we can then make an appeal to direct actions, however rare, and interpret our faults not as 'habitual corruptions, or settled practices, but as . . . single lapses.' The practice is evil simply because it involves self-deception. For self-delusion, of whatever sort, tends to grow rather than diminish; there are always 'so many more instigations to evil, than incitements to good.' But the practice of substituting acts for habits, in our estimate of ourselves, is almost universal. If men differ here, the difference is largely one of degree. Even those whose intention is comparatively pure forget the difference between abstract agreement and conduct, 'between approving laws, and obeying them.' So willing is 'every man to flatter himself,' that, by acknowledging 'the obligations of morality, and . . . enforcing them to others,' he 'concludes himself zealous in the cause of virtue.' [11]

In this light, Johnson also discusses slander and most gossip. We do not usually recognize the less attractive feelings that gossip releases, as he suggests, until we find ourselves the subject of it. Often we unavoidably snatch at gossip because of a 'vacuum' or lack of acquaintance with anything else to say. In fact, even among the more intelligent, it is understandably dragged out as a stock resource. But if gossip serves as a helpful means of enlivening neutrality — we may think of the wits he pictures as glaring at each other and then returning to less challenging and more receptive company, where they are free from the sense of rivalry and 'recover their good humor' — it also provides opportunities for displaying a sort of spurious superiority. Like the countryman who returns from London, eager to mention names with which the villagers are unacquainted, or have heard only indirectly, some are always pushing into the foreground of conversation a 'real or imaginary connexion with a celebrated character,' and 'desire to advance or oppose a rising name.' Johnson's almost obsessive dislike of gossiping or telling stories should be regarded as a conscientious attempt to carry out the opposite of a practice he so distrusted. In all the recorded conversations, there are few remarks that can be interpreted as gossip. When pressed to give an account of someone, he would make a clear, concise statement, and then try to turn to other matters. *Rambler*, No. 188 — written when Johnson was at work on the *Dictionary* — provides a perceptive analysis of the eagerness to be accepted that leads us to recount stories or incidents about others, although even here a large arch of sympathy reaches out to recognize the hunger for acceptance and the need of the heart not so much to be 'admired' but to be 'loved.' And one of the ways in which Johnson differs from those romantics of his own period and a generation later who extol a primitive state, is in pointing out that, if rural or solitary people seem to escape this temptation, it is not from superior virtue but only from lack of opportunity.

But the need to be loved, to be accepted, can awaken desires of which we are not always completely aware, and which no longer permit us to be a 'free agent.' Gossip, for example, rarely remains in that uneasy neutrality in which we are able to avoid commitment while trying to 'disburden the day.' It may quickly become a way of 'disburdening' *ourselves,* of giving outlet to that 'ill-humour or peevishness' which is usually 'the symptom of some deeper malady' and suggests an inner poverty that cannot afford generosity.[12]

For example, most falsehoods, especially those that are successful, are really the result of vanity. In lies inspired by malice or the hope of gain, 'the motive is so apparent, that they are seldom negligently or implicitly received; suspicion is always watchful.' But vanity pleases itself 'with such slight gratifications' that its unconscious stratagems are less obvious. Also it takes so many forms that he who would watch her motions can never be at rest: 'fraud and malice are bounded . . . some *opportunity* of time and place is necessary . . . but scarce any man is abstracted one moment from his vanity.'[13] The hidden hunger in this case is not so much to 'impose on others as on ourselves' — to replace our sense of inadequacy by recounting incidents that give us a more vital sense of our own importance. Again, we see how rarely secrets are kept. And yet 'the negative virtues at least' — such as the ability to keep another's confidence — are theoretically within everyone's power. Though it may be difficult for a man to speak or do well, it is 'still easy for him *not* to speak.' But the explanation is simple enough. 'Most men seem rather inclined to confess the want of virtue than of importance,' and 'the vanity of being known to be trusted with a secret, is generally one of the chief motives to disclose it.'[14] The reactions that lead us to betray another's trust ultimately sprout from our sense of our own inadequacy. Speaking of the habit of projecting guilt on others — of acquiring excuses for what he elsewhere calls the 'general hostility, which every part of mankind exercises against the rest' — Johnson states that 'No man yet was ever wicked *without secret discontent';* and the method of easing this chronic discontent must be either to 'reform' ourselves or else to lower others.[15]

4

As the aim of morality is to 'reform' or redirect human appetites and needs toward healthful ends, *envy,* as Johnson treats it, suggests the opposite — the destructive result that occurs when human desires, left to themselves and lacking healthful satisfaction and development, begin to turn into an appetite for 'lowering others.' This desire to relieve 'the sense of our disparity by lessening others, though we gain nothing to ourselves,' is easily the principal 'treachery of the human heart' discussed by Johnson. In fact, the theme of envy crawls like a tortoise through the moral essays, giving way at times to other subjects, but always emerging at the end. In the *Rambler* alone, fifty-seven issues — or well over a fourth — contain either the word itself or the idea. It appears in every context, from the ingrown rancor of rural and village life to the 'stratagems of well-bred malignity' in fashionable life. In professional life, the discussion ranges from the mutual animosity of rival callings — such as the 'malignity of soldiers and sailors against each other,' often 'at the cost of their country' — to the far more alert and individual envy among writers, scholars, and critics. In a sense, the frequency of the term alone becomes almost comic. Even the first paragraph of the *Preface to Shakespeare* is unable to avoid it. That praises are lavished on dead rather than living writers is one of the consolations of those who feel that 'the regard which is yet denied by *envy,* will be at last bestowed by time.' And in the second paragraph following, the idea again shows up: 'his works support no opinion with arguments, nor supply any faction with invectives; they can neither indulge vanity, nor gratify malignity . . .'

But the large place given envy by Johnson is perhaps logical. For the bottle from which this genie is ready to spring and grow is always open. All vices except indolence and envy, as he says, at least need special opportunities. But just as 'to do nothing is always in every man's power,' so envy can operate 'at all times, and in every place.' The direct pursuit of self-interest, if it is to get very far, usually requires 'some qualities not universally bestowed.' It demands some perseverance or effort. 'But envy may act without expense or danger. To spread suspicion . . . to propagate scandal, requires neither labour nor courage.' The ease with which almost every stir of pride or discontent can begin to turn into envy explains its universality, not only among all people, in different ways, but in every stage or aspect of one individual's life. Even in the innocence of the Happy Valley, where all desires are satisfied, Rasselas — in the chapter called 'The Wants of him that Wants Nothing' — finds himself envying the animals if only because, unlike them, he has nothing 'to desire.' The very frequency of envy 'makes it so familiar that it escapes our notice.' Only when a man, who has 'given no provocation to malice, but by attempting to excel,' and who finds himself pursued 'with all the implacability of personal resentment,' and discovers how his habits and misfortunes, or those of his family have been discussed or laughed at, — only then does he learn to 'abhor those artifices at which he only laughed before,' and discover 'how much the happiness of life would be advanced by the eradication of envy from the human heart.' [16]

But most of us are fortunately spared such experiences; we struggle with the effects of envy piecemeal, without knowing our opponent, fencing with it as it appears behind different masks. Thus in professional as well as social life, Johnson notes the motives that create the cult of mediocrity — that smooth the path for those who make us better 'pleased with ourselves,' who never 'harass the understanding with *unaccustomed* ideas' — and, at the same time, the antagonism felt toward those whose strong commitment to ideas, or whose probing queries or skills in argument, disturb our complacency.[17] Our acceptance of those who make us pleased with ourselves, and our resistance to others who do not, may be easily rationalized: we may justify our response in terms of stability of institutions, conventions, or principles. But in the conservative Johnson the treacherous ability of the human imagination to project or rationalize is never forgotten. There is always the salutary reminder — in our moral judgments or in the criticism of literature — that what we may be rushing forward to defend is not so much institutions in society, in literature, or in anything else, as it is ourselves. Perhaps inevitably, Johnson's sensitive insight into the innumerable 'stratagems of self-defense,' to which all of us devote so much of our time, pauses most often for examples among authors and philosophers, scholars or critics. To some extent, his own personal experience vivifies his consideration of this, which contains as much bitterness as Johnson was ever to show. The strong phrasing occurs repeatedly: 'so universal is the dread of unconscious powers'; critics 'whose acrimony is excited mostly by the *pain of seeing others pleased, and of hearing applauses which another enjoys';* people of genuine wit, unless they have enough reputation to shed luster on their hosts, are seldom re-invited to social gatherings, 'being dreaded by the pert as rivals, and hated by the dull as disturbers of the peace'; *'merit rather enforces respect* than attracts fondness'; such is 'the unwillingness of mankind to admit transcendent merit' that, to 'malice and envy,' a single failure 'gratifies'; he pleases most whose talk is full of *'unenvied* insipidity.' The Emperor Seged, in the *Rambler* allegory, innocently hoping 'to avoid offense,' awards liberal prizes to everyone, greater than any had ever expected. But all the recipients found their own 'distinction' unhonored, and 'wanted an opportunity to triumph in the mortification of their own opponents.' We see how commonly even the 'slight mistakes' and personal habits of great men, who may be completely unknown to us personally, are still singled out and dwelt on with obvious relish. If in this, as in other respects, 'mankind is in general more easily disposed to censure than admiration,' it is partly because 'more can detect petty failings than can distinguish or esteem great qualifications.' [18] Others hope to shock their hearers or simply to 'fill the moment' more vividly for themselves. But underneath, in most cases, there is at least some desire to lessen 'the sense of our disparity.' The logical and drastic result of envy is finally to feel an uneasy rivalry with everyone in every way.

Explaining his early life to Rasselas, who is still in the Happy Valley, Imlac tells how his companions, when he first joined a caravan, exposed him to frauds, and led him into situations where he had trouble with officials, 'without any advantage to themselves, but that of rejoicing in the superiority of their own knowledge.' Rasselas cannot believe that man is so depraved as to wish to 'injure another without benefit to himself.' Also, though men are certainly pleased by feeling superior, yet Imlac's ignorance and naïveté being 'merely accidental,' could afford his fellow merchants 'no reason to applaud themselves; and the knowledge which they had, and which you wanted, they might as effectually have shown by warning, as betraying you.'

Something of Rasselas' incredulity seems to persist in Johnson himself, joining with the surprise that men can treat each other so in a world 'bursting with sin and sorrow,' where all of us await the same doom. Nor can Imlac give any answer except to say that 'Pride is seldom delicate, it will please itself with very mean advantages; and envy feels not its own happiness, but when it may be compared with the misery of others.'[19] The most blatant pursuit of self-interest is in a sense preferable to envy. Self-interest simply disregards the rights or feelings of others. But envy leads us into something worse and essentially more destructive — into a state of actually desiring to 'pull others down' for no other reason than that they are not already down. 'I have hitherto,' says Johnson in one of the *Ramblers*, (No. 183), 'avoided that dangerous and empirical morality, which cures one vice by means of another. But envy is so base . . . that the predominance of almost any other quality is to be preferred. . . . Let it therefore be constantly remembered, that whoever envies another, confirms his superiority, and let those be reformed by their pride who have lost their virtue.' Almost every other 'crime,' as he says, is carried out by the help of some quality which *might* have produced esteem or love, if it had been well employed; but 'envy is mere unmixed and genuine evil.' If only on the basis of a higher, more demanding pride, envy can be resisted if we wish 'to maintain the *dignity* of a human being.' Yet, as Johnson's misgivings about the Stoics show, to overturn one form of pride by means of another, and then stop at that point, is not a final or satisfactory solution. Its value is only as a last resource or as an aid or inciter which should then be quickly supplemented with other more lasting aids. But we are not to disregard any help provided the means we use does not take over and create worse complications. 'The cure for the greatest part of human miseries is not radical, but palliative.'[20]

5

Yet there is always the charitable tug back to recall that 'the cold malignity of envy' — the nearest approach to 'pure and unmixed evil' — is projected from our own 'secret discontent.'[21] Johnson reminds us how adolescents, because of

their uncertainty about themselves, are ready to regard everyone who approaches them as 'an admirer or a spy,' confident
that every motion or word is remembered.[22] So with those
professions that, in any external reward they offer, seem to
depend solely on 'reputation.' Johnson speculates how easily
men of genius and learning could control the world if only
they joined together, especially since the anti-intellectualism
of the public is always present to stimulate them into making
such a union. But the friendship of scholars — except among
the most generous — is often like that of celebrated 'beauties';
'as both depend for happiness on the regard of others, on that
of which *the value arises merely from comparison,* they are
both exposed to perpetual jealousies, and both incessantly
employed in schemes to intercept the praises of each other.'
Hence scholars, for example, often end owing little to their
colleagues 'but the *contagion* of diligence,' and 'a resolution
to write, because the rest are writing.' The merchant is fortunate in being able to judge his success by income, and the
physician by cures, but mere 'reputation' is too uncertain and
fluid a measurement of success to give any rest or satisfaction:
it can never be securely held to a fixed standard, especially
among scholars and writers where the reputation desired is
intellectual, arising 'solely from their *understanding,*' and can
hardly be sensed, as Johnson says, except as is involves direct
comparison with others.[23]

Much of the argument — fortunately not all — that we
self-righteously seem to base on principle really arises from the
automatic impulse of human nature to ward off another's
threat to our opinion of ourselves. The pathetic tenuousness
of our own self-confidence is shown by our quickness to defend not only what we think we believe, but what we may
have said casually or argued for only because we had previously lacked anything else to say at the moment. Hence a
dispute on a subject, 'regarded with careless indifference' a

moment before, 'is continued by the desire of conquest, till *vanity kindles into rage,* and opposition rankles into enmity.'[24] And yet a personal reassurance, a more open and generous exchange of personal esteem, would at once collapse these awkwardly colliding balloons. Hate, when it is not produced by the fear of obvious and direct threat, is the product of vanity colliding without such reassurance. And envy is the unsatisfied 'hunger of imagination' as it seeks excuses and further motives for hate.

The purifying of the motives that otherwise create most of the evil and unhappiness of the world is one final theme of all Johnson's work. Not the least of his success is the concrete example of his own compassion, which sees the whole vast network of man's 'stratagems of self-defense' for what it is — as a self-made prison, or web, built largely by projections, fears, or wants, in which the desire is not so much 'to impose on others as on ourselves,' and in which, as 'helpless man' becomes enmeshed with it, his faculties begin to 'serve only for his torment.' The somber elevation already apparent in *The Vanity of Human Wishes* joins with a close empirical charity that never fails to rise above envy and extinguish it by clearly realizing that '*there are none to be envied,* and surely none can be much envied who are not pleased with themselves.' And Johnson at once goes on to add:

> Such is our desire of *abstraction from ourselves,* that very few are satisfied with the quantity of stupefaction which the needs of the body force upon the mind. Alexander himself added intemperance to sleep, and solaced with . . . wine the sovereignty of the world; and almost every man has some art by which he steals his thoughts away from his present state.[25]

The remark is almost a caricature of his thinking. For the word 'stupefaction' at once puts the situation in a surprising, almost comic light. Yet there is also implicit the same charity — the same inability to remain closed to all the possible fears and hopes that can swerve the heart — that led him, as we have mentioned before, to turn on Mrs. Williams when, complaining of men drinking, she wondered 'what pleasure men can take in making beasts of themselves': *'I wonder, Madam, that you have not penetration enough to see the strong inducement to this excess; for he who makes a* beast *of himself, gets rid of* the pain of being a man.'

6

When you feel that your own gaiety, said Imlac to Rasselas,

is counterfeit, it may justly lead you to suspect that of your companions is not sincere. Envy is commonly reciprocal. We are long before we are convinced that happiness is never to be found, and each believes it possessed by others, to keep alive the hope of obtaining it for himself.[26]

The injunction is not one of despair but an injunction for the use of the heart. It is a plea for the cleansing of illusion through compassion, and through the outward reach to sympathetic understanding: an understanding that demands both range of mind and sincerity of feeling, and can never become complete with either alone. In his own practice, exactly this use of the heart is what gives base and reassurance to his thought. Considering how frequently such subjects as envy and hostility recur, it is tempting to turn for explanation to his own long struggle. But it appears that they were something he had to face in others more than himself. The further we go into Johnson's life, the plainer it seems that his aggressive struggle and sense of rivalry had pitched itself so sincerely on the desire for understanding, that it completely avoided the pitfalls of personal jealousy. The success is a tribute to the ability of awareness, however fitfully or aggressively obtained at first, to act formatively, when it is sincerely desired, on one's own experience. Unquestionably, the unhappy youth, caught in the bleak little school at Market-Bosworth, must have felt a sort of general envy of others; and there may have been occasions when it became sharper in the twenty years that followed. Moreover, although Johnson's habit of 'talking for victory' indicates a desire to clarify, to achieve greater certitude, it also discloses a keen sense of rivalry. Indeed, the idea of asserting 'superiority' dodges about and appears in the most unpredictable and amusing ways. Boswell teased him to study the Scottish dialect in the pastoral, *The Gentle Shepherd,* by Allan Ramsay, and offered to help him do so: 'No, Sir, I won't learn it, *you shall retain your superiority by my not knowing it.*' 'Do not,' he once said to Mrs. Thrale, indulge in 'the *superiority* of inattention . . .' We may also feel that here is a certain compensation, or bending over backward, in Johnson's strong Tory regard for social rank. Certainly he disliked those who project their political and social envy so that they wish to 'level *down* as far as themselves; but they cannot bear levelling *up* to themselves.' But it is healthful to recall that there are different ways of compensating, and that they vary in the final result and value. It is as possible to be governed or controlled by compensation as by simpler and cruder motives. But it is also possible to use compensation rather than be used by it — to use it as an aid or a temporary stabilizer, and then in turn to correct or modify it. Johnson might feel it sane and healthful to give a nobleman his due, and yet take issue with others who laughed when Oliver Goldsmith complained of being snubbed by Lord Camden, and state, 'Dr. Goldsmith is in the right. A nobleman ought to have made up to such a man as Goldsmith; and I think it is much against Lord Camden that he neglected him.'

There is a state, in other words, in which pride, however dangerous, has not yet passed into envy, and there is a largeness of perception that can prevent its doing so. No matter how rough his replies, as Reynolds and others stressed, there was never anything that could be called 'little or mean' about him. As compared with Swift, there is something childlike, perhaps humanly reassuring, about even Johnson's most extreme outbursts of pride. Mr. W. B. C. Watkins has cited one of the more marked instances of Johnson's defensive pride that at once links him with and separates him from Swift. We may think of Swift's entry in the *Journal to Stella*, when he talks of sitting next to Lady Godolphin, and trying to talk to her: 'but she would not give me one look or say a word to me . . . *She is a fool for her pains, and I'll pull her down.*' While Johnson was writing the 'Life of Pope,' Boswell spoke to Lord Marchmont, who had known Pope. He officiously made an appointment for Johnson without his permission ('tomorrow at one o'clock') and then bustled off to tell the news to Johnson, who was out at Streatham. Johnson, surprised, taken off-guard, astonished Boswell by suddenly saying:

> '*I shall not be in town to-morrow. I don't care to know about Pope.*' MRS. THRALE: (surprised as I was, and a little angry.) 'I suppose, Sir, Mr. Boswell thought, that as you are to write Pope's Life, you would wish to know about him.' JOHNSON. 'Wish! why yes. If it *rained knowledge* I'd hold out my hand; but I would not give myself the trouble to go in quest of it.' There was no arguing with him at the moment. Some time afterwards he said, '*Lord Marchmont will call on me, and then I shall call on Lord Marchmont.*' [27]

The innocence of the opening statement is increased when we remember not only that it was Boswell who had made the appointment, but that Johnson — restive in his conscience — later called on Lord Marchmont, talked with him, and said afterward, 'I would rather have given twenty pounds than not have come.'

Remembering the struggle to excel, which had become rooted in Johnson's behavior, it is moving to see him, as he grows older, increasingly urging the need for 'good humor.' He turns to the first demand of the human heart: *'it is always necessary to be loved, but not always necessary to be reverenced.'* 'Good humor,' which he defines as *'a habit of being pleased'* will draw people to us when more positive and difficult virtues will not. Without it 'learning and bravery can only confer that superiority which swells the heart of the lion in the desert, when he roars without reply, and ravages without resistance.' [28] Consequently, despite illness and the liabilities of his own temperament, he struggled, as we have noted in the first chapter, to develop a habitual 'willingness to be pleased,' and experienced a high, almost diverting satisfaction on those rare occasions when he could feel that the habit had been acquired. For example, he once turned to Boswell as they were riding in a carriage, stating

> 'It is wonderful, Sir, how rare a quality good humour is
> in life. We meet with very few good humoured men'
> . . . *Then, shaking his head and stretching himself at
> his ease in the coach, and smiling with much compla-
> cency,* he turned to me and said, 'I look upon *myself*
> as a good humoured fellow.' [29]

This valuing of 'good humour' is impressive because it is unillusioned but still active and formative. The moral essays, taken as a unit, contain an almost frightening analysis of the reasons why 'good humour' appeals to the human ego. There is, for example, the little portrait in *Idler*, No. 83, of the man liked by all, whose only problem, when his acquaintances are present and arguing, is 'how to be of two contrary opinions at once,' but who has learned the 'art of distributing his attention and his smiles in such a manner, that each thinks him of his own party.' *Rambler*, No. 188, takes up the reason why the telling of stories is so popular. For one thing, everyone has 'some real or imaginary connexion with a celebrated character, some desire to advance or oppose a rising name.' But ultimately it is because stories are heard 'without envy'; for they imply no 'intellectual qualities above the common rate. To be acquainted with facts not yet echoed by plebian mouths, may happen to one man as well as to another.' But stories wear themselves out; an inexhaustible stock is impossible to attain. Yet 'such is the kindness of mankind to all, except those who aspire to real merit and rational dignity,' that everyone can find some way of exciting benevolence 'if he is not *envied*.' And the irony that Johnson was always trying to check in himself sharply switches to the 'good-natured man,' — whose benevolence largely proceeds from 'indolence' and lack of commitment, who follows the stream of talk wherever it leads, bears jokes without retaliation, and 'retires rejoicing at his own importance' — down to the 'modest man . . . whose only power of giving pleasure is not to interrupt it,' and whose silence his companions interpret as 'proceeding not from inability to speak, but willingness to hear.' In short, Johnson recognizes with trenchant clarity that 'good humour' appeals to men by not '*condemning* them to vigilance and caution,' [30] to insecurity and doubt of their worth.

Yet, seeing all this, Johnson at the same time saw more deeply, returning to the ultimate need, in all individual development, of open receptivity, of the capacity for '*being pleased*.' With a certain personal desperation, perhaps, there is the reminder that, if the passive or opportunistic can appear to be pleased, then it is also possible for the intelligent to be genuinely pleased. It is not only a matter of being loved or accepted — though this is of primary importance to the human heart. It is ultimately that awareness, knowledge of things as they are, and therefore development, result from a largeness of response touched and led by generosity and sympathy. Surely, as he said to Mrs. Thrale, 'delicacy' of taste — which so many seemed eager to show by negative reactions — does not consist in *impossibility to be pleased.* And he ended by feeling that perhaps argument itself was not so valuable after all; that it aroused too many differences, or perhaps stemmed from defenses equally impure. Perhaps more was to be said for the quiet 'interchange' of opinions. Considering Johnson's life and habits of sixty years this final admission was one of the greatest tributes to his capacity to revise himself. The success was not complete, of course. But the old man who, dying, cried out for *new* topicks of merriment, or *new* incitements to curiosity' — who had written to Boswell a few months before, 'Be well when you are not ill, and *pleased* when you are not angry' — is still the opposite of the old man in *Rasselas* to whom 'the world has lost its novelty,' and who feels that 'nothing is now of much importance; for I cannot extend my interest beyond myself.' It is safe to assume that there would have been differences in earlier years too. The first would have been in the quality of sincerity which in Johnson not only included the sense of sharing life with others but involved an inability to think or feel otherwise.

7

The uninhibited Boswell once amused his fellow-spectators during a dull play by lowing like a cow. But he, like almost everyone else, seems to have been puzzled by the quick unpredictability and variety of Johnson's sense of comedy. All of Johnson's friends agreed with Mrs. Thrale that 'No man loved laughing better, and his vein of humor was rich, and apparently inexhaustible.' But what seemed to strike them were just two aspects of it. One was his imaginative play of wit. The other was his surprising delight — virtually forgotten after the nineteenth century began — in farce and playfulness that made him, as the Irish playwright Arthur Murphy said, 'incomparable at buffoonery,' and an 'admirable mimic' despite his 'inflexible' appearance. Certainly a part of the constant delight, as at least two of his friends implied, lay in the contrast of this ready mimicry with the 'inflexible features,' and also with the large brooding majesty of Johnson's face in repose. Even the dour Sir John Hawkins thought that 'In the talent of humour there hardly ever was his equal, except perhaps among the old comedians, such as Tarleton, and a few others mentioned by Cibber'; and Hawkins goes on to add how much this side of Johnson 'disconcerted' grave people, like the scholar, William Warburton.[31] Also, it is plain, from a contemporary account, that some of the antics that the rather prim Miss Reynolds interpreted and passed on to posterity as mere neurotic explosions — such as suddenly turning and seating himself on the back of his chair — have a different context from the one she suggests. They are outbursts of a 'childish playfulness,' quite on a par with his imitation of the kangaroo in Scotland, or the morning when he surprised Boswell by imitating Lady Macdonald, 'leaning forward with a hand on each cheek and her mouth open.'

By sheer infection, this active exuberance could be caught and shared by others. But there are occasions when, instead of acting it out, Johnson seems to stand aside, almost as a passive spectator. Then it is that, in place of mimicry and playfulness, we have simply the 'immoderate laughter' that so puzzled his friends. This quick leap of the comic sense into a dimension that they could not reach appears to result when the enormous pressure in Johnson's effort at self-control and self-direction momentarily suspends the excuse he is usually finding for human motives, and instead the shams and self-deception in human nature are suddenly seen, as in slow motion or a still picture, with terrible clarity, and with something of the uncanny and huge mockery of Swift. One such instance is told by Boswell, who was at a loss to account for it, but thought it made an interesting contrast to what 'might be expected from the author of "the Rambler."' Forcing himself out into company, though he 'continued to be very ill,' Johnson visited the eminent lawyer, Robert — later Sir Robert — Chambers at the Temple. He seemed to feel better as the conversation grew more animated. The talk turned on male succession in noble families, which Johnson defended with enthusiasm, and it then switched to the will of Johnson's friend, Bennet Langton, which had been drawn up that day by Chambers, and which left Langton's estate to his sisters — whom Johnson called 'three *dowdies*' — in preference to the nearest male cousin. Then the account continues:

I have known him at times exceedingly diverted at what seemed to others a very small sport. *He now laughed immoderately, without any reason that we could perceive,* at our friend's making his will; called him the *testator*, and added, 'I daresay, he thinks he has done a mighty thing. He won't stay till he gets home to his seat in the country . . . he'll call up the landlord of the first inn on the road; and, *after a suitable preface upon mortality and the uncertainty of life,* will tell him that *he* should not delay making his will; and here, Sir, will he say, is *my* will, which I have just made, with the assistance of one of the ablest lawyers in the kingdom . . . (*laughing all the time*). He believes he has made this will; but he did not make it: you, Chambers, made it for him. I trust you had more conscience than to make him say, 'being of sound understanding;' ha, ha, ha! . . . *I'd have his will turned into verse, like a ballad.'*

In this playful manner did he run on . . . Mr. Chambers . . . seemed impatient till he got rid of us. Johnson could not stop his merriment, but continued it all the way till we got without the Temple-gate. He then burst into such a fit of *laughter, that he appeared to be almost in a convulsion;* and, in order to support himself, laid hold of one of the posts . . . and sent forth peals so loud, that in the silence of the night his voice seemed to resound from Temple-bar to Fleet-ditch.[32]

It is all there, though the context is rather grim and extreme. The long habit of meeting vanity and self-deception by immediately piercing through them now lunges out almost automatically, under the pressure of illness and accumulated past effort. Also, Johnson's life-long struggle against the mere idea of death is suddenly stirred awake by the thought of the death of a close friend. Here both the obsession and recoil from death are instinctively controlled by focusing on one related aspect, the making of a will, plucking it out into the bright air of comedy, and then pushing it, as with a giant's hand, farther ('laughing all the time'), as he piles one image on another. Here is the picture of Langton 'filling the *vacuities* of life,' '*disburdening* the day,' momentarily feeling more alive and significant as 'the *testator,*' gratified at his magisterial power to bestow or deny, and doubtless imagining to himself the waves of gratitude or dismay he will have caused by this 'mighty thing.' Then, we have Langton, impressed with his own act, speaking gravely, in stock terms, about 'mortality and the uncertainty of life' (one thinks of the ominous line about self-deception in *The Vanity of Human Wishes*, 'The secret *ambush* of a *specious prayer*'), and advising others to follow his example. The whole sense of the meaningless and 'incessant competition for superiority' — which will satisfy itself with the most trivial advantages — is also brought into play here. There is the picture of Langton 'invigorating' his own new significance still more by mentioning, to the open-mouthed innkeeper, that his own will has now been drawn up 'with the *assistance* of one of the ablest lawyers in the kingdom' ('everyone has a real or imaginary connexion with a celebrated character'). Pushing still farther, we have the merry Langton — now sobered and enlarged in his new role as '*testator*' — fast feeling it was he himself who has made this document ('but he did not make it: *you*, Chambers, made it *for* him').

Behind it all is the vast, fatigued sense of *The Vanity of Human Wishes*, of the flurry, the ultimate waste and triviality of hypocrisy and self-deception throughout every part of life. Only, at this moment, Johnson's almost endless capacity for charity seems partly suspended. Instead, the realization condenses itself into the final, puzzling tag: 'I'd have his will turned into *verse*, like a ballad.' It is like the spritely, macabre lines in ballad meter, made up on the spur of the moment, that Johnson cried out to the young daughter of the Thrales as she deliberated solemnly with a friend about a new gown and hat that she was to wear to an assembly:

> Wear the gown, and wear the hat,
>   Snatch thy pleasures while they last;
>   *Hadst thou nine lives like a cat,*
>   *Soon those nine lives would be past.*[33]

When the young Fanny Burney, now a frequent visitor at the Thrales' house at Streatham, brought out her novel, *Evelina*, her main interest for some months seems to have been in recording the constant flattery that the fashionable and intellectual showered on it, and their persuasions that she should now devote her satirical power to *dramatic* comedy. So suffocating and persistent does this flattery become in reading her diary, especially that which she quotes from Johnson, who so rarely 'read books *through*,' that we feel a sense of relief in finding him admit to John Opie the painter — when asked whether he really thought *Evelina* so good: 'I never read it through at all, *though I don't wish this to be known.*[34] Finally, one morning after breakfast, occurs a scene when all at once the whole superstructure of pointless flattery and the polite protestations with which we are all led to 'fill the day' and 'vivify importance' are viewed as a dramatic comedy; and a comedy in which Johnson sees himself as clearly as anyone else could — 'disburdening the day' in his own way, bandying flattery with the young authoress, grotesque and lonely, fretful at being left when the women went to a ball, and insisting on going with them, ill and deaf as he was, rather than stay alone. But Fanny Burney's only comment is, 'How little did I expect from . . . this great and dreaded lord of English literature, a turn for burlesque humour.' But it is not burlesque only. Behind it, as Mr. Watkins said, is 'a more devastating laughter of intellect from a man who saw through all pretense and hypocrisy, even his own, with a terrible clarity.' After breakfast at Streatham, the talk again flowed 'copiously,' said Fanny, urging her to 'produce a comedy.' While Mrs. Thrale was in the midst of her 'flattering persuasions,' the two women suddenly noticed that Johnson,

> see-sawing in his chair, began laughing to himself so heartily as to almost shake his seat as well as his sides. We stopped . . . hoping he would reveal the subject of his mirth; but he enjoyed it inwardly, without heeding our curiosity, — till at last he said he had been

struck with a notion that 'Miss Burney would begin her dramatic career by writing a piece called *Streatham.*'

He paused, and laughed yet more cordially, and *then suddenly commanded a pomposity* to his countenance and his voice, and added, 'Yes! *Streatham — a Farce!*' [35]

8

That Johnson is so far from being a comic writer is a fact of some significance. For most of what makes up the comic sense is abundantly present. To begin with, there are the strong accumulated pressures of which Freud speaks, built up throughout a lifetime of precarious effort. Mr. Watkins, in quoting Boswell's account of Langton's will, with its bewildered description of Johnson's violent and prolonged laughter, aptly appends the great lines from *King Lear:* 'O! how this mother' — this welter and surge of feeling —

> swells up toward my heart;
> *Hysterica passio!* down, thou *climbing* sorrow!
> Thy element's *below!*

But the subjective need for outlet is only one element; for it is met and matched at the same time by the perceptive intelligence, by the close notice of detail and the immediate ability to generalize, which are necessary to make the comic sense into something more than a mere outlet for pressure. There is also a third element, which is particularly relevant in considering Johnson. It involves his own intimate and honest participation.

We cannot deal with morbid and destructive fears and impulses, as he told Boswell, simply by suppressing them ('to think them down is madness'). Part of the relief we find in comedy is that, instead of blocking feelings that disturb us, it joins with them, and allows them to propel themselves by their own momentum while it steers them around into a new context. Even mere mimicry can serve as a way of deflecting our reactions or getting them under some kind of control. Hence the tendency of people to mimic those whom they resent or fear, or to enjoy watching them mimicked by others. Reduction through caricature is, in fact, one of the common means by which fear or resentment can be turned into something less threatening and more manageable. Unquestionably the temptation for Johnson to use ridicule in this way was strong. His inability to yield to the temptation is one of the fascinating things about him. His habitual ways of meeting threat or pressure of any kind involve the courage of direct encounter, and the attempt to bring a fuller knowledge to bear.

But mimicry can also serve less malicious purposes, where what we are instinctively trying to control is not so much the threat of others as the pressure of our own desires, or our dissatisfaction with something in ourselves. Here we may simply burlesque what we are feeling, if we are histrionically inclined. Or, more commonly, we enjoy watching, in the expressions or actions of others, an exaggerated counterpart to what we are feeling, put on another stage, and made harmless beneath a comic light. Seeing it in this outside context, embodied in what Santayana calls a 'correlative object,' we can then view it with more detachment. And there is the further relief, of course, in discovering that we have companionship. The great comic characters in literature affect us in exactly this way. They do — only more openly — (as Johnson said of Don Quixote and his day-dreams) what most of us are half afraid we do anyway, or else what we should like to do if we only dared. This use of comedy, kept generous and therapeutic as long as one's own participation is acknowledged, is always present in Johnson. It lends the sharp notice that only direct personal acquaintance can give, while remaining honest about itself. What Sir John Hawkins said about Johnson's gift for innocent mimicry — that despite his bad sight and inflexible features he could 'discriminate' with the nicest exactness the character of those whom it concerned, in a way rivaled only by the 'old comedians' — also applies to the humor that lurks in the moral essays, and breaks out in the satiric portraits scattered through them. For the exactness and fidelity with which Johnson senses motives, blows them up, and then punctures them after edging them into the absurd are largely based on his own self-perception; but they persuade because the admission of his own participation is so honestly implicit. The obsessive desire for 'change of place'; the dreams of primitive romantic love, mocked in the little Eskimo Idyll he wrote for the *Rambler*, while years later Bishop Percy could still find him avidly reading 'romances of chivalry'; the appetite for fame — the newly published author steeling himself to bear adverse comments on the book no one has ever noticed, while those who have arrived, or think they have, are seen as now 'oppressed by their own reputation' — in almost every aspect of the 'hunger of imagination which preys incessantly upon life,' and which is 'always breaking away from the present moment,' Johnson's latent sense of the comic involves a self-burlesque.

Even in the episode of Langton's will, the direct sharing is present, though less obvious. The picture of Langton as now 'the *testator*' plucks up, from the ill and fatigued Johnson, and burlesques all the self-conscious weight of statement that he himself brings to bear, whether in the legal briefs he dictates to Boswell, or in the great opening paragraphs of the *Preface to Shakespeare* with their finality of phrase and their conscious sense of being bequeathed to posterity. As for Langton giving the inn-keeper a 'suitable preface upon mortality and the uncertainty of life,' what writer has composed more of them than the author of *The Vanity of Human Wishes?*

And no one was more aware of this than Johnson himself, who begins a letter to the *Rambler* (No. 109) by saying 'Though you seem to have taken a view sufficiently extensive of the miseries of life . . . you have not yet exhausted the whole stock of human infelicity.' He then goes on to picture the author of the *Rambler*, delighted at receiving this letter, locking the door, and sitting down to 'enjoy a new calamity without disturbance.' There is self-perception also as he cuts through pretense in human institutions, even those he strenuously defends with his informed and vital conservatism. Certainly his Tory sympathies were not a whim. They were based on real reasons. But he was still able to see these reasons for what they were — as tentative, uncertain, perhaps groping, always incomplete. He could disarmingly admit that he thought he had certain merit 'in being zealous for subordination and the honours of birth; for I can hardly tell who was my grandfather,' and at the same time he could reproach the elder Pitt for 'feudal gabble.' It is significant that the background to the incident of Langton's will was Johnson's defense of male succession, his dismissal of the women who were to receive the estate as 'three *dowdies*,' and his spirited talk about keeping up noble families. As he plunges into the subject, the perception of himself and the whole scene immediately triggers the explosive laughter that follows — the irritable, ailing Johnson, so 'zealous' for the 'honours of birth,' when he could 'hardly tell who was my grandfather,' bringing out his stock shibboleths, and using strong talk out of all proportion to the subject, as he sits there in the Temple, with the prim, professional Chambers and the open-eyed Boswell. It is like the incident, years before, when he visited Plymouth with Sir Joshua Reynolds. A new, rival town, 'Dock-Yard' (now Devonport), was being built two miles off, and was petitioning to use the water-supply of Plymouth:

Johnson, affecting to entertain the passions of the place, was violent in opposition: and *half-laughing at himself* for his pretended zeal . . . exclaimed, 'No, no! I am against the *dockers:* I am a Plymouth man. Rogues! Let them die of thirst. They shall not have a drop!'

And at the beginning of the long cascade of laughter about Langton's will we can see something of the self-burlesque we find three months later when, on the tour through Scotland, he strutted grotesquely about with a Scottish warbonnet on, or when MacLeod of Skye playfully offered to give Johnson the little island of Isay, on condition Johnson would live there one month a year. Johnson grew increasingly merry: 'I have seen him please himself with little things, even with mere ideas . . . He talked a great deal of this island — how he would build a house, how he would *fortify* it.' And then, immediately seeing himself as he really was, and delighting in the title, *Island Isay,* which he said he would assume, he went on, telling

> how he would have cannon . . . how he would sally
> out and *take* the Isle of Muck; *and then he laughed
> with a glee that was astonishing, and could hardly
> leave off.* I have seen him do so at a small matter that
> struck him, and was a sport to no one else. Langton told
> me that one night at the Club he did so while the com-
> pany were all grave around him; only Garrick in his
> smart manner addressed him, 'Mighty pleasant, sir;
> mighty pleasant, sir.' [36]

This self-participation of Johnson provides relief not so much by blunting the effect of ridicule as in diffusing its effect through general sharing. The writer or comedian who includes himself in comic exposure, who himself shoulders much of the weight of its impact, makes less of a demand. We ourselves are less on the defensive, and are readier to follow the contagion of example. The rather fatiguing effect of what is easily the most intricate and brilliant satire in literature, Swift's *Tale of a Tub*, may be partly explained in this light. Ultimately its audience consists of critics or other writers; it is a scholar's or writer's satire; and few scholars or writers have really found it very laughable. In the last of its many levels, it may be satirizing satire, including itself. But Swift — who supposedly laughed only twice in his life, once when he read Fielding's *Tom Thumb*, and another time in watching a juggler — is present, if at all, only as a lynx-eyed and sardonic observer, who holds all the cards. Comic relief, like any other, involves repose and reassurance as well as release. For mere release, by itself, cannot last very long.

Bergson has a point, however, in saying comedy rests on a 'momentary anesthesia of the heart.' Concern, if it is too avid, can blot out the comic sense, replacing it either with mere earnestness or else with a sympathetic identification that is too intense to permit laughter. And in Johnson the participation is so strong that burlesque is only a temporary thing. He seems instinctively to realize that, if we dwell too long on the incongruity between reality and appearance, between human motives and the pretense, the exuberance will soon pass. In its place will be a state of mind essentially destructive — a state the opposite of a 'willingness to *be pleased*' — which will begin to rationalize and project its discontent. If Swift's letters offer any evidence, said Johnson, 'he was not a man to be either loved or envied. He seems to have wasted life in discontent, by the rage of neglected pride and the languishment of unsatisfied desire." [37] What Johnson says is true enough. But his instinctive recoil from Swift — and partly because he was in some ways temperamentally akin — was strong enough to warp his whole estimate of Swift's work. This is rare for Johnson. Despite casual statements about other writers, torn out of context and repeated by Victorian critics, we now believe that Johnson is really unfair, in his total judgment, to only one author, Swift. The reaction to Swift illustrates why Johnson could never be a comic writer in the strict sense of the word. He had an 'aversion,' said Mrs. Thrale, 'to general satire' of any sort. So honest and experiencing a nature was too much aware of the force of circumstances which comedy — almost by definition, in so far as it is a 'momentary anesthesia of the heart' — must disregard when it unclothes and exposes hypocrisy and self-delusion.

Still, the compassion of Johnson does not so much destroy the comic sense as fill it out, for the moment, in a richer form, and then afterward gather it back into sympathetic understanding. Nothing so much distinguishes him from the greatest of satirists as his own immediate sympathy for anything from which his intellect tears away the veil, and his endearing willingness not only to acknowledge that he shares in it but actually to plunge in, voluntarily, and increase it. The object is never a 'you' alone, but a 'we,' as in the little imaginary playlet, *Streatham — a Farce*. Resolving repeatedly to rise in the morning, despairing of his own lack of will in failing to do so, he could still, when friends dropped in during the morning, sense the grotesque contrast between his own cluttered room and a royal levee in a palace chamber; and the laughter that followed could include the comedy of self-awareness. This was the Johnson whose nights, as he approached seventy, were 'full of misery,' and yet, when Boswell stopped by before he was up, called him to his bedside, crying out 'in the gaiety of youth,' to Francis Barber, 'Frank, go and get coffee, and let us *breakfast in splendour.*' And there is the little scene during the tour through Scotland, when he is told one morning that a friend has received a pension.

Sitting bolt upright in bed, a knotted handkerchief crowning his head, he clapped his hands at this regal news, and — using 'a peculiar exclamation of his when he rejoices' — cried out happily, 'O brave *we!*'

IV

THE STABILITY OF TRUTH

FREEDOM IS THE HARMONY of the inner life with truth. If we consult our hearts honestly, we find that most of the obstacles that prevent us from attaining this harmony come not from the difficulty of discovering what the truth is but from the resistance we ourselves make. Hardly a day passes, for example, without our hearing or reading something to which we assent as true. Yet at the very moment our own lives will be contradicting our assent. The pull of our feelings, with their subterranean swell from one hope or fear to another, will still be sweeping through us in the same way as before. We may agree to what we hear, and recall 'single acts' if not 'habits' of our own that support us. But at the same time over half of our mind may be secretly agitated in 'shortening the way to some new possession' or in ruses to protect what we think we already possess. To say that the reason is that we do not really care enough is only superficially true. In fact, it is precisely because the desire for both light and happiness presses so strongly on us that we are led to defeat our own hope. Our eyes strain so hard in one particular direction, and we become so engrossed in what we hope to get from one particular means, that the dim shape of this expectation hangs over our attention and magnetizes our imagination, and we

THE ACHIEVEMENT OF SAMUEL JOHNSON

have room to give only passive assent to more abstract truths.
Nor is this conscious hypocrisy. We always feel, as Johnson
says, that there will be some later opportunity to give them a
fair try when the immediate interest claiming our attention
is satisfied. As critics or educators, we may make an occupation of studying the precepts and methods of moralists, and
yet repeat, embroider, and confute them primarily to 'advance reputation or to keep it.' Not that this is a weakness
of intellectuals. They simply use a more elaborate vocabulary
in the process. Those less verbal can be equally occupied in
invoking, for ulterior purposes, principles and virtues they
themselves do not follow. Unlike thinner moralists, Johnson
not only takes such incentives into account. He expresses
and even protects them; they are a part of the forward,
propulsive movement of life itself.

2

The truth is that *'reformation'* — the re-molding and developing of human nature — 'is seldom the work of pure virtue or *unassisted* reason.' [1] Repeatedly Johnson recurs to the
salutary principle that 'activity' carries within itself its own
possible 'reformation.' [2] To paraphrase his own favorite illustration, the man who is walking north, for whatever reason,
may more easily swing about and start moving west, if that is
the desirable direction, than the man whose legs are paralyzed
or who is still debating whether or not to leave his arm-chair.
The 'hunger of imagination which preys incessantly upon life'
wakes up and keeps prodding motives and desires that gradually weave the whole superstructure of the 'vanity of human
wishes,' with its complex webs of envy, fear, and projection, of
ambition and the craving for novelty and change. But this
same glancing 'before and after' also underlies everything
that gives man superiority over other animals. Hence the prob-

lem is to use this capacity, which distinguishes us from the 'torpid insensibility' that 'lacks nothing of the carcase but putrefaction,' rather than to *be* used by it as it accidentally latches itself to 'fancied ills' or 'airy goods.' We work through and by means of the immediate experience of our senses and imaginations. To disregard them — to put them, with their piled store of experience, erroneous or not, on the defensive — is futile, even if we wished to do so. They would remain just as active if the door were closed against them. But instead of moving toward a salutary end, their 'chase,' in Dryden's phrase, would then have 'a beast in view,' in any of the numberless shapes that fear, envy, or desire can project. So, when Boswell tossed off the suggestion that morbid fears or compulsions could be dealt with by trying to 'think them *down*,' Johnson replied that 'to attempt to *think them down* is madness,' and that the '*management of the mind* can be acquired only gradually,' by experience and habitual exercise.[3]

3

'We are more pained by ignorance, than delighted by instruction.' With a kind of fascination, Johnson recurs to the way in which we automatically begin to disagree — at least in feeling — whenever we are put on the defensive. We may think how Johnson's friends, simply by praising anyone or anything too much, could always goad him into taking a different stand. So if our past experience and feelings are brushed aside or disregarded by what we are trying to learn, there will be no welcome assimilation or growth, no excited and open inner agreement between ourselves and what we are experiencing. One issue of the *Rambler* (No. 87) discusses the reasons why we fail to react eagerly to knowledge, incorporate it quickly, and start to build on it. Johnson begins, in characteristic fashion, by citing the resistance our own vanity and sense of rivalry throw out against what we are learning. For example, the 'vanity of giving advice' — simply because of its 'appearance of superiority' — arouses in us an even greater vanity to resist the advice, 'without any very accurate inquiry whether it is right.' But then we also find that, in some people, 'the softest language or most humble diffidence' can still arouse resentment, 'since scarcely any degree of circumspection can prevent . . . the rage with which the slothful, the impotent, and the unsuccessful, *vent their discontent upon those that excel them,*' even if they do so only in the quality of 'modesty.' Also, we might suppose that, in the *reading* of books, at least, 'many temptations to petulance and opposition, which occur in oral conferences,' could be avoided. An author, after all, cannot '*obtrude his services unasked,* nor can he be often suspected of any malignant intention to insult his readers' by showing his superiority. But 'so prevalent is the habit of comparing ourselves with others' that books are rarely read with complete impartiality except when the writer is safely dead. Yet even in this case we see how 'a student may easily exhaust his life in comparing divines and moralists' without this influencing his conduct in the least, and how, for most scholars and critics, the purpose is 'either to consume those hours for which they can find no other amusement' or to 'gain or preserve that respect which learning has always obtained.' Now in this case the writers studied are not directly obtruding *themselves* 'unasked.' But something else is plainly doing it for them, and we become inwardly indifferent to the real human significance of what we are reading. For example, the ulterior motives that push us to study them in the first place are obtruding the writers on us in a way hardly likely to open the heart.

We also find that we can actually throw before ourselves ideals or principles that we know to be completely valid. They will not only seem abstractly right to the intellect, but we can also see that they allow for our own emotions and past experiences — that they even shelter and clarify them. And yet we can still fail to feel personally involved and interested in the way we believe we should be. One has only to think of Johnson himself, after the nine-year period during which the bulk of his moral writing was done, falling into a painful apathy, increasing with every year as he delayed the work on Shakespeare, until finally '*Such a torpor had seized his faculties,*' according to Hawkins, 'as not all the remonstrances of his friends' could penetrate: 'Johnson felt them not.' The obvious conclusion is that something in human nature is mulish, rebellious, or sealed over with protective armor, if only because we are on the defensive against what we expect from ourselves. For something, in such a case, is plainly 'obtruding' itself on us; and, if everything else has been fully allowed for, it can only be a part of ourselves that is doing so. The resistance to the advice of others is only a more obvious counterpart — perhaps largely a result — of the deeper resistance, within our divided selves, to our own demands. We become most antagonized by others, as Johnson reminds us, when their advice or criticism confirms what we suspect or fear in ourselves.

The primary resistance, in other words, comes from ourselves, and this includes not only the way in which we resist what others demand but also what we expect or furtively hope from ourselves. This is not to say that the principal driving-force of all human beings is self-admiration. It is only to say that the desire to assert or participate, as Johnson realizes, winds through all our feelings. The balking or misuse of this need to declare ourselves through the stability of action, through some form of assertion, may spawn most of the evils of life, including the desire to dominate others. But the constructive use of this need for recognition and activity is still necessary to all achievement. The greatest evil of poverty — what makes it an obstacle to virtue — is that the pain of destitution, as Johnson saw, can prevent us from thinking of any other need or value. So with the cravings not only of our own egos, of our own sense of importance, but of all primary feelings. If squelched or neglected, they leave us little leisure to think of anything else. But if they are actively used, permitted to contribute, and thus find their own reassurance, they then free the caged aspiration of the spirit to lift its need for reassurance to another and freer plane.

4

The 'hunger of imagination,' with all it means, and the 'stability of truth,' thus form the twin poles between which Johnson's practical insights into human life and destiny move back and forth. Characteristic of the former is the theme of *The Vanity of Human Wishes* itself; and his exploration of it, in the great moral writing of the following decade, could be described as an expansion of the book of Ecclesiastes. More specifically, it is patterned after one of the most powerful books on practical religion and conduct since Pascal — William Law's *Serious Call to a Devout and Holy Life* (1728). This, as Johnson said, was the first work to turn his thoughts seriously to religion. He had picked it up at Oxford, 'expecting to find it a dull book (as such books generally are,) and perhaps to laugh at it. But I found Law quite an overmatch for me.' The procedure of Law's *Serious Call* is to touch, one by one, upon the particular hopes or ambitions which the restless imagination of man creates, to note how every possession grows stale or turns to 'ashes in the mouth,' and to illustrate, step by step, how the human heart can find repose and final direction only in religion. So, following the prototype of Law — which in turn follows the pattern of Ecclesiastes — Johnson, with more perception than Law, moves from hope to hope, and through every form of life, domestic or professional. This sharp and spacious view has in it something of the intention of ancient Stoicism to bring a lynx-eye to all human pretensions and hopes — to note, as Marcus Aurelius said, that the purple senatorial robe, with all its pomp, is only the wool of a sheep dyed with the blood of a shell-fish.

But as this long ebb-tide recedes, laying bare the weak and sandy foundation of what we build our hopes on, we also find rising into prominence the second major theme of Johnson's moral writing: that despite the transitoriness of things, despite the chronic lack of satisfaction our ambitions bring, the first need of the heart is to turn outward and avoid paralysis and self-concentration. 'In order to *regain liberty*' — in order to free human capacities toward an end that will give them fruition and development — man must still exploit every 'means of flying from *himself;* he must, *in opposition to the stoick precept,* teach his desires to fix upon external things; he must adopt the joys and the pains of others.' [4] The ability to turn outward is to be kept alive at all costs. We have little else to work with, and, like hope, 'its frustrations, however frequent, are less dreadful than its extinction.' The plea is for the use of human interests and desires; and the confidence is that knowledge and sincerity can prevent them from becoming permanently caught on any one rock, and can lead them to further and freer channels.

Thus the desire for fame, which is one form of our need for reassurance and recognition, is to be 'regulated rather than extinguished.' Needless to say fame brings disappointments once it is attained and frustrations if it is not. Far from minimizing them, Johnson dwells on them with amusingly vigorous perception. As a writer, he is naturally most tempted, of course, to focus on what he calls the 'epidemical conspiracy for the destruction of paper,' the results of which, after a short flurry (and a flurry, very often, only in the heart of the writer himself), repose, undisturbed and forgotten, in a few libraries. But the symbol applies universally to anyone who 'places happiness in the frequent repetition of his name.' Like those who console themselves that their names will be kept alive by gravestones, by their children, or by institutions they have started, the writer whose hope is sewn to the image of his name printed on the back of a book 'lives only in *idea*.'

But when a man makes '*celebrity* necessary to his happiness, he has put it in the power of the weakest and most timorous malignity, if not to take away his satisfaction, at least to withold it.' Also, we forget how little renown is possible anyway in the world, and how preoccupied other people are with their own fears and hopes, and engaged 'in contriving some refuge from calamity, or in shortening the way to some new possession.' Johnson, as a critic, is great partly because he never forgets this. It tempers the clean incisiveness and moral humanism with which he looks at literature. In addition to everything else that can be said of them, the *Lives of the Poets* are a final chapter in Johnson's tragic exploration of man's destiny. In this 'literary biography of England,' for a period of more than a century, the writers of England appear, as on a stage, each animated by hopes, fears, and ambition for a short while, and then give way to others. Every 'catalogue of a library' — crowded with 'names of men, who, though now forgotten, were once no less enterprising and confident' — is a reminder that names which 'hoped to range over kingdoms . . . shrink at last into cloisters and colleges.' Nor, even in 'these *last retreats of fame,*' these cemeteries or death-registers, is the attention more than casual of the 'few solitary students' that copy or glance at a name. For few scholars 'extend their views beyond some particular science'; and the greater part of these 'seldom inquire, even in their own profession, for any authours but those whom the *present mode of study happens to force* upon their notice.' [5] Certainly one dominant theme of the moral essays, therefore, is the text, 'Lay not up for yourselves treasures upon earth, where moth and rust doth corrupt, and where thieves break through and steal.'

But hardly any theme is single in Johnson. It is always being subsumed within a larger harmony. So this particular one is joined by the practical reminders that constantly acknowledge and make place for the need of every individual to assert himself, to share, and to be recognized. He that is struggling to reach any point 'must frequently turn his eyes to that place which he strives to reach; he that undergoes the fatigue of labour, must solace his weariness with the contemplation of its reward.' It is almost unavoidable that the reward craved for should be partly thought of in terms of the world in which we are living. The reward may mean little when it comes. Johnson mentions how close we all are to Don Quixote in forming expectations, always living in the future, exaggerating and coloring rewards in imagination which inevitably turn out to be disappointing: 'our hearts inform us that he is not more ridiculous than ourselves, except that he *tells* what we have only thought.' On the other hand, as Johnson at the same moment reminds us, few enterprises that involve labor or risk would ever be undertaken to begin with if we did not magnify the importance of what we are doing, and the effect it might produce on others. For this reason if for no other, the desire for fame is to be 'regulated rather than extinguished.' [6]

Again, if the desire for fame often remains a 'last infirmity' to intelligent minds that can disregard other rewards or possessions, it is because the craving for 'celebrity' at least involves a use of the imagination that is potentially valuable. The desire for fame, as Johnson says, is primarily the 'desire of *filling the minds of others.*' [7] In jumping ahead from our present sensations into an imaginary or ideal realm — anticipating and dwelling in the minds of others — we employ a form of sympathy that is really a part of the function of an intelligent being. The object may be ourselves, to be sure. But still the procedure of 'living in *idea*' in this way at least involves a kind of detour, or circuitous route, through the minds of others; and it is one of the ways in which we differ from the animals whom Rasselas envied, who crop the grass, and are at once filled and then lie down. It is indeed remarkable how much of our lives are spent vicariously, through what is at least a kind of rudimentary sympathy with others. 'The greater part of mankind,' as Johnson said, 'are gay or serious by infection.' In most ambitions, behind almost all affectation, the desire is to live more vitally through 'filling the minds of others,' and therefore of ourselves.

The vanity that tempts people to give a false impression to others, whom they meet casually in travel or social gatherings and never expect to see again, provides a touching as well as comic example of the need to live vicariously. In a brief satiric sketch (*Adventurer*, No. 84), Johnson pictures six travelers entering a coach, greeting each other with 'supercilious civility,' then settling back in silence, 'all employed in collecting importance into our faces, and endeavouring to strike reverence and submission into our companions.' After an oppressive silence of some hours, they stop at an inn for a meal. One of them speaks of a similar inn where he and two titled friends, whose names he mentions, had stayed; but he scarcely has time 'to congratulate himself on the veneration which this narrative must have procured for him from the company,' when one of the women begins to mention the inconveniences of traveling if one is accustomed to have a number of servants at home. 'A general emulation seemed now to be excited.' One of the men, who has been silent till now, calls for the latest newspaper, scans it pensively, shakes his head over the unpredictability of stocks, and mentions ruefully an investment of his a week before involving twenty thousand pounds. And so the 'general emulation' continues for four days, with each suspicious of the other and not too delighted with himself. At the end it turns out that the man who prates of his noble friends is a butler, the speculator is a stock-broker's clerk, and the woman who missed her servants keeps a small eating-place. No obvious utilitarian benefit is gained by such deception; we know that what we are pretending to be — or whom we are pretending to know — is imaginary. But so alluring is this momentary identification with others that by means of it the imagination is able to slip, through a kind of play-acting, into a more vivid semblance of what we wish to be.

This outward jump of the imagination, this capacity to take on, as it were, by infection, may not automatically serve as the basis for all improvement. But though it may be used to serve vanity or other motives, it is indispensable in every step of growth that ever takes place in a human being. 'Activity,' to repeat Johnson's memorable insight, contains within itself the means of its own reformation. The same forward thrust of the imagination to our own future condition, as we fear it or wish it to be — the same exercise of imagination that pictures our present or future importance as it 'fills the minds of others,' — is also able to catch at other objects and develop other desires. 'All joy or sorrow for the happiness or calamities of others,' said Johnson, 'is produced by an act of the imagination . . . placing us, for a time, in the condition of him whose fortune we contemplate.' [8] As Hazlitt later said, we could not love ourselves unless we could also love others. We could not project ourselves forward, that is, into our future condition — which exists only as it were in blueprint and in our imagination — and bend our efforts to secure it unless we were equally able to turn outside our present sensations in another way, and lose the sense of our 'personal identity' in some *other* object. It follows that selfishness and malice, however common, are not inevitable, but that we are 'free agents.'

5

Human development, then, involves not the rejection but the use of primary human capacities — an active 'concord and harmony,' as Plato said, 'of definite and particular pleasures and appetites.' Furthermore, almost all of these pleasures or appetites have within themselves a *potential* yearning — perhaps too blind to be called desire — to reassure themselves, and to work toward reality. As Johnson said, the 'heart naturally loves truth' — it wants, at least, the security which truth alone can give. We may dislike particular aspects of the truth, and greatly prefer it to be otherwise. But we do not remain happy for long if we know that what we imagine or desire is only an illusion, and that it can have no possible counterpart at all in reality. We see how desperately, in order to reassure themselves that they are not dwelling solely in illusion, people will wrench reality to fit the imaginative pattern they have in mind. Finally, men commonly dislike insincerity, even when they are led to practice it. Though we are ready enough to 'impose on ourselves,' as Johnson says, yet all of us are quick to note insincerity when we find it in others, particularly when we are concerned with their attitude and behavior toward us.

In a very real sense, therefore, human feelings, at least potentially, work outward toward reality, hoping to re-enforce and secure themselves by the 'stability of truth.' To this extent, they contain their own tension upward and outward, if only in their need for reassurance, for external justification and support. But in order to use this to advantage there must first be some sort of exposure to what will arouse or satisfy us; our desires cannot clarify themselves or find objects to satisfy them unless we know or suspect the existence of such objects. Unless we have first tasted what we desire, hunger often remains only an uneasy and painful sensation, without a clear object. Accordingly, as a contemporary of Johnson pointed out, very young babies, suffering from physical hunger, often fight against food unless they have already experienced the taste of it. Almost all our primary desires for satisfaction and recognition — unless they have already hopelessly projected themselves toward a destructive end — can provide some opportunity of acquiring such an exposure, however brief. The need is for the intelligent and progressive use of such an exposure.

Here we are touching on the nature of human experience itself. Thought — if it is to be more than floating impressions or abstract agreement — must be incorporated within ourselves, must coalesce with the activity of desire or interest that is already stirring or ready to stir within us, and then be used to carry that desire or activity even farther. Thought 'must proceed,' as Johnson states, 'from something *known*, done, or suffered; and must *produce* some action or event.' [9] In so far as it is genuine, in other words, thought really ministers to growth. And growth or experience involves at least two necessary stages, each of which depends on the other. It must, first of all, take hold on what has already been experienced. It must reach down among all the accumulated longings of the heart — which linger as dim, unexpressed pain, or as brief glimpses of pleasure remembered only in nostalgia as fragmentary satisfaction. In this deep anchorage, from which all human motivation stirs and rises again, the new perception can touch base, open reserves of desire, and arouse that interest which can be stimulated only by recognition or past familiarity. At the same time that it reaches down to the reservoir of our past experience, anything that comprises a genuine and meaningful experience in the present also lights up a further landscape of possibilities that somehow carry or clarify further what we have already known and felt. The incorporation of knowledge into feeling thus contrasts with the light verbalizing of the philosopher in *Rasselas* who spoke 'with great energy on the *government of the passions,*' including grief, and then immediately crumpled and gave up all interest in life when he heard of the death of his daughter. The point is the shallowness of the common metaphor that compares the various 'passions' to an unruly horse that can be mysteriously prodded or bridled by something we call 'reason' or 'will.' Will is neither a spur nor a bridle. It is itself a need felt with enough strength to lead us to move in such a way as to start fulfilling that need — to carry it out through 'some action or event,' whether the action be to walk across the room for the mere sake of moving, or to take a stand based on a principle that means a great deal to us. The 'art of the management of the mind,' which can be attained only through 'experience and habitual exercise,' involves among other things *increasing* both the breadth and durability of what is desired.

'Truth, such as is *necessary to the regulation of life,* is always to be found *where it is honestly sought.*' [10] 'Honestly sought': — to attain this concern, this caring, almost every resource and tension of the human heart can and should be 'put to use.' Sincerity, the active desire that wants sincerity and works by means of it, is the first requirement, clearing its own path as it proceeds, creating its own health. So, in *The Vanity of Human Wishes,* the answer to the question '*Must* helpless man, in ignorance sedate, Roll darkling . . .' is the honest and 'supplicating' desire: 'Pour forth thy *fervours* for a healthful mind.' 'Sincerity,' as Confucius wrote, when it is carried far enough, will be found to 'result in intelligence,' just as 'intelligence,' if it strikes deeply enough, leads to 'sincerity.' For the heart can find durable satisfaction only through 'seeing things as they are.' 'Let us endeavour,' Johnson wrote to his friend, Bennet Langton, in 1758,

> *to see things as they are,* and then inquire whether we ought to complain. Whether to see life as it is, will give us much consolation, I know not; *but the consolation which is drawn from truth, if any there be, is solid and durable;* that which may be derived from errour, must be, like its original, fallacious and fugitive.[11]

A few years later, after the severest psychological struggle — including the exhausted despair in which the Thrales found him — Johnson recurred to this assertion in the noble premise on which the great *Preface to Shakespeare* builds:

> The irregular combinations of fanciful invention may delight a-while, by that novelty of which the common satiety of life sends us all in quest; but the pleasures of sudden wonder *are soon exhausted, and the mind can only repose on the stability of truth.*[12]

6

Behind the uniquely personal figure of Johnson, therefore, — from the time he first frantically tried to take his destiny in his own hands, up until his friends finally saw that incredible and 'most awful sight' of Johnson stretched out on his bed 'without life' — looms the greatest of classical discoveries and generalizations. It is the discovery that human nature is able to remake and remold itself, and that this re-creation — this liberating and educating or leading out of human potentiality — can be carried through, not by denying or cutting off impulses, but rather by constantly broadening and enriching the quality of the *objects* to which they are reaching. It is the realization that the process of doing this can color and refashion the act of desiring or wanting itself, just as other habits, based on accident, or custom, can narrow or deflect it. Habit, in other words can be used as an ally rather than an enemy. 'We have only,' as Pythagoras said, 'to pitch upon that course of life which is the most excellent, and habit or custom will then render it the most pleasureable.' The process involves an actual meeting of desire halfway, and — far from denying its claims — joining with it, breaking through the self-constricting molds of personal projection, custom, and stock response, and asserting the claims of human needs even more strongly. It is, indeed, a spreading or fanning out of desire into a still larger and more searching demand, by seeking within the object desired what will satisfy the intellect as well as the accumulated, uneasy reservoir of past *eros*. In doing so, it integrates and brings into an active — if uncertain and perilous — unity the resources of the human heart and mind.

The result may not be completely serene and harmonious. 'A fallible being will fail somewhere,' especially if he be a 'creature whose motions are *gradual*,' for whom 'the present is in perpetual motion' and 'leaves us as soon as it arrives.' But there will at least be an extension or refinement of those tensions of desire, of those unfulfilled gaps of satisfaction that make up 'will,' and that serve as motives or incitements to action. In such a way, a progressive craving can be induced for the 'stability of truth' itself — which includes the flexible openness to revise and to refuse to remain satisfied with any pat formula, while at the same time it also uses and satisfies the restless hunger of the mind by raising the curtain to what we have not yet experienced.

Hence Johnson's antagonism to any form of the belief, such as that popularized by Hobbes a century before, that human motives are determined by a mechanical, inner calculus of pleasure that ministers to our own egos. In one of the first

issues of the *Rambler*, he turns at once upon Swift's statement
that men are 'grateful to the same degree that they are re-
sentful':

> This principle, with others of the same kind, sup-
> poses man to act [solely] from a brute impulse . . .
> without any choice of the object . . . *It is of the utmost
> importance to mankind, that positions of this tendency
> should be laid open and confuted.*[13]

The 'laying open' and 'confuting' of all determinism, of all
thinking that seals over man's hope for freedom of choice, is
carried through every aspect of Johnson's writing on human
life, on literature, and everything else, even when the grandeur
of his writing becomes most tragic. Its authority comes not
from comfortably denying the 'treachery of the human heart,'
and all that leads to it, nor shrinking from it ('Madam,' as
he far too hastily rebuked the abbess of a convent, 'you are
here, not for the love of virtue, but the fear of vice'); the
authority comes from having gone through it, with the complete sense of what produces it, and then coming out on the
other side. His own life is an exemplum. In his strenuous assertion of free-will there are by-products that are forgivably
comic. One is his obsession with excuses based on the weather
('imagination operating on luxury'). Gray's belief that the
weather affected his writing is 'fantastic foppery' (any man
'may write at any time,' said Johnson, 'if he will set himself
doggedly to it'; and we should remember that no one has
spoken more feelingly than Johnson of the sheer torture of
forcing oneself to write with the imagination 'breaking away'
every second to more 'delightful pursuits'). Milton, in his belief that he could write fluently only in autumn or spring, is
treated with no more sympathy than Gray. Once, when Boswell and Johnson attended church in the country, Boswell
stated that the beautiful weather joined with the effect of

the church service to make him feel that he now wished to be 'benevolent to all mankind': Johnson, he said, was kindly enough in his reaction, but added:

> Do not, Sir, accustom yourself to *trust to impressions*. . . . By trusting to impressions, a man may gradually come to yield to them, so as not to be a free agent, or what is the same thing in effect, to *suppose* that he is not a free agent. . . . There can be no confidence in him, no more than a tyger.[14]

More poignant are the resolutions, in the *Prayers and Meditations*, to 'renovate' incentives; and the word, or others like it, recurs throughout Johnson's work. 'The great art . . . of piety, and the end for which all the rites of religion seem to be instituted, is the *perpetual renovation* of the motives to virtue.'[15] Moral writing is powerless unless it incites in us the ability 'to *remember* what is commonly forgotten, even after it is noticed.' 'Men more frequently require to be *reminded* than informed.' We have noted his chronic dislike of Swift. The line in *The Vanity of Human Wishes*, 'And Swift expires a driveller and a show,' comes to mind when we find Johnson stressing, in the *Life of Swift*, that as Swift grew older his ideas were 'neither *renovated* by discourse, nor increased by reading,' but 'wore gradually away, and left his mind vacant to the vexations of the hour.'

The man who welcomes and seeks out 'every new object' will find in the 'productions of nature an inexhaustible stock of materials upon which he can employ himself, without any temptations to envy or malevolence.' Selfishness and malice become inevitable only to the degree that 'discontent' alerts and sharpens vanity and makes it paramount to other interests.[16] The point of Johnson's quotation from Spinoza, 'Nature abhors a vacuum,' applies here, as to almost everything he touches. Discontent is not simply to be plucked out of the heart; it can be dislodged and replaced only by positive and outgoing interest. The interests and activities into which people throw themselves may vary in value, and some may bring their own frustrations. If Johnson follows out their dangers and failures, he also recognizes their innocence and possible aid to the mind, even if they serve only as another version of Johnson's own use of mathematics, to which, as Mrs. Thrale said, he habitually turned when he 'felt his fancy, or fancied he felt it, disordered.'

7

Few men of conscience can consistently bestow on themselves the compassion they give to others, even though they may be quick to defend their particular actions. For we have to live with ourselves. We know our own secret hopes, as Johnson said, better than others do; they are with us every minute; and our disappointment therefore strikes home more constantly as well as more sharply. 'Reasonable with regard to others,' as Mrs. Thrale said, Johnson 'had formed vain hopes of performing impossibilities himself.' [17]

Immediately after Johnson's death, Thomas Tyers, writing for the *Gentleman's Magazine*, said that 'His imagination often appeared to be too mighty for the control of his reason,' and mentioned Johnson's lifelong fear of insanity. After reading this, Mrs. Thrale wrote in her diary: 'Poor Johnson! I see they will leave *nothing untold* that I laboured so long to keep secret; & I was so very delicate in trying to conceal his fancied Insanity.' [18] From then until the present, the pathology of Johnson, as an individual, has been a magnetic subject, serving as a source of grotesque, amusing anecdotes, and more recently as a happy hunting-ground for clinical diagnosis. If the diagnosis sometimes seems one-eyed, part of the explanation is simply that Johnson is so well known and fascinating. Examples both of his chronic sense of guilt and of his eccentricities are readily available in Boswell and Macaulay; and they stand out so picturesquely, that we are tempted to single out those that first strike us and, without looking farther, build from them alone. Among recent psychiatric interpretations, the most convincing is a fragmentary discussion, based on Carl Jung, which suggests that Johnson's personal distress can be construed as an unresolved conflict between an exacting rationalism and strong emotional drives of a general sort.[19] Less satisfying is an interpretation — based largely on the facts that Johnson drank a lot of tea and sometimes bit his nails — that deciphers his whole character in terms of oral eroticism, but without much hint how we then distinguish Johnson from innumerable other mammals.[20] Nor need we take seriously the belief that Johnson's chronic melancholy was a result of being sexually impotent because so much of his libido had been directed toward intellectual achievement. The principal evidence used here is Johnson's casual, pessimistic remark, 'I never wished to have a child.' It is construed as an unconscious rationalization of 'I never *could* have a child.'[21] To the routine use of psychoanalytic concepts, we may apply Coleridge's wise statement about the fashionable psychology of his own day, which had been interpreting everything according to the mechanical association of ideas. Its attraction, said Coleridge, is in enabling 'a man to talk *about* . . . anything he likes, and to make himself and his hearers as wise as before': 'Association in philosophy is like the term stimulus in medicine; explaining everything, it explains nothing; and above all, leaves itself unexplained.' Too often, by invoking the quick answer of sex, we show ourselves children of the later nineteenth or early twentieth century. As Bunyan's *Grace Abounding* illustrates, we can feel a painful sense of guilt in wishing to play bowls on Sunday, if bowling on Sunday is strongly enough condemned.

A further moral to be drawn is the advantage, in interpreting a great writer, of looking for more material than the mere statement, by the biographer, of a few personal habits.

We can hardly agree with Mr. Watkins that Johnson's paralyzing sense of guilt is explained by his indolence. Rather, the fits of apathy result from the feeling of guilt. But Watkins, in his brilliant discussion of Johnson, does not push this thesis; he merely implies it while dealing with other concerns. This is not the place to discuss the most detailed interpretation of Johnson's melancholy, that of Miss Balderston, who suggests that the basis of Johnson's conflict was not only erotic but actually masochistic; and that it led to his being voluntarily fettered, and perhaps flogged by Mrs. Thrale.[22] A complete answer to Miss Balderston would not only cite other considerations, but would also have to scrutinize, step by step, every implication of the circumstantial evidence she cites. The present concern is indeed with those other considerations. But the specific evidence on which Miss Balderston builds can be only rapidly and lightly touched on. The startling note in Latin, in the Hyde collection ('Insane thought about foot-fetters and manacles') suggests fear rather than desire. Chains, references to being shackled or dragged down, are not an uncommon figurative expression of Johnson,[23] especially when he refers to being enslaved by indolence and undesirable habits. We know how cleverly the assiduous Boswell — not to mention others — tried to find out about Johnson's private life. But the most that he could disclose is far different from what Miss Balderston suggests. Even his unpublished interview with Mrs. Desmoulins suggests, to me at least, the tension between Johnson's exacting ideal of conduct and a pathetic desire for affection.[24] Perhaps the most informative part of the account is the way Burke dismissed it as 'common human nature' when Boswell told him of it. As for the foolish purchase of the padlocks and fetters, which Johnson later surrendered to Mrs. Thrale, there is every explanation for the weariness and despair from self-struggle that led to it.

The subject of Johnson's psychological distress cannot be by-passed, if only because of its personal fascination and the amount of speculation given it. Moreover, it adds another dimension for evaluating Johnson's reassuring grasp of human life. For it provides an example of the most direct and concrete sort of the way in which the human heart, however crushed by guilt or sealed over by accumulated fear and defense, can still drive shafts to the outer air.

8

To make the conscience captive to complete honesty can be a fearful as well as a noble thing. The need and fatigue of making a continual choice seem to rear themselves behind every sentence of Johnson; and it is easy to infer how much they towered over his own personal life. We have only to think, for example, how afraid he was of introspection; how clearly he saw the way in which it could unnerve effort, turn attention solely on oneself, and end in bitter or peevish self-absorption. With this must be placed his emphasis on turning outward with open and eager curiosity. On the other hand, there is his firm belief that knowledge is nothing except as we carry it out in our own conduct; and that without such an awareness the imagination can always be unconsciously projecting itself, in any form, without our knowing it. If we care honestly enough, therefore, our conscience must necessarily turn on our own conduct; and the result is hardly consoling. Einstein, speaking of the effects of psychoanalysis, cited the fable of the centipede who was asked to explain how so many different legs could all work together. The self-conscious centipede then found he could no longer get all his legs to work in unison. If one probes through every fallacy to which the 'hunger of imagination' worms its way, continually measuring one's own feeling and conduct by the 'stability of truth,' how does one avoid a destructive self-absorption?

Again, if 'seeing things as they are' leads to a Stoical perception of the emptiness of human wishes — that the end of most ambition, for example, is hardly more than to have the syllables of one's name repeated generations later in a college, or the letters of it copied in a library catalogue — then how does one avoid a final, hopeless cynicism, and still manage to turn outward ('in *opposition* to the stoick' philosophy), with active relish, in the state of '*being* pleased' that Johnson rightly prized as the end of an evaluating and aware being? True enough, as he says on several occasions, if life is uncertain, if the imagination is so easily misled, this at least means that most '*fears*' as well as 'hopes' may prove to be imaginary. So, in our apprehensions about our relations with others, Johnson reminds us that we should worry less about what others think of us if we knew how little time they spent doing so. Though this consolation may calm our worst fears, it is fundamentally negative. It only reaffirms the statement from *Rasselas* that 'Life is a state in which much is to be endured, and little to be enjoyed.' Or assume that we have too close and scrupulous a sense of the way in which we all tend to mistake 'single acts' for 'habits' of virtue. If we apply this too honestly and rigorously to ourselves where shall we draw the line between our impulsive, isolated acts, however numerous, and 'habits'?

It is significant that the most serious mental collapse of Johnson came after the great decade of moral writing (1750–60) which put before him the most exacting ideal of conduct — exacting not because it was based on a rigid formula, but because it carried with it almost too close a knowledge of every pitfall into which the imagination can tumble. 'Nothing is more unjust, however common,' he could argue with a part of his mind,

> than to charge with hypocrisy him that expresses zeal for those virtues which he neglects to practise; since he *may be sincerely convinced of the advantages of conquering his passions, without having yet obtained the victory;* as a man may be confident of the advantages of a voyage . . . without having courage or industry to undertake it, and may honestly recommend to others, those attempts which he neglects himself.[25]

And there are the outbursts in the recorded conversations — 'are you so grossly ignorant of human nature as not to know that a man may be very sincere in good principles, without having good practise?' [26] But this charity, so ready in defense of others, he could extend to include himself only in moments of fitful self-defense. Even then he suspected it immediately to be rationalization, watching himself, as Mrs. Thrale said, 'with a solicitude destructive of his own peace, and intolerable to those he trusted.' Now, in the 1760's, after thirty years of 'resolving,' the contrast between his own life and the high aims he had himself written about so fully during the previous decade seemed hopelessly irreconcilable.

The feeling of helplessness and guilt which seemed almost overpowering at this time naturally had a long previous history. And we should continually bear in mind that a strong sense of guilt is not evidence that one is actually more guilty than other people. One may merely be overscrupulous. It is, of course, a commonplace that the aggression which starts the minute we are born is aroused further by every deprivation; and if it is checked, the usual reasons, at least in infancy, are fear of punishment or of losing love. But in the case of a child put much on his own, the fear can quickly become the dread of failing to live up to his own expectation. It is typical that Johnson, who always thought of insanity as the loss of self-responsibility, so early posed his own problem to himself in terms of 'self-*management*,' solitarily taking the long walks, and writing the Latin statement of his case for Dr. Swinfen. At least the strong aggression and self-pride are abundantly present. There is the story of the infant Johnson, aged three or four, returning from school, so near-sighted that he crawled to peer more closely for the way, and rising to beat back the schoolmistress when she tried to help him; and, later, he spoke of the year at Oxford as a battle in which he tried to '*fight*' his way by his 'learning and wit.' Certainly the aggression in fighting back brought its own sense of guilt. His adolescent pride in refusing to sell books at the Uttoxeter market for his father had 'lain heavily' on his conscience for fifty years until his only recourse was to club even the memory of that pride by forcing himself, late in life, to stand on the spot for an hour. And the phrasing in the story, which we have already cited, is significant: he stood bare-headed in the rain, '*exposed to the sneers* of the standers-by.' Again, there are the accounts of tears starting to his eyes when he made a rude remark; the bending over backward to apologize ('I'll make it up to you twenty different ways'); the close of the fiery argument with Bishop Percy that began with Johnson's defense of a dull book, Pennant's *Travels* ('I am willing you shall *hang* Pennant'). Ultimately, this pervasive sense of guilt grew still more as a side-result of his own conviction that the responsibility of an aware and moral being is to 'put to use' his awareness and moral sense. It was therefore strongest after the comparative failure, in his own eyes, of the most strenuous period of his life, when he had tried to clarify motives and ideals as fully as possible and seemed unable to abide by them.

Worst of all, there is now the dread that to lose the

sense of guilt itself after one has so long lived with it, might remove an incentive necessary to spur one into activity or 'reform.' There is the note, for example, that he wrote on a blank leaf in the diary of his journey to Wales: 'Faith in proportion to Fear.' 'No disease of the imagination,' he said in *Rasselas*, 'is so difficult of cure, as that which is complicated with the dread of *guilt; fancy and conscience then act interchangeably upon us*, and so often shift their places, that the illusions of one are not distinguished from the dictates of the other.' If the imagination presents images obviously not moral or religious, we can always try to drive them away. But when melancholy images or notions 'take the form of *duty*, they lay hold on the faculties without opposition, because we are *afraid* to exclude or banish them.'[27]

9

A vicious circle, in other words, creates its own by-products. These, in turn, simply provide further hurdles, which, if not overcome, harass and complicate the feeling of inadequacy even more. Johnson's spells of blank and tired apathy are an example. Another is the swarm of attractions, always arising by contrast from the mere effort to control feeling. One of the least explored tendencies of the mind, if only because it is so pervasive and can take any form, is the problem posed by Plato as the *generation of opposites*. Psychologically, this may be described as the tendency of the mind to react defensively against what another part of it is reacting toward. While it loves, it also resists; while it says yes, it generates a no; while going in one direction, it finds itself sensing the attractions of another. So 'labour and rest, hurry and retirement,' and all other opposites, said Johnson, 'endear each other.' As eighteenth-century scientists were the first to point out, even the physiology of the human organism reacts in this way. Thus, in what has since become a common-place of optics, if we stare long enough at a red object, when we close our eyes we see a green appearing; or if we do the same with blue, it will be yellow. And Erasmus Darwin, the grandfather of the great evolutionist, put into his *Zoönomia* (1794–6) illustrated plates to allow the reader to test this for himself. Again, if we exercise certain muscles for a given end, others are inevitably stalled or held back in order to permit the desired end to be attained. Accordingly, they in time flex themselves or make a spasmodic assertion.

The channeling of effort toward achievement, in other words, constitutes a certain limitation: to be one thing is, by definition, not to be another. It is limitation, at least, when compared with what Santayana calls 'vacant liberty,' even though this blank liberty to drift without purpose in the dark is meaningless until it is again channeled into specific aims and renewed efforts. The history of human achievement is strewn with com-pulsive by-products — and with by-products that become, if not more pronounced, at least more striking, in proportion to the degree of concentration on the end desired. Too often, of course, we find a tendency to interpret the achievement as either the flowering or else the compensation of the secondary traces that accompany it, putting the hoof-prints before the horse, and regarding them as a pre-determined path. We are never unwilling to 'lessen our disparity.' We all feel disturb-ing psychological quirks in ourselves; and it is not unpleas-ing to imagine that if we allowed them to be a little more pressing, the achievement we are interpreting could be our own.

Again, if the lives of saints or ascetics commonly show them struggling with powerful temptations, it is no answer to say that they started out by feeling these temptations more strongly than others do, and then simply compensated by trying to overcome them. An example is Tolstoy's suppressed impulse, while preaching Christian brotherhood so fervently, to slap the face of anyone who ever disagreed with him. Now Tolstoy was no more belligerent than any number of people who have felt such a desire far less strongly. The difference arises from the effort to live up to an ideal that was exactly opposite, and then self-consciously trying to guard against any feeling that departs from it. As the comparative history of religions illustrates, the temptations most strongly felt by ascetics are always those most frowned upon by the given code of *mores* which the particular religion synthesizes. For the western hemisphere, a classic example is Governor Bradford's *History of the Plymouth Plantation*, which is concerned with sex in such a way as to suggest that, in the tiny and bleak New England of the time, a seventeenth-century Babylon or Nineveh had arisen. In the case of Johnson, the opposition takes the form not only of fatigue and inner resistance, but also an attraction to anything that contrasts with whatever the occasion demands. One example out of many is the antipathy he felt to writing, and his uneasy, almost explosive guilt when he was pressed to write more. Writing was associated first with necessity and poverty, and later with the demands of duty and conscience. By continually having to do something, or feeling we have to do it, a 'habitual dislike,' as he says, steals over any occupation. But when it came to writing prefaces or dictating for others, which he was always ready to do, the weight of obligation immediately disappeared; and he then wrote rapidly and with apparent pleasure.

10

Ultimately the symptoms that have most caught the imagination of his commentators fall into four rough categories: the sense of guilt, which we have been discussing; the compulsive tics and similar mannerisms; the obsessive fear of death; and especially the horror of insanity. Any interpretation misleads which concentrates on just one or two. The symptoms flow back and forth through each other. Even when taken as a unit, they are still only a part of the total picture of Johnson. And any conclusions must be further tested by the extent to which they illuminate and are in turn explained by the more important aspects of Johnson's character and thinking.

The tics and other eccentric mannerisms are, of course, common symptoms of what today would be known as a compulsion neurosis. Examples would be his touching the posts as he passed; adjusting his steps so that his foot would cross the threshold or a particular line at a given moment; or making patterns with his feet, putting together his heels or sometimes his toes, said Miss Reynolds, 'as if endeavouring to form a triangle or some geometrical figure.' In all such cases — and there are many others in Johnson — the compulsion is transparent. They make up part of the gallery of habits and mannerisms by which the human mind, if it is beset with a strong enough anxiety, is always unconsciously or semi-consciously trying to *order* experience, to divide it up by steps or stages, to complete, round it off, and give it pattern. If these instinctive attempts to steady feeling or experience were more extreme in Johnson than most people, so were the tensions and anxiety. They were always within his control, as Reynolds said; and they were characteristically matched by his dislike of gestures (he once reached forward and impulsively held down the arms of a friend who was gesticulating too much), and by the resolution, inserted among others in the *Prayers and Meditations*, 'To avoid all *singularity*.' Again, the habit of talking to oneself — unless one is in a state of irresponsible psychosis — is usually a joint product both of the need to 'vivify the moment' and also to steady or control it — to give it pattern and settlement in words. We should note that, when Johnson did talk to himself, he was not simply muttering prayers, as some acquaintances assumed, but was apparently either quoting passages that seemed to stabilize or bring to a head strong feelings of his own, or else, as Bishop Percy said, he was forming sentences — distilling experience down into words, into firm and expressive form. In their own way, such mannerisms simply repeat — half-consciously transferring to a side-dimension of human behavior — the more general drive toward finality that is always at work in Johnson.

The 'scruples' that were always stealing over him are just one more form of compulsion, like touching the posts. On the day after Good Friday 1770, he wrote: 'I had nothing but water once in the morning, and once at bed-time. I refused tea *after some deliberation* in the afternoon.' But still more important for understanding Johnson's character is the constant effort, recorded in the *Prayers and Meditations*, to overcome scruples by a larger, more intelligent self-demand:

> Good Friday, 1766: '*Scruples* distract me, but at church I had hopes to conquer them.' March 29, 1766: '*Scruples* still distress me. My resolution, with the blessing of God, is to contend with them . . .' Easter Day, March 30, 1766: 'I prayed in the collect for . . . *deliverance from scruples;* this deliverance was the chief subject of my prayers. *O God, hear me. I am now trying to conquer them.*' Later, undated: 'Enable me to break off the *chain* of my sins . . . and to *overcome and suppress vain scruples* . . .'

A half-mad clerk once haunted Johnson for five weeks. It turned out, according to Mrs. Thrale, that he was in the habit of taking paper and packthread from his employer for his own use. Johnson reasoned with him, but to no effect. Finally, learning the man left his business at seven o'clock and retired at twelve, he burst out that, in this case, five hours of the four-and-twenty are enough for a man to *go mad in;* so I would advise you, Sir, to study *algebra,* if you are not an adept already in it; your head would get less *muddy,* and you will leave off tormenting your neighbours about paper and packthread, while we all live in a *world that is bursting with sin and sorrow.*[28]

As if to keep reminding himself, he 'quoted this scrupulous person with his packthread very often,' said Mrs. Thrale, and applied it once to a friend who, looking out of the window at Streatham, lamented the wickedness of the times because some bird-catchers were on the common one fine Sunday morning:

> While half the Christian world is permitted to dance and sing, and celebrate Sunday as a day of festivity, how comes *your* puritanical spirit so offended with frivolous and *empty* deviations from exactness. Whoever *loads life with unnecessary scruples* . . . incurs the censure of singularity without reaping the reward of superior virtue.

It is plain that, even in this little instance, the final compulsion is not toward the specific 'scruples' that his biographers have stressed. Instead the final compulsion is to something beyond them. It is toward a cleansing, and informing of the mind in such a way that it may actually push aside 'scruples' — push aside the localizing of the imagination upon specific acts — in terms of a larger 'scruple' or demand.

11

The need for certitude and control through order and pattern, is more than matched by the exhausting compulsion to be awake to every detail, and the fear lest something relevant

is being disregarded or self-deceptively given a false importance. Indeed, the two compulsions are constantly conflicting.
As distinct from sudden worries that occasionally prevent
sleep, we know that chronic insomnia arises from a con-
straining need to keep, as it were, all guards posted: to anticipate new emergencies, and be prepared for the next, unexpected calamity. We have only to think of the years Johnson stayed up till four or five in the morning, the ruses he
resorted to in order to keep others awake for company, and
the activities, particularly his chemical experiments with
which he would try to busy himself when alone at night. The
character of Sober (*Idler*, No. 31) is largely a self-portrait:
his 'chief pleasure is conversation,' which frees him 'for the
time from his own reproaches.'

> But there is one time at night when he must go home,
> that his friends may sleep. These are the moments of
> which poor Sober trembles at the thought. But the
> misery of these tiresome intervals he has many means
> of alleviating. He has persuaded himself, that the man-
> ual arts are undeservedly overlooked . . . and supplied
> himself with the tools of a carpenter, with which he
> mended his coal-box very successfully . . .
> He has attempted at other times the crafts of the
> shoemaker, tinman, plumber, and potter; in all these
> arts he has failed. But his daily amusement is chemis-
> try. He has a small furnace . . . draws oils and waters
> . . . which he knows to be of no use; sits and counts
> the drops as they come from his retort, and *forgets
> that, whilst a drop is falling, a moment flies away.*

The fear of relapse into an unconsciousness that could no
longer deal with experience, and 'manage' it, is the final aspect
to be noted. The obsessional fears of death and insanity are
extensions or counterparts of the chronic insomnia. We should

ing return from Oxford at the age of twenty, and even more in the dark twenty years that followed, the raw material with which he had to work was anything but promising. The gain of dwelling on the more painful details of Johnson's life is not that they furnish the seed from which his final character develops. The real value in stressing them is precisely because they did not do so.

12

The working toward control, toward order and steadiness of pattern, which the scruples and compulsive mannerisms mirror in their own unimportant but picturesque way, is what gives the marked centripetal character we find in Johnson's thought. His Tory politics provide a clear-cut example. For he never turned much thought to the subject of politics, at least in written form. It is not, therefore, complicated by the innumerable qualifications Johnson makes to whatever he states about more general problems of morality and human nature. At times, one even suspects an element of Thoreau in Johnson, and a feeling that all government is equally unfortunate, though necessary. At least there is the belief, expressed in the lines he wrote for Goldsmith's *Traveller:*

> How small, of all that human hearts endure,
> That part which kings or laws can cause or cure.

Accordingly, Johnson's political expressions seem to come from only a part of his mind. We have little to go on except oral remarks, usually made under the pressure of argument, and the rapidly written and not too serious political pamphlets. The pamphlets themselves often read like a man 'talking for victory' at the moment. In *The False Alarm,* for example, he says that petitions got up among the masses mean nothing: 'One man signs because he hates the Papists; one because it

165

will vex the parson . . . one to show that he is not afraid; and another to show that he can write.' As for the complaint that the American taxes are unprecedented, 'the longer they have been spared, the better they can pay.' Burke may have thought that, if Johnson had only turned his mind to politics early enough, he would have been the 'greatest speaker' the Commons ever had; and Johnson himself in later years wished he had entered the law. But whatever he really thought or could have thought, the extant remarks and writings — simply because he was not moved to supplement or modify them — remain as a kind of side-assertion (capable of some depth and ramification, like everything else in Johnson) reflecting his centripetal drive toward order and continuity.

Nor is this stress on the need for centrality and control a mere stock sanction of the established order. As Mr. Bronson has shown, Johnson's position is partly one of revolt against the economic *status quo*, which by his own time had become the *laissez faire* of the Whig merchants.[32] His Toryism, in other words, swings against prevailing doctrines, and reasserts the old Tory ideal of King and Commons — of responsible central authority for the good of the commonwealth — in place of what seemed to him the interests of a small group. By later nineteenth and early twentieth-century standards, such a protest against the *status quo*, against *laissez-faire* mercantilism, might even seem radical, though it advocates the use of traditional forms. To Johnson, Whiggism was ultimately a direct expression of self-interest, and thus — to cite a remark often misinterpreted as mere petulance — it involved 'a negation of all principle,' a surrender of general responsibility. Characteristically, Johnson's own stand is always for greater social responsibility and humanitarian reform — reform of laws that permit imprisonment for debt, radical change of the death-penalty that was so freely handed out for minor crimes ('To equal murder with robbery is to reduce murder to robbery . . . and incite the commission of a greater crime to prevent the detection of a less'), and, above all, abolition of slavery and the slave trade. ('How is it,' as he wrote in *Taxation no Tyranny*, 'that we hear the loudest yelps for liberty among the drivers of negroes?'). It was the Whig, Lord Monboddo, who sided with slavery in the famous trial of an escaped Negro in Scotland. It was the Tory Johnson who dictated an eloquent defense for this Negro which Boswell records. In fact, Boswell goes on to say how misguided he thought Johnson was, since 'To abolish a *status*, which in all ages GOD has sanctioned, and man has continued, would not only be *robbery*' of the owners, but 'extreme cruelty to the African Savages, a portion of whom it . . . introduces into a much happier state of life.' Here Johnson's dynamic conservatism, with its emphasis on responsible authority, could make place even for rebellion, as in the sudden toast with which he startled a company of 'very grave men at Oxford' — 'Here's to the next insurrection of the negroes in the West Indies.' [33]

Again, to touch briefly on the delicate problem of Johnson's religious convictions, we should note the almost desperate manner in which he both asserts and clings to the order and settlement of orthodox Christian doctrine. This in no way reflects on the sincerity of his belief that in religion the need of the heart for certitude finds its surest answer, although happier and more serene natures might assume this. But while holding to beliefs, one still can be harassed by feeling that one's faith is not complete enough, and then try to assert it all the more firmly and literally. But once this firmer assertion is made, the disparity in one's own eyes between the actual faith felt and the degree expected can, of course, seem even greater. Certainly something like this familiar pattern of guilt, so plain in other aspects of his life, appears here. He did not forget that he had been a 'lax talker against religion' before he went to college. Later there is the repeated self-laceration in the *Prayers and Meditations* because he was not going to church — whether because he rose too late, was too indolent, or, with very human rationalization, wondered whether he would be properly 'receptive.' Nor should the evidence of the *Prayers and Meditations* be minimized. In fact, even what survive of these private jottings, edited and published a year after Johnson's death by the Rev. George Strahan, still contain deleted portions. The researches of Donald and Mary Hyde, now in progress, suggest that these deletions were not made by Johnson himself but by the Rev. Strahan. Also, as they have kindly informed me, the passages crossed out often refer to Johnson's own 'doubts' and to his struggle with them and with unnecessary 'scruples.'

The point is certainly not that Johnson's religious convictions were a variety of compensation. To say this is as foolish as to say that the beliefs of St. Augustine were a compensation for his doubts and struggles. The point is only that there was a struggle; that to create a clean-cut, two-dimensional alternative between 'doubt' or 'belief,' and then apply either singly, is a rather simple-minded procedure; and that, in an extraordinarily exacting and scrupulous nature which tries honestly to disregard nothing, the struggle toward belief can involve pain and apprehension. 'His incredulity' in most things, said Mrs. Thrale, 'amounted almost to a disease.' The self-protective, insomnia-like need to anticipate and be awake to every qualification is able, in his other thinking, to unite with the equally powerful need to extract stable meaning, and to 'surmount' the clutter of conflicting reactions. But the absolute criteria of religion represented another sort of finality, different from that he was accustomed to struggle up to empirically, and one in which so much had to be taken, as it were, on trust. There is no reason to think that Johnson's general habit of 'incredulity,' which once led Boswell to say that he came 'near Hume's argument against miracles,' could be wholly anesthetized, or put as it were in cold storage, the minute he approached religion. The resolution, as the *Prayers and Meditations* show, was far from simple. Even in the *Life of Johnson* there are the uneasy outbursts. Thus, when Lord Lyttelton's prediction of the time of his death is mentioned, Johnson states: "I am so glad to have every evidence of the spiritual world, that I am willing to believe it." DR. ADAMS. "You have evidence enough . . . which needs not such support." JOHNSON. *"I like to have more."* '

It was during the same visit with Adams at Oxford, six months before Johnson's death, that an unusual, rather dreadful scene occurred which indicates how fearfully he could doubt his own sincerity, and how demanding was the standard by which he measured it. Adams suggested that he compose some family prayers. Johnson was reluctant, but said he had thought of collecting prayers from various sources, perhaps adding a few, and prefixing a discourse on prayer. 'We all now gathered about him,' said Boswell, and two or three of us 'joined in pressing him to execute this plan.' Suddenly, to everyone's surprise, Johnson

> in great agitation called out, 'Do not talk thus of what is so awful. I know not what time GOD will allow me . . . *There are many things which I wish to do.*' Some of us persisted, and Dr. Adams said, 'I never was more serious about anything in my life.' JOHNSON. *'Let me alone, let me alone; I am overpowered.'* And then he put his hands before his face, and reclined for some time upon the table.[34]

Nothing more was said, of course. But the matter must have remained on his conscience. Five months later, just before his death, he saw Adams again, mentioned the request, and said he thought he was 'now in the right frame of mind' to try to carry it out. Johnson's strenuous assertion of orthodoxy must be partly seen in the light of this sensitive self-struggle and apprehension. Yet even here, if not too aroused, he could at times bend over backward to be fair, as when he stood up against the attack on Samuel Clarke for departing too much from the Trinity, or, despite his rooted adherence to the Anglican Church, defended the Catholics against the old lady in the coach. He could even go so far as to ask, in talking about faith with Mrs. Knowles, 'have we heard all that a disciple of Confucius, all that a Mahometan, can say for himself?'

13

It is in Johnson's great moral and critical writing that we find the need both for centrality and for empirical openness most fully answered. By comparison, the political thought, because he did so little with it, and the religious beliefs, because he felt them beyond controversy, tend to be less open to development and qualification. The style at its best is a synthesis of these needs. To begin with, Johnson's style more than reflects, it carries out into finished form the centripetal working toward control, the grasping for final certitude that is always pushing through everything he says. In the famous letter to Lord Chesterfield, rebuffing Chesterfield's offer of patronage, Johnson significantly uses an image suggesting danger of drowning: 'Is not a Patron, my Lord, one who looks with unconcern on a man *struggling for life in the water,* and, when he has reached ground, encumbers him with help?' The whole body, so to speak, is involved in Johnson's style, as though he were trying to pull himself above the surface. Partly because of the stamp they receive from so drastic an effort, even the mere side-remarks that come from treading water or grasping at the shore seem final convictions based on a lifetime of experience. For this reason, he is so aphoristic and quotable. But this quality has operated to his disadvantage simply because such statements, dredging up particles of our own experience and putting them at once in so new and alluring a setting, are remembered as separate units. Or even if we do not agree with such side-remarks, we find them provocative. Hence the common statement about Johnson's literary criticism that — even when Johnson is plainly in the 'wrong' (and in all such cases people are thinking only of particular quotable remarks isolated from their context) — he tells us more, he incites more thought, than critics who are or seem to be in the 'right.'

On the other hand, Johnson himself is always the first to supplement such incisive thrusts — however applicable they may be at the moment — by giving justice, indeed actual mercy, to the claim of other details and motives, just as he could speak of gambling in a way one would never forget ('*rattling* dice and *shuffling* cards') and yet begin his excuse for an habitual gambler by saying, 'Why, life must be *filled up* . . .' His exposing of the lures of novelty is matched by recognizing the need for novelty, and the perception of the final emptiness of riches by the recognition of the evils of poverty. Curiosity is the first and last passion in great minds; yet much of the waste and evil of life result from unleashing curiosity to petty or destructive ends. Some suspicion is necessary in a world where we are surrounded by envy and malice; yet suspicion destroys happiness, saving life without saving what makes life worth living.

This active balance of his thought is, in fact, the secret of his formal prose style. For Johnson's is the most symmetrical, as well as one of the most vigorous, of the great prose styles in English. It moves back and forth, with every form of balance and antithesis, always settling, always making order. With vigorous finality, one element is given its due, appearing

171

permanently stabilized; and then its counterpart receives the same justice and permanence. The union of vigor and order is significant. The strength of Johnson's style, which Burke found absent in all Johnson's imitators, is illustrated by the number of verbs. In the great English prose styles, verbs average about 10 per cent to at most 14 per cent of the total words. In Johnson, they begin at about 13 per cent and go up, in his later work, to 17 per cent. This is partly because, as T. S. Eliot says, Johnson, instead of writing in the long periods of the orator, writes like a man 'talking in short breaths.' The verbal clauses are brief, each with a life of its own. Speaking of a man who had been kind to him in the early days at Lichfield, Johnson, now in his old age, writes:

> Of Gilbert Walmsley, thus presented to my mind, let me indulge myself in the remembrance. I knew him very early; he was one of the first friends that literature procured me, and I hope that at least my gratitude made me worthy of his notice. He was of advanced age, and I was only not a boy; yet he never received my notions with contempt. He was a Whig . . . yet difference of opinion did not keep us apart. I honoured him, and he endured me. . . . His belief of Revelation was unshaken; his learning preserved his principles: he grew first regular, and then pious.[35]

And so the passage continues, in short breaths, until it begins to swell through larger forms of parallelism, and culminates in the famous tribute to the dead David Garrick whom Gilbert Walmsley had also befriended. The impression that Johnson's style is Latinate (and the proportion of words of Latin origin in his writing as a whole is not much above average for English prose) rests solely on two facts: his understandable use of out-of-the-way words in the writing he did around the time he compiled the *Dictionary;* and his predilection for abstract nouns, usually of Latin origin. It is the latter that concerns us. It is a part of the strong habitual urge, which we have already noted, especially in his poetry, to distil experience into a general and stable permanence. But what is surprising is to find these abstract nouns, in his prose style, sometimes jostled and always invigorated by the most frequent use of verbs in English prose: 'employed in *collecting importance* into our faces'; '*diseased* with vain longings'; '*dissolved* in listlessness'; the belief that weather and change of seasons affect invention is 'imagination *operating* on luxury.' Moreover, Johnson's habitual use of vivid metaphor in conversation gradually spread throughout his prose, which was censured by Lord Monboddo for this very reason. Finally, as Mr. Wimsatt has brilliantly shown,[36] Johnson's abstract nouns, however flatly conceptual some of them may now seem after almost two centuries of domestication, were far from static as he used them: they are charged with latent metaphor, drawn from the various sciences, still carrying the force of active and empirical observation as they are brought back to moral and psychological interests.

Indeed, in the union of apt concrete illustration with incisive, logical presence of mind Johnson is hardly excelled by any prose writer since the mid-seventeenth century except Burke. It is salutary to remember that the prose of each is concerned with large human or public issues, and is anything but cloistered, academic, or private. Each, of course, proceeds differently. Johnson advances step by step, with power of concrete illustration and sharpness of distinction joining hands at every pause: it moves from thesis over to antithesis and then into synthesis, as if in some parody of the Hegelian dream of the perfect dialectic. That of Burke throws out sweeping and sinuous arms, moving back more slowly, through larger patterns and more circuitous routes.

The significant feature of Johnson's style, then, is the vitality that is always supplementing and even feeding the compulsion toward finality and general certitude. In Johnson's style, at his best, the abstract nouns and the symmetry of balance act only as a governing-wheel, a controlling and ordering of a restless and energetic activity. One almost unique characteristic of his style especially illustrates how this twofold demand can effectively express itself through literary form and in turn vitalize that form. It is the way in which the centripetal pull back to secure, tamped-down finality can join with the outward centrifugal thrust — reaching out, expanding, or qualifying, and then reincorporating. Even when the thought is not plainly advancing, the structure which so many of the sentences almost automatically assume illustrates the beginning stability, the expanding, and then the recurring to the original ground before proceeding further. Thus, in the *Life of Pope*, he falls into balance, but gradually expands it. Pope, he says, had not only 'good sense,' but genius — that is, 'a mind active, ambitious, and adventurous':

> always investigating,   always aspiring;
>   in its widest searches still   in its highest flights still
>   longing to go forward,   wishing to be higher.

Or again:

> Of genius,
>   that power which constitutes a poet;
>   that quality without which judgment is cold and
>   knowledge is inert;
>   that energy which collects, combines, amplifies, and
>   animates —
>   the superiority must, with some hesitation, be allowed
>   to Dryden.

174

Or, from the *Preface to Shakespeare:*

This therefore is the praise of Shakespeare,
    that his drama is the mirrour of life;
    that he who has mazed his imagination . . . may
        here be cured . . .
        by reading human sentiments in human lan-
           guage,
        by scenes from which
           a hermit may estimate the transactions of
           the world, and a confessor predict the
           progress of the passions.

To works, however, of which the excellence is not
                absolute and definite
                    but
                gradual and comparative;
to works
           not raised upon principles
                demonstrative and scientifick,
                  but
         appealing wholly to
                observation and experience,
no other test can be applied than length of duration
                    and
              continuance of esteem.[37]

The central problem of literary form is surely the extent to which form can express, and give redirection to, human needs. We may forgivably stop short of discussing this large problem, and simply italicize the general premise that expression mirrors — in a sense completes and fulfills — not only more general psychological needs but especially larger achievements of thought and feeling. Specifically, in the case of Johnson, we are concerned with a compelling need for order and finality. We are also concerned with the way in which this need is always being matched and invigorated, in fact uses and capitalizes on a dynamic experience and empirical openness. The centrality, the drive toward conviction and certitude, is perhaps more obvious. But its strength is finally genuine not because it excludes familiarity and openness but because it reaches out and assimilates them.

V

Johnson as a Critic:

The Form and Function of Literature

'The great differences that disturb the peace of mankind are not about *ends*, but means.' [1] Certainly the greatest of classical legacies is the ideal of the richest possible development of human nature as the goal by which to measure the value of what we do. No one, of course, openly denies this ideal unless he is hard pushed for something to say. Our denial comes in practice. 'We seldom deviate far from the right,' as Johnson said of literary criticism, 'but when we deliver ourselves up to the direction of vanity.' [2] Yet whether we call it 'vanity' or not, the need to 'attach ourselves to life' — to find something particular to say or do — is always stirring within us; and what is far more distracting, we also find it at work in others. Almost inevitably, therefore, our attention slips away from the obvious and gets caught up in details — either because details reassure us with their familiarity, because they give a prospect of change by appearing new, or, worst of all, because they provide an opportunity to point out the slips or ignorance of others.

Even when our motives are fairly pure, we hardly know what to do with obvious ends when we have them in front of us. We cannot always remain content simply to point at them and say they are there. We soon go blank if we do. We want to participate in some way; and if we cannot contribute our mite, as Johnson suggests, the next temptation is to remember that we can at least withold it. Almost every writer, as he states, finds it 'not only difficult but *disagreeable*' to dwell much on things 'really and naturally great.' He becomes subtly 'degraded in his own eyes by standing in comparison with his subject, to which he can hope to add nothing from his imagination.' [3] Also, we live in a world where practical choice faces us every day. Thus Imlac, who is certainly aware of ends, finally tells the youthful Rasselas, 'while you are making the choice of life, you neglect to *live*.' The need to qualify and choose among particular means is a part of the process of living. Yet there is always the cleansing reminder that, in disputing over means, ends may become shaded out or forgotten; that the process of forgetting ends in favor of means is, in practice if not theory, one of the principal ways in which 'helpless man' seeks to 'vivify the moment,' and creates issues that 'engross' the mind without improving it.

What we really want, of course, is a grasp of ends that will give full weight to the means and to the variety of human needs they express, while it is trying to clarify them. We naturally want a sense of order and significance. In fact, we want it so badly that we all develop a consuming need to simplify life in one way or another. But unless we are very desperate, we are not satisfied by any preaching of ends, forms, or values that arbitrarily imposes itself on literature — or on our own experience — and, like a cookie-cutter, stamps out a flat, stereotyped product. At least we are not permanently satisfied if the preaching comes from others ('We are seldom tiresome to ourselves'; and 'that will always seem best to every man which he himself produces'). Instead we want the recognition that a work 'may be varied,' as Johnson said, 'a *thousand* ways with equal propriety,'[4] while at the same time it reminds us that 'propriety' and principles of excellence do exist, that they vary in value, and are possible to attain. Above all, what we wish is an understanding that will have gone over the same steps we have taken, sharing in the same attractions and fears we ourselves feel, and which is then able to go further in such a way as to take us with it.

Whatever special qualities or refinements literature may develop from time to time, the first premise in thinking about it as a whole is plainly that it springs from human life, that it expresses life in widely differing ways, and that it can be used for almost any purpose. Most of the thin, specialized approaches to literature that war with each other in a library twilight are able to release so much militant energy because of the extraordinary ability of people to forget this fundamental premise. And yet any attempt to simplify literature in a way that does forget this runs the risk of triviality — not in intention, perhaps, which may be painfully earnest, but in result — and we then get what Johnson describes as 'the cant of those who judge by principles rather than perception.' Characteristically, the first major point in his defense of Shakespeare — the extent to which Shakespeare's appeal has continued for a century and a half despite the different technical criteria that critics have applied to his work — stops to underline Johnson's favorite distinction between the exact sciences and the humanities — between works 'raised upon principles demonstrative and scientifick' and those that appeal to accumulated 'observation and experience.'[5] This is a commonplace that we repeat when it occurs to us. But we too often forget it in our hurry to diagnose or to construct the special demands by which, as Johnson says, men in every profession seek to 'fright competitors away.' The natural temptation of critics, as he says elsewhere, is to select 'out of various means by which the same end may be attained . . . such as happened to occur to their own reflection,' and then to give them 'the certainty and stability of science.' But 'since life itself is uncertain, nothing which has life for its basis can boast much stability.' The urge to limit or 'circumscribe poetry by a definition,' therefore, 'will only shew the narrowness of the definer.' [6] In fact, the more fully anything is connected with human life and experience, the wider is the spectrum of opinion and disagreement. As any question

> becomes more complicated and involved, and extends to a greater number of relations, disagreement of opinion will always be multiplied; not because we are irrational, but because we are finite beings, furnished with different kinds of knowledge, exerting different degrees of attention, one discovering consequences which escape another, none taking in *all* the concatenation of causes and effects . . . each comparing what he observes with a different criterion, and each referring it to a different purpose.

Hence 'he who differs from us, does not always contradict us'; and we 'have less reason to be surprised or offended when we find others differ from us in opinion, because we very often differ from ourselves.' [7] Nor should we forget that the more fluid and less clear-cut a subject is (like literary taste and most politics) the more quickly personal disagreement flares into animosity. In fact, discord, for this very reason, 'generally operates in little things; it is inflamed to its utmost vehemence by contrariety of taste, oftener than of principles.' [8] Certainly if Johnson had ever written the 'History of Criticism . . . from Aristotle to the present age' that he projected — a strangely novel ambition to find in any writer before the later nineteenth century — the work would have focused on the ways in which criticism, in its desire to find issues and make stands, becomes prematurely exclusive. It would follow the pattern of Johnson's other writing, which, in trying to find what can be 'turned to use,' starts out by probing first the over-simplifications that the human imagination is always constructing. Repeatedly, in his own criticism, he comes back to the healthful reminder that performance in literature comes before precept. If the neo-classic rules of the drama conflict with the achievement of Shakespeare, it is they that are inadequate, not Shakespeare.

2

The statement in which Johnson begins to lift the criticism of Shakespeare above the rule-mongering of lesser neo-classic critics could be taken as the starting-point of all his critical writings: 'There is always an appeal open from criticism to nature.' In criticism as in everything else, the first duty of a thinking being is to 'distinguish nature from custom; or that which is established because it is right, from that which is right only because it is established.' [9] Criticism, in one of its main functions, is therefore the evaluator of conventions. In Johnson the distinction between 'nature' and 'custom' remains limber and convincing because it starts from the principal fact of experience: the fact that genuine experience is an activity which touches home to what we already feel, starts out by taking hold of it, and then carries it farther into meaning.

Experience is a process, in other words, involving the interplay of familiarity with novelty, and with it the leading out of human resources through an expression or form which is meaningful because it rests on the 'stability of truth' or includes some sort of 'congruity' with 'things as they are.' 'Happiness' he once described as 'the *multiplicity of agreeable consciousness.*' Happiness, unless one is content to call euphoria 'happiness,' thus implies an objective awareness of

something outside us; it also implies massiveness, variety, fullness; and finally it involves the 'agreement' of this awareness
with the inner life. This strong grasp of the active nature of
experience, which we have been noticing in his other writing, constantly carries over into Johnson's criticism, lending
it suppleness and perspective. So the key-words that we find
in his critical writing, if we take them together as a unit, apply equally to the mind's own reactions and also the object of
its consciousness. On the one hand, there are 'novelty,' the
'familiar,' what 'fills' the mind or gives it 'repose'; and, on
the other, 'nature,' 'truth,' 'propriety,' 'observation,' and 'generality.' Of course it is very easy to say abstractly that experience is a process, and then go on to add that the purpose
of literature, at its best, is to deepen and extend this active
process of experience. Appropriate words that put across the
point are not hard to find; much of the effort of nineteenth-
century critical theory was to develop and domesticate them.
But accumulated practice is more convincing. The force of
Johnson's example is not that he abstractly describes the obvious process of experience as it applies to art, but that he is
unable to forget it in his actual practice. That later critics and
historians of criticism have not stressed this in him is nothing to the purpose. Practice is always less easy to pigeon-hole
than theory. For in theory, we have more than half the work
done for us, and we also have the advantage that it already
provides a ready-made vocabulary to help us classify it.

Johnson's procedure thus manages to by-pass the false dialectic with which the criticism of literature and art forces us
to think in terms of polar opposites — of classicism and
romanticism, realism and formalism, subjective and objective.
In fact, most of the 'intestine hostilities' of literary criticism,
which are always needlessly adding to the complexity and
mutual antagonism of human life, come, as he implies, from
forgetting the dynamic character of experience, dividing it

up arbitrarily, and then arguing for one or two aspects of it to the exclusion of others. For example, one of the particular issues that the criticism of art raised in Johnson's own lifetime, and has since 'kept up to the disturbance of the world' — to use one of his own remarks about critical quarreling — came from making too strong a distinction, in experience, between the human mind and what is outside it — between the act of experience and what is being experienced. Of course, criticism, as it started to do this, was only following the lead of European philosophy itself. Critics might take it for granted, as an abstract theory, that experience is a two-way process, and that you cannot separate the act of knowing and feeling (and especially the value of it) from the nature and value of what is being known and felt. But in actual practice the mind seems to find it painful or at least difficult to remain in a state of dynamic equilibrium. Sooner or later the eye begins to waver and then sink for rest on one side or the other. Few critics really rationalized their positions in a thoroughgoing way, or carried them to a logical extreme. This was left to the field of abstract aesthetics, where the knowledge of the variety of art was less pressing and therefore less embarrassing. But the division showed itself in the actual practice of criticism, in piecemeal argument, and in temporary *ad hoc* justifications summoned up for the occasion. Again in practice, if not in real theory, twentieth-century criticism has continued to split itself in the same way, and to imply that we can do only one of two things. We can take, as our starting point, human reactions, in all their variety, or else we can jump over and start with the formal, objective qualities of art.

Accordingly, if we say that art is better for having the quality of 'familiarity' — for having a direct appeal that touches or builds directly on common human experience — this is often pigeon-holed as a plea for a naïve realism — for something that 'gives us back the image of our mind' and will simply reassure us by stirring up our stock responses. Or at very least it can be taken to mean that we are starting to judge art, not in terms of qualities that characterize its 'form,' but solely in terms of personal human reactions. On the other hand, when we find a critic stressing qualities that do apply to the special forms of art, we are tempted to make the opposite simplification. If we like his approach, we find in it a refreshing ability to get away from the subjective relativism, the messy — and apparently, to many critics, frightening — clamor of restless human interests. We feel that it shows an appreciation of art as a 'craft,' and that since art is plainly not life and uses very special materials, the greatest mistake is to start thinking of it too much in terms of life. But if, like many writers of the nineteenth century, we are reacting against formalism, we then view any such approach as an attempt to withdraw art from the arena of common interests, wall it off from the fluid and organic nature of life, and to become thin-lipped and frozen before the individual variety of human feelings.

Simply because he takes so many different aspects of experience into consideration, we can find in Johnson's criticism almost anything we want to find, and then use it as a basis or support. There is nothing wrong with doing this. The harm comes only if we isolate what we find and use it either as a straw man to knock down, or else as a means of consuming paper to attack the interpretation of others. So with the variety of methods that Johnson uses as well as his more general aims. The different approaches to the study of literature that have since become more mutually exclusive — the approach through intellectual or social history, psychology, and the formal analysis of style — can each be plentifully substantiated from Johnson's own interests and writing. Nor are we speaking only of commendatory remarks — the praise of Thomas Warton's *History of English Poetry* that it 'set a noble example,' or his belief that Burke's *Sublime and Beautiful* is 'an example of true criticism' because it tries to show how tragic terror 'is inspired in the human heart.' It is rather Johnson's ability to draw on detail or method of varied sorts for the larger purpose of evaluating literature in terms of general human experience. *The Lives of the Poets,* for example, were not written as an experiment in biographical criticism. Commissioned primarily to write 'a concise account of the *life* of each author,' he almost instinctively stretched these biographical prefaces into a form of literary criticism. They are biography turning into criticism, not criticism withdrawing into biography. But neither would have seemed exclusive. The interest in either case is in informing and supplementing human experience.

3

Certainly Johnson provides a refreshing protest on behalf of the familiar and of direct human interest. 'That book is good in vain which the reader throws away.' The remark is comforting coming from a critic with Johnson's formidable knowledge and power of analysis. For the sentiment is common to all human beings in their more honest moments; and yet it is one of the premises that criticism is often led to forget or feels that it ought to forget. 'Alas!' as he said once to Mrs. Thrale, 'how few books are there of which one ever can possibly arrive at the *last* page!' Shakespeare, at his best, accomplishes 'the *first* purpose of a writer, by exciting . . . him that reads his work to read it through.' Prior's long poem, *Solomon,* may fit into special tastes current at the time but it lacks that quality 'without which all others are of small avail . . . *Tediousness* is the most fatal of all faults.' [10] So, in speaking wearily of the heroic tragedies fashionable in his own day and the generation before, with their stilted declamation and stereotyped characters, Johnson swings back to the desire we all feel for a direct application of literature to life as our own experience gives it to us, even though we vary, with others and within ourselves, about what aspects of our experience are most important. Nor was his own youthful play, *Irene*, an exception. When told that a certain Mr. Pot thought it unrivaled among modern tragedies, there was no affected modesty in the reply: 'If Pot says so, Pot lies.' Characteristically, his own taste in acting — and Boswell seems amply justified in saying that he 'had thought more upon the subject of acting than might be generally supposed' — was for *'natural* expression of character.'

'Few are engaged in such scenes as give them opportunities of growing wiser by the downfall of statesmen or the defeat of generals. The stratagems of war, and the intrigue of courts, are read . . . with the same indifference as the adventures of fabled heroes.' [11] Remarks like this are frequent and betray a very human exasperation. Like his reaction to pastoral poems or his weariness with the routine lyric poems common in his own period ('after so many inauguratory gratulations, nuptial hymns, and funeral dirges, he must be highly favoured by nature . . . who says *anything* not said before' [12]), such remarks are so staple and exaggerated that they begin to become amusing, like the automatic responses of a character in Dickens. They are amply justified, of course. They show a spilling over of irritability about the sort of stylized heroic tragedy that had swelled English drama for almost a century. Dramatists too often

> seem to have thought, that as the meanness of personages constituted comedy, their greatness was sufficient to form tragedy; and that nothing was necessary but that they crowd the scene with monarchs, and generals and guards; and make them talk, at certain intervals, of the downfall of kingdoms and the rout of armies. [13]

This healthful exasperation cuts through a way of thinking about literature that, far from being dead, remains one of the principal obstructions between human beings and the intelligent use of their own literature. It is easy enough, when we look over the literature of a period that is safely removed, to see how the pressure of affectations, and the desire to cultivate some special quality to the exclusion of others, defeated their own hope and ended up in a side-branch of evolution that had limits in the sheer interest it could sustain. Even when we are led to foist such works on students, and encourage them to plow in that ground as virgin soil (as though our principal interest in soil is not whether it is fertile but whether it is chaste and untouched), we have a certain uneasiness; we half-sense what we are doing. But when it comes to dealing with our own contemporaries, or writers just before our own generation, we are more timid. Here our critical taste (if we have some conscience) becomes cagey, while at the same time it wants to seem selective. In our search for qualities that will show our selectivity, and will link us with others occupied in the same endeavor (and no moralist has more amusingly exposed the process of doing this than Johnson), we may even become frightened lest, if we ask for immediacy and breadth of interest, we seem unsophisticated or Philistine.

In Johnson there is always a refreshing ability to remain free from all this. He seems unable to be intimidated. This unfearing humanity, so cleansing as an example, shows itself especially in the ease with which he walks through the preoccupations and stock responses that dominate the literary taste of his own day. But we know that it would be the same at any other time. *Avant-garde* or *arrière-garde* clichés about literature during the nineteenth or twentieth centuries would have been viewed in the same way whenever the desire for experiment (which Johnson so strongly supports) or for conserving (which he also supports so sympathetically) loses sight of the first aim of art. The weight of prestige does not seem to matter very much to him. There is always the reassuring ability to master prestige or fashion, prevent it from paralyzing, keep it at arm's length, and, while following out the technical issues, bring common human interests to bear at the same time.

We can see this inability to be intimidated when he discusses even the greatest writers. While giving complete due to whatever else they offer, the memory of what makes up direct human interest is always alive, always assertive. Of Milton's *Paradise Lost*, for example, he stated the bald fact that 'the want of human interest is always felt': 'The reader finds no transaction in which he can be engaged, beholds no condition in which he can by any effort of imagination place *himself*; he has, therefore, little *natural curiosity or sympathy*.' Johnson even went so far as to say, 'None ever wished it longer.' It is not surprising that such remarks have been plucked out of context with real or assumed shock. But we find them reassuring to frail human nature when we remember that Johnson also wrote the first great critique of the poem; that he at once puts his finger on what is most distinctive — its sublimity and power; and that he could quote Milton with a *verbatim* knowledge that would be hard to match. *Paradise Lost*, again, is not 'the greatest of heroic poems, only because it is not the first' — only because it had Homer before it as a predecessor; and the critic who can put the 'faults of that wonderful performance' into a balance with its virtues is to be 'pitied for want of sensibility.' The fact remains that 'human interest' is not the principal virtue of *Paradise Lost*; and that even its 'images' lack that 'raciness,' as Johnson said, which only the direct turning to nature supplies. 'We must confess the faults of our favourite,' as he says elsewhere, 'to gain credit to our praise of his excellencies.' [14]

Yet Johnson's appeal to a directly familiar interest is shot through by the desire for novelty and variety that invigorates all his writing, at times assuming almost comic impatience. 'Mere obvious nature may be exhibited with very little power of mind.' 'The highest praise of genius is *original* invention.' The conscious elegance of Latin literature, which critics of Johnson's own period were always extolling, exacted a price. By following the 'inventions of the Greeks,' Latin writers frequently lost 'that power of giving pleasure which *novelty* supplies; nor can we wonder that they excelled so much in the graces of diction, when we consider how rarely they were employed in search of *new thoughts*.' [15] As we go through the *Lives of the Poets,* we find the phrases recurring; 'He that courts his mistress with *Roman imagery* deserves to lose her . . . Hammond has few sentiments drawn from nature, and *few images from modern life.* He produces nothing but frigid pedantry.' We should note here that Johnson habitually uses the word 'image' more than any other critic before the twentieth century; there is always a craving for what will give a direct, concrete impression to the mind. Matthew Prior, again, may have 'correctness and industry,' which were qualities that poets and writers of the earlier eighteenth century were avid to display; but 'his greater pieces are only tissues of *common thoughts*.' 'Of these images,' he says of Waller's mythological allusions, '*time has tarnished the splendour*.' 'The judgement of the public was not erroneous,' as he says of Thomson's poem, *Liberty;* 'the *recurrence of the same images* must tire in time.' [16]

In fact, as Johnson roams through the poetry from the middle seventeenth century until his own day — despite his antagonism to any 'gloomy' or 'credulous confidence' about the superiority of the past — we can sense the accumulated weariness that bursts out suddenly in Boswell's *Life,* when the now-forgotten poems of John Ogilvie are mentioned. Johnson could find 'no *thinking* in them':

BOSWELL. 'Is there not imagination in them, Sir?'
JOHNSON. 'Why, Sir, there is in them what *was*
imagination, but it is no more imagination in *him,* than
sound is sound in the echo. . . . We have long ago
seen *white-robed innocence* and *flower-bespangled
meads.'* [17]

He even planned to write — perhaps in a moment of burlesque
— a work that would 'shew how small a quantity of REAL FIC-
TION there is in the world,' and how most writers use 'the
same images, with very little variation.' [18]

And yet 'originality' and 'novelty' are not used quite as battle cries — as they have been used by so many critics — for
downing any large group of writers wholesale. This is one
reason why, during the nineteenth century, Johnson was
viewed as a kind of watch-dog defending the conventional
neo-classic taste of his own century. This impression still lingers on, though it lacks whatever original raciness it probably
possessed for writers of the age of Victoria and Edward VII.
'A few, a very few,' as he said, 'commonly constitute the taste
of the time; the judgement which they have once pronounced,
some are too lazy to discuss, and some too timorous to contradict.' There are other possible reasons, of course. Johnson
lived in the eighteenth century; the conventional taste of his
century was plainly not that of the nineteenth; and he must
have shared in it since he did not devote his efforts to attacking it as a unit. Also, remarks could always be snipped out of
context to substantiate this assumption. There is a famous
scene in Boswell where Johnson, in David Garrick's presence,
praises a passage in Congreve's *Mourning Bride* and says that
he 'recollected none in Shakespeare equal to it.' This incident
seems to have become permanently engraved on the minds of
some of Johnson's critics. Yet he told Mrs. Thrale how he 'used
to *teize* Garrick' by saying just this, adding, 'These fellows

know not how to blame nor to commend.' Though it is clear that Johnson was really fond of this particular passage in Congreve, and in fact went on to defend the justice of his remark before Mrs. Thrale, she adds that she 'forced him one day, in a similar humour,' to prefer a description in Edward Young to similar ones in Dryden and Shakespeare, although he felt compelled to add that Young's eloquence, in general, was the noise of a 'tea-kettle' compared with the 'roar of the ocean.' [19] A few of the *Rambler* essays try to explain to readers who are not critics, or who at least did not spend their time writing formal criticism, why the stylized poetic diction of the period takes the form it does; and these can be cited, if one wishes to forget his other criticism, as a final expression of his taste. Also Johnson uses the critical vocabulary of European criticism before the romantic movement: he uses words like 'reason,' 'nature,' 'propriety,' and 'wit,' though he gives them a far larger meaning than others did at the time. Of course, all of us make a bow to semantics when writing abstract criticism. But when it comes to practice, we still seem to forget, as Johnson said of Cowley, that 'words being arbitrary must owe their power to association, and have the influence, and that only, which custom has given them.' [20] Another explanation for the stock notion of Johnson as a high priest of neo-classic taste is that the *Lives of the Poets* began, as the booksellers requested, with the middle of the seventeenth century. It could be perversely argued, therefore, that Johnson thought English poetry started, to all intents and purposes, only with the death of Milton, and the beginning of English neo-classic literature as we ordinarily think of it.

But ultimately the reason is that Johnson did not openly condemn the literature that the nineteenth century itself rejected in its desire to assert its own independence. Instead, with the charitable desire to be fair that we find in almost all of Johnson's criticism — not all, but almost — he bends over backward to find in the neo-classic literature of his own era virtues that would permit it to stand on its own feet, and, with quick notice, searches out every contribution a writer makes, however small, to diversify literature. Though not over-fond of Thomson's poetry, and feeling that his diction 'sometimes may be charged with filling the ear more than the mind,' he notes the relative novelty of Thomson's work: 'he is entitled to one praise of the highest kind: his *mode* of thinking and of expressing his thoughts is *original*.' Even where other desirable qualities seem to him absent in a writer, Johnson tries to note what he did that was original or new. The stylized, witty comedies of Congreve, for example, certainly fail to present human nature vividly and richly as it reacts to the most immediate problems of life. Also, their happy unconcern with any moral values tended to go against the grain in Johnson. The dialogue is too often 'a constant reciprocation of conceits . . . in which nothing flows necessarily from the occasion'; Congreve's characters become 'intellectual gladiators; every sentence is to ward and strike.' But having said this, his ability to seize on what is distinctive in a writer at once appears (and he had not read Congreve in many years: his own capacious memory was sufficient). Congreve, he begins, 'has merit of the *highest kind;* he is an *original* writer'; the plots and the 'manner of his dialogue,' however 'artificial' the characters, were not 'borrowed' but are the 'works of a mind replete with images and quick in combination.' [21]

Nothing so quickly illuminates Johnson's conservatism as this constant appetite for 'novelty' and 'originality' which still refuses to let these fluid and subjective concepts serve as a final basis for critical judgment. There is always the reminder that they are incomplete as descriptions of experience; that more enters in; that, as slogans, they may be used to support anything. The value of the familiar is as a means, a basis from which to move; the new is also a means, an incitement or arousal. Change for the sake of change alone may simply wander from one dead-end alley to another unless it is pursuing something capable of intrinsic development and variety —just as the certitude and reassurance of the familiar, when clutched at solely for itself, can become regressive or static rather than a starting point. The distinction, in short, is once again between the mere desire for 'novelty,' which may defeat itself in what it turns to, and what is really capable of 'filling' that desire. Of the innumerable 'novels and romances that wit or idleness, vanity or indigence, have pushed into the world, there are very few of which the end cannot be conjectured from the beginning.' But in nature itself there are 'stores inexhaustible by human intellects' if only the mind can be 'quickened' by habit and interest to note them.[22] Johnson's indictment of the common run of escapist romances is not solely that they fail to represent life, but that they also do not much help to 'endure' it. The ways in which the human mind tries to escape life are limited in kind, however extreme in degree, and the soil in which such an escape tries to root itself is ultimately thinner than the variety that nature itself provides. Exactly this distinction pervades the *Preface to Shakespeare*. The permanent 'originality' of Shakespeare springs from his own grasp of 'the living world,' and the fact that it replenishes itself by the 'inexhaustible' variety of truth. The theme is similar to Goethe's remark that the 'subjective' writer, who departs from objective reality in the attempt to be original, has 'soon talked out his little *internal* material, and is at last ruined by *mannerism*,' by stereotyped repetition, whereas the writer whose mind has become a window to reality 'is inexhaustible and forever new.'[23]

4

It is easy enough to grasp the point as it applies to romances. At a time when the split between popular and sophisticated art seems almost unbridgeable, we can even think the issue elementary. But there are other methods of abstracting ourselves from 'the living world' (to use a favorite phrase of Johnson) besides open and popular fantasy, though they may exact more ingenuity and may appeal to less direct interests. As Johnson moves rapidly toward the subject of Shakespeare's distinctive greatness, Shakespeare's fertile and direct 'power of *nature*,' the refreshing surprise is to find three principal shibboleths of extreme neo-classic formalism — the 'unities' of time and place, the fear of mingling comic and tragic elements, the stylized 'types of character' — all fall into place, and rub shoulders with the routine conventions of the average romance as just one more species of abstraction from reality, though of a more demanding sort. This is not a protest against selectivity in art. That Johnson still remains the greatest critical exponent of English neo-classicism, despite all his reservations about it, is ready enough proof. The writer should not indiscriminately 'number the streaks of the tulip.' Selectivity, economy, unity of impact, 'decorum' (or 'propriety') are taken for granted; some of the most memorable statements on behalf of them have been made by Johnson himself. But 'propriety,' as he said, can still take a 'thousand' forms. 'There are qualities in the products of nature yet undiscovered, and combinations in the powers of art yet *untried*.' [24]

The protest is against taking one particular *mode* of selectivity or 'form' and then following it literally — against following anything, in art, criticism, or scholarship, so closely that it can shut us off from the suggestive variety and healthful 'amplitude' of experience. Writers who can use the neo-classic rules of the drama to advantage, without sacrificing more important qualities, deserve genuine praise, as Johnson states. But there is a point at which the rules give 'more trouble to the poet, than pleasure to the auditor.' The ideal that Johnson has in mind is not to toss aside special conventions of art in favor of 'mere obvious nature,' but to protect conventions from the arbitrary dominance of any one variety. Moreover, conventions differ in value; and Johnson simply reminds that they need to be very firmly grounded in general human experience and capable of genuine elasticity in their application, if they are to be held up as patterns for literature or used as practical devices for judging and rejecting a work.

Hence Johnson's procedure, as he defends Shakespeare's neglect of the particular 'rules' of the drama that had cowed the imagination of so many European critics since the Renaissance, is to swing back to his premise of distinguishing 'that which is established because it is right, from that which is right only because it is established.' Behind the neo-classic rule of the 'decorum of type' in portraying character dramatically was the commendable desire to concentrate on what is most generally true of a character, and to present him, during the brief time that a play allows, in a vivid and consistent way. But in trying to get at the general 'type,' and to exclude irrelevant personal idiosyncracies, neo-classic theory often focused on very special aspects of human character — on what Coleridge called their 'exterior' rather than 'interior' nature. A Roman should always appear to be typically Roman; a miser should be a prototype of a miser and not allowed to act otherwise. Thus such critics as John Dennis or Thomas Rymer, said Johnson, think that Shakespeare's Romans are 'not sufficiently *Roman;* and Voltaire censures his kings as not completely *royal.*' Dennis thinks it violates decorum for Menenius, a senator of Rome, to play the buffoon; and Voltaire objects that Hamlet's uncle, as King of Denmark, should prove, at times, to be a drunkard:

> But Shakespeare always makes nature predominate over accident . . . He knew that Rome, like every other city, had men of all dispositions; and wanting a buffoon, he went into the senate-house for that which the senate-

195

house would certainly have afforded him . . . that kings love wine like other men, and that wine exerts its natural power upon kings. These are the petty cavils of petty minds.[25]

In other words, there are different kinds of generality in portraying human nature, and some are more important than others. Shakespeare is amply justified in disregarding 'the casual distinction of country and condition, as a painter, satisfied with the figure, neglects the drapery.'

5

The plea is really for a more dynamic conception of form: the intention is not to reject the classical ideal of decorum but to root it in a soil from which it can replenish itself. As such, it typifies an approach to literary form which is implicit in all of Johnson's writing about literature, and which remains one of its principal virtues. If this fails to seem obvious at first glance, the reason is that Johnson, as we have noted, uses a traditional vocabulary rather than terms that became current in the nineteenth century. The 'drapery' of local customs is something given and hung upon us by a particular time and place. Current customs may express human needs. Also, the way we react to them can certainly become a part of our character. Still, it is not they themselves but our reaction to them and by means of them that is the essential thing. We are justified in reverting to Johnson's moral thought here; we can never dissociate his more general thinking from his criticism without violating his own precept and especially his example. We have here the same distinction that pervades Johnson's moral writing — the distinction between the 'hunger of imagination,' or the act of desiring, and the 'objects,' so often accidental and so soon transcended, to which desire latches itself. We cannot build our generalizations about human nature solely on the *objects* it pursues: the objects can so easily change; and the sheer welter of them can cloud the issue. So, in literature, if we are portraying human nature, the concern is rather with 'the passions of men, which are uniform, than their customs, which are changeable.' [26] We do not, for example, build pyramids at the present time. But the various motives that led to building the pyramids are still urgently present in human nature, though they may have become disentangled from each other and have wound themselves into new 'modes and combinations.'

We certainly want the recognition and use by literature of these changing 'modes'; anything that poses as fiction simply repeats earlier fiction and treads 'a beaten walk' otherwise. This is one of the principal premises of Johnson's criticism; it is also one of the least understood. Johnson repeatedly stresses the new 'combinations' that motives, thoughts, or images can always offer to the writer. The possibility not only of novelty but of inventive originality is associated with it. 'Wanting *combination*,' as he says of Shenstone's subjects, they 'want *variety*.' [27] And to what he calls the 'cant' of critics or writers that all the important topics have already been 'exhausted' by writers of the past, and that only comparatively minor subjects of special interest remain untouched, Johnson's answer is to stress

> the alterations which time is always making in the modes of life . . . Avarice has worn a different form, as she actuated the usurer of Rome, and the stockjobber of England; and idleness itself, how little soever inclined to the trouble of invention, has been forced from time to time to change its amusements, and contrive different methods of wearing out the day.

> Here then is the fund, from which those who study

mankind may fill their compositions with an inexhaustible variety of images and allusions . . . The complaint,
therefore, that all topics are pre-occupied, is nothing
more than the murmur of ignorance or idleness, by
which some discourage others and some themselves;
the mutability of mankind will always furnish writers
with new images . . . [28]

There is, of course, a point to the complaint that great examples of the past can intimidate. Edward Young had urged
this in his *Conjectures on Original Composition* (1759), which
used to be regarded as an early herald of the romantic movement. Johnson himself was surprised to find Young 'receive
as novelties' what were 'very common thoughts.' He would
have especially agreed with Young's maxim that the writer
who imitates the *Iliad* is not imitating Homer. Certainly much
of the intimidation we feel from past models is unnecessary.
It comes, as Johnson implies, from isolating the particular
details of life that a writer portrays, or special mannerisms of
style, rather than following his example and noting those
'modes of life' that are available to our own experience. But
the changing modes, it should be repeated, are still not the
basis of the universality, of the persistent general qualities of
human character. Johnson liked Butler's *Hudibras*. But he
rightly points out that this satire on the Puritans concentrates
heavily on manners and customs that have receded in importance. The generality is certainly there underneath; the wit
is genuine and agile; but the objects obscure the generality,
weigh down the wit, and the poem has dwindled from notice,
whereas Homer, by contrast, survives because 'his positions
are general . . . with very little *dependence* on local or
temporary customs.' [29] It is not a matter of blotting out particular details, special customs, or current beliefs and symbols, then, but of managing them and preventing them from

taking over completely. Johnson, it is true, permits Imlac, in *Rasselas,* to say that the poet should 'divest himself of the prejudices of his age and country . . . he must disregard present laws and opinions, and rise to general and transcendental truths, which will always be the same.' The present writer has been particularly guilty in using this statement as a key to Johnson's critical thought.[30] But Imlac's remark is simply strong phrasing; it is preceded by other remarks that qualify it; and to this noble and sincere statement of the function of the poet, there is the very human reply of Rasselas: 'Enough! thou hast convinced me that no human being can ever be a poet.'

Johnson's position, in short, avoids the usual monotonous quarrel over the issue of generality versus particularity in art. It avoids this debate by subsuming it within a larger framework. [What is wanted is detail — the familiar, the concrete, the vivid, and sensory — for the sake of the form; and what is desired in the form is the ability to apply not only to the particular details that serve as the immediate vestibule or conductor to it, in a work of art, but also to others that are cousin to them.] It is a safe guess that few of us live in precisely the same circumstances that Lear did. Yet they permit a universality that is painfully obvious. The 'general nature' desired is thus a species of symbolic value; it proceeds through the concrete detail, but the test is still how applicable it is beyond. So, in the plays of Nicholas Rowe, the generality is never brought into point by 'accurate discriminations.' There is no 'display of passion in its [concrete] *progress; all is general and indefinite.*' [31] We are not far from the idea that Keats has in mind when he says that the 'intensity' desired in art — perhaps we should now call it simply 'tension' — is a state that is 'capable of making all disagreeables evaporate from their being in close relationship with Beauty and Truth.' The detail, the part, or however we may describe it, is empirically present, but dynamically relevant or 'agreeable' to other details, each contributing to that 'swelling into reality' whereby 'truth,' in the process of becoming clarified and 'intense,' is felt as the 'beautiful.'

6

In enlarging on this point, we are departing somewhat from the letter of Johnson's criticism in favor of the spirit. Our justification is that the spirit is large, and that it is tentative, and empirically demanding and restless, while still seeking the most humanly pertinent generality. Nor do we need to dwell so much on the way in which Johnson, in the *Preface to Shakespeare,* reconsiders and supplements the other neo-classic rules of the drama. The arguments that had underlain them were only superficially diverse; and Johnson's answer is all of a piece. The claim that Shakespeare's Romans were not sufficiently Roman, nor his kings consistently regal in their manner, is vulnerable on two accounts (although both of them interlace): it is neither based on anything essentially true about human nature, nor does it appeal to any human interest that is not very special and soon exhausted. As in the portrayal of human characters, so with the plot or form of a play. The neo-classic rule against mingling tragic and comic scenes in the same drama was based on two arguments. The first was that economy, and the straightforward development of a theme, demand that a tragedy, for example, exclude comic scenes in order to attain the unity of impact that is fundamental to all experience. And the second closely followed: comedy and tragedy, in their effect on the spectator, cancel each other out, or create unnecessary distraction. Here again Johnson's guiding perception is that 'the basis of *all* excellence is truth' — the truth about what is, and the truth about the way we react. In crisp, telling phrases, he again recurs to the common experience of life. Reactions we feel as tragic or comic are always intermeshing; and how can any presentation of life be condemned because it depicts this? The belief that comic and tragic scenes destroy the effect of each other impresses no one except those who wish to be impressed: it is repeated by critics who 'in *daily experience* feel it to be false,' and who also forget that 'all pleasure consists in *variety*.' The principal aim of the drama is to 'instruct by pleasing.' It is plain that the 'mingled drama' can potentially both 'instruct' and 'please' more massively than the drama in which the comic and tragic are cautiously plucked apart. That Shakespeare should exemplify so effectively ways in which each can be combined is not something to apologize for, as Johnson wrote more than ten years before the *Preface to Shakespeare;* rather we ought to 'pay new honors' to him for it.[32]

Johnson, it is true, wavers from the very principles he is espousing here when he is faced with the convention of 'poetic justice,' according to which the good should be rewarded and the bad punished. His undeniable attraction to it is always being cited; and it does show a rather pathetic tug toward wish-fulfillment. But it is never permitted to serve as a primary critical principle by which to accept or reject. The statements on behalf of it are amply counterbalanced by his vigorous reaction from any attempt to make it into such a principle. Dryden 'petulantly' denies that Milton's Adam can be a hero 'because he was overcome; but there is no reason why the hero should not be unfortunate *except established practice,* since success and virtue do not necessarily go together.' As for Dennis's censure of the lack of poetic justice in Addison's *Cato,* if dramatic poetry is 'an imitation of reality, how are its laws broken by exhibiting the world in its true form?' [33] It can be said, of course, that Johnson felt the situation of Lear with powerful empathy, whereas he cared

nothing about Cato and failed to be caught up in the character of Adam. But empathy is a tribute to a critic, especially
in an era when the fear of direct emotion in art or criticism
becomes itself emotionally overpowering. Our need is that the
empathy should be used with illumination rather than allowed
to release special personal reactions that cloud the issue.
That Johnson is able to prevent so strong and immediate a
feeling from elevating itself into principle is what is really
the important thing. The fact remains that any number of
plays that observe 'poetic justice' are rightly seen by him as
little more than 'chill declamation,' whereas the praise of
Shakespeare is that he presents 'the real state of sublunary
nature,' and that at the same time 'the reader . . . finds his
mind more *strongly seized* by the tragedies of Shakespeare
than of any other writer.'

As with the rule against mingling comic and tragic scenes,
so with the 'unities' of time and place — the rule that the
action a play covers should not last longer than a day, and
that the scene of the action should not be switched from one
place to another. Otherwise, the argument ran, the play ceases
to be probable to us as spectators, as well as becoming less
clean-cut. If we are asked to believe that the scene we are
watching is laid in a particular time and place, then, after this
first admission, we have done enough: the drama should go
forward and build on this alone. In opposition to 'the minute
and slender criticism of Voltaire,' which found Shakespeare
'barbaric' in his disregard of the 'unities,' and similar criticism
by others with only a fraction of Voltaire's ability, Johnson
subjects the 'unities' of time and place to a searching analysis
of 'dramatic illusion.' So far as truth or credibility is concerned, the real leap of imagination is made at the start. If
once we are asked to believe that we are at Alexandria, we can
surely go on, in the next act, and imagine ourselves at Rome.
As for time, the imagination, as we all know, can as easily

conceive 'a lapse of years . . . as a passage of hours.' No more heed of time and place need be given by us, if we are watching a play, 'than by the reader of a narrative, before whom may pass in an hour the life of a hero, or the revolutions of an empire.' [34]

The issues are not really as dead as they seem. Or we may put it another way, following Johnson's own example, and say that, while the objects of argument have dropped by the way-side, the motives that lay behind it are surprisingly vital and persistent. The difference is that the desire to simplify and exclude can attach itself to different aims: the cultivation of the 'powers of dislike,' and of 'elegance *refined into impatience,*' is frighteningly persistent. The importance of Johnson for the history of criticism during his own era is a sort of gloss to his larger importance for the practice and history of criticism in general. Johnson's appeal to the total nature of experience as the basis for the evaluation of form, as it rises from the special context of eighteenth-century criticism, is a salutary reminder that the passion for form, if allowed to reign unchecked, may, like any other passion, latch itself to simplified and rigid fixations. Moreover, the fixations, unfortunately, do not always remain with the individual. They occasionally become epidemic. One of the functions of intellectual history, indeed of all history is to discover how this happens. The historical context that provides a background to Johnson's criticism can be described in several ways depending on whether we use from one century to twenty-five in our consideration, on how much we want to distinguish aims from methods, and on what aspect of either we take as a starting point. We may follow convention and suggest the prevailing mode of criticism through which he moves as 'neoclassicism.' Nor are we departing far from the truth if we say that critics from the Renaissance down to Johnson's own day, in their attempt to rival the challenge of classical antiquity, had for some time tried to systematize art into a 'new classicism.' We are speaking, it should be stressed, of critics — of those whose interest or task it is to discuss the aim, function, and practice of literature; and we are also speaking of neo-classic theory as an abstract unit, omitting not only refinements but qualifications and antagonisms.

From one point of view, the critical effort of neo-classicism, starting with the Renaissance, may be described as an attempt to build primarily on one side of experience — the demand for order, arrangement, and unity. The hope or ideal was to turn the purely objective content of experience into a stylized, general product. Art, as Aristotle had said, is an 'imitation' of nature. What is most essential in nature is the persisting, universal forms and principles which work through it, and which reason can objectively find if it proceeds on a general enough plane. Art comes closest to imitating nature when it discloses a clean-cut pattern, washes out details that are not strictly relevant to the pattern, and presents only those that are most relevant in close interconnection. There were exceptions, of course. But we are speaking of the general character of neo-classic theory. The ideal aim, in short, is a rational unity of impact, free from distractions or from needless supplement. This sounds well enough. Most things do, as Johnson implies, when still in the form of a general credo. But in our consuming need to simplify life, in criticism as in everything else, we concentrate on a few facts or intuitions, and then start to extend 'the same train of reasoning, to establish some collateral truth, to remove some adjacent difficulty, and to take in the whole comprehension of our system.' [35] He compares the process to a prince who tries to secure his first conquest by adding another, until he is over-extended or defeated. It is possible, as Burke says, to love system more than truth. The weakness of system is that the desire for order can begin to release in us the passion for uniformity. It may come to disregard the human sympathy for vivid, concrete detail, and the need for 'that novelty,' as Johnson said, 'which is always necessary to procure attention'; and it may also begin to overlook or even discourage the accidents and insights of the creative process. The passion for order can also restrict the range or area which art can touch, as the romantic and realistic movement of the nineteenth century stressed when they were thinking, not about the limitations of some of their own aims, but about those of European neo-classicism.

By the middle of the seventeenth century, the literature of Europe had become strongly affected by this deliberate and self-conscious critical effort. There were advantages, of course, But one result of self-consciousness is anxiety. And the effect of the pinch of anxiety, as Johnson is always pointing out, is that we begin to look for safety — as a sick man is 'looking after ease' — and to narrow our sights. This applies as much to the history of art as to the life of an individual. The point here is neither an attack on neo-classicism, nor a defense, nor even a definition of it. The nineteenth century is strewn with all the attacks we need if we care to resurrect them; and the twentieth has sufficiently answered them with defenses and with detailed redefinitions. Also, both the nineteenth and twentieth centuries have been intimidated by their own anxieties, some of which are very similar. The point is only that the large and impressive body of systematic critical writing which the eighteenth century inherited — the 'rules' of the drama are only the most graphic example — is principally, not solely but principally, an appeal to just one aspect of human experience: the need for order, arrangement, and unity, which is a need that has been known to become frightened and militant in other eras of criticism. Without discarding this need — indeed taking it for granted and building on it — Johnson's use of it is a reminder that the sheer passion for formalization can never by itself serve as the principal basis for evaluating form or for inflicting it on others. It is a motive or desire that is constantly able to betray its own final satisfaction, just as in daily life we fix obsessively on riches, prestige, or change of place as the sole answer to our happiness, and then find them inadequate. The durable satisfaction of form will not be apart from what is being formed, either for us, in the materials that a work of art is using, or else within us, in the 'multiplicity of agreeable consciousness' to which all experience aspires.

7

We are dealing with a conception of form that is altogether functional, and in a massive and reassuring sense of the word. In fact, it evolves from Johnson's conception of the function of literature itself, and is completely dependent on it. And the principal function of literature, as Johnson said, is to 'instruct by pleasing.' The growth in awareness, the process of enlightenment, is not apart from the process of 'pleasing,' but rather by reason of it. So the generality that we want in literature — any meaning, order, or point — is not apart from the details that appeal to both 'familiarity' and 'novelty,' but rather a deepening and clarification that proceeds by means of them.

We are justified in dwelling on Johnson's own phrasing — to 'instruct by pleasing.' For he conservatively uses a traditional vocabulary; yet he at once reshuffles the elements, and alters the chemistry of it, so to speak, with the result that it becomes more dynamic, while at the same time it permits a superior unity. Horace's injunction, that poetry should either 'instruct or delight,' had passed into the vocabulary and to some extent the thinking of European criticism during the Renaissance. There the sense of division or mutual exclusion — 'instruct or delight' — became gradually modified by the phrasing that poetry should both 'instruct *and* delight.' But the suggestion still remains that what 'delights' is in some way added on to what 'instructs,' the first sugar-coating the second. The significance here is simply that Johnson's altered phrasing is so casual and automatic. He does not write manifestoes on behalf of some aspect of 'pleasing' for its own sake, which is something critics have frequently done; but the plea for direct human interest, whether in terms of the 'familiar' or the 'new' is seen in terms of growth, or further extension and 'instruction.' We can over-strain at the phrasing perhaps. For Johnson, on other occasions, may also put the matter in a more traditional way. Nor are we saying that no one else used such an expression before, however undeveloped it may have remained in practice. But the context of his remark, 'instruct by pleasing,' does give it a special claim. For he is in the midst of meeting the sort of challenge that most called up his abilities — the defense of Shakespeare's neglect of certain criteria of form that had made up part of the stock-in-trade of criticism for two centuries. Also it is the cumulative practice of his criticism, meshed with the larger context of his writing on human life and experience itself, which must provide the basis for evaluating the labels or terms that we extract from his criticism.

The active dawning into meaning that Johnson so relished — the activity in which life at last is felt to 'go *forwards*,' in which events can be 'managed' and seen in perspective, while at the same time they stimulate, replenish, and stabilize the mind — gives this conception of the function of art, 'to instruct by pleasing,' a human vitality and conviction that we can find in no other critic. In this function or activity, the total resources of the mind are called out: both the intellect and the emotions are '*filled*,' to use his favorite term. Speaking of poems of his own day that tried to imitate Spenser, Johnson states that they 'presuppose an accidental or artificial state of mind. An Imitation of Spenser is nothing to a reader, however acute, by whom Spenser has never been perused.' [36] Such works appeal only to 'memory,' not to *reason or passion.*' The exercise of either 'reason' or 'passion' would perhaps be enough. But the joining of 'reason' and 'passion' is especially what is desired. We should also note how frequently Johnson prefers to use the word 'mind' rather than terms that express separate faculties. The idea foreshadows T. S. Eliot's protest against the 'dissociation of sensibility.' Nor is this implicit search for what unites the mind and emotion, for what 'fills' and gives them satisfaction, a narrowly or purely psychological premise. It does not become so preoccupied with the mental processes of the poet or the reader that it forgets to prize the fullness of what is being experienced, of what is able to provide the satisfaction and integrate the mind. The corollary is that no *pure* aesthetic experience — pure in the sense of removed and abstract — is desirable, even if possible, as the general aim of art. For by definition so 'pure' an experience would touch only special aspects of mind, while shutting off others. It would then work against the harmony it preaches, not merely by impoverishing the area of opinion to which it can apply, but also by thinning attention rather than arousing and organizing it.

So with the language of poetry, and indeed the entire problem of style. The form desired is one in which details, images, or allusions are valued within a process of dynamic decorum in which both over-all point and the particular allusion sustain each other, but always in such a way as to open the mind to other allusions and other images. This may explain the drop in Johnson's enthusiasm as he approaches the didactic and descriptive poems current in the late seventeenth and much of the eighteenth century. He accepts the *genre*, of course. Yet, despite the number he had read, if not 'read through,' few of them get extended notice or admiration.

Didactic poems do not generally permit any real, intrinsic form or development. The subject of Pope's *Essay on Man* is 'perhaps not very proper for poetry.' The poem relies on a condensed presentation of separate premises, sentiments, and hopes. Even the *Essay on Criticism* — and we have here the verdict of a critic who is not bristling with defensive apologies but easily takes precedence over every critic of English neo-classic verse — is not, in its argument, capable of structure:

> Almost every poem, consisting of precepts, is so far arbitrary . . . that many of the paragraphs may change places with no apparent inconvenience; for of two or more positions, depending upon some remote and general principle, there is seldom any cogent reason why one should precede the other. But for the order in which they stand, whatever it be, a little ingenuity may easily give a reason.[37]

We are speaking not of Johnson's estimation of Pope but of his reaction to one type of poetry. Again, in longer scenic poetry, where one description follows another, 'The defect,' as he said of Thomson's *Seasons,*

> is want of method; but for this I know not that there was any remedy. *Of many appearances subsisting all at once, no rule can be given why one should be mentioned before another;* yet, the memory wants the help of order, and the curiosity is not exercised by . . . expectation.[38]

It is not a matter of condemning such poetry — though critics of the past century have done so — but of simply noting what it does not permit, taking it for granted, and then viewing the poetry in question accordingly. Yet Johnson's impulse to mention the lack of possible structure should be noted. What is sensed as missing, in general descriptive or didactic poetry, is the occasion or event, which the drama can especially provide — the over-all unity, that is, whereby circumstances, actions, characters, or even language are coalesced, in that reciprocal and active 'combination' which Johnson most prized; where the 'natural and the new,' the general and concrete, begin to shuttle back and forth, increasing each other's vitality and meaning. So, in the plays of Shakespeare, we might collect maxims for human conduct, as Johnson said. Yet Shakespeare's 'power of nature' is

> not shewn in the splendour of particular passages, but by the *progress* of his fable, and the *tenour* of his dialogue; and he that tries to recommend him by select quotations will succeed like the pedant in *Hierocles*, who, when he offered his house to sale, carried a brick in his pocket as a specimen.[39]

The equation of the 'power of nature' with the direct ebb and flow of dialogue and the actual process of events is fundamental. The desired form does not impose itself arbitrarily: it arises intrinsically, from and through the materials, as Homer's characters remain living because they are not 'described' so much as they are made to 'develop themselves.' [40]

Certainly most of Johnson's strictures on poetic style are really reactions against the use of what we now call stock devices — the use of allusions, phrasing, and images that have no active and functional value, but simply make up the 'pomp of machinery' of which he speaks in writing of Thomas Gray's formal odes, where Gray acquires a 'strutting dignity and is tall by walking on tiptoe.' Hence Johnson's antagonism to the 'ready and puerile expedient' of sprinkling a poem with allusions to classical mythology. John Gay's poem, 'The Fan,' is

> one of those mythological fictions which antiquity delivers *ready to the hand;* but which, like other things

that lie open to every one's use, are of little value. The *attention naturally retires* from a new tale of Venus, Diana, and Minerva.[41]

So with Johnson's dislike of the 'easy' use of archaic language, common at the time, in order to give atmosphere. His grumblings about blank-verse usually have to do with the monotonous blank-verse imitations, ostensibly imitations of Milton's special style, that were current in the eighteenth century. The reaction is against one more stock mannerism. Such imitations are another form of Collins's mistake in putting his words 'out of the common order, seeming to think, with some later candidates for fame, that not to write prose is certainly to write poetry.' The result, as in the case of Somerville, is '*familiar* images in *laboured* language.' Speaking of Thomas Warton, he made up a parody with the phrase, 'Wearing out life's evening gray.' '*Gray evening*,' Johnson added, 'is common enough; but *evening gray* he'd think fine.'[42] Johnson's affinities with recent criticism of poetic language are obvious. He does not, of course, offer a militant platform to modern poets or critics reacting against Victorian or Georgian poetry. Neither had he offered, for that matter, a credo for the romantic poets. And yet Stendhal had virtually translated part of the discussion of the neo-classic rules of drama from the *Preface to Shakespeare* and published it as a 'romantic' manifesto. The fact would have surprised Johnson. Certainly, from his own point of view, Johnson was only recurring to the testimony of common experience, and reconsidering the relevance and dignity of form as it was able to meet the claims of experience rather than flee from them. So on other problems of style, as they relate to language, metaphor, or imagery, Johnson's premises are not couched in the form of a manifesto, or a categorical thesis. They are once again the by-products of his practical criticism.

8

'Lonely in his life,' as T. S. Eliot says, 'Johnson seems . . . still more lonely in his intellectual and moral significance.' As in his other writing, so in his criticism, including the more technical problems of style, Johnson is of no easily bracketed school. There are the same values of immediacy and concrete suggestiveness that we later find advocated in both nineteenth and twentieth-century criticism. There is also a desire for the presence of 'intellect' and of 'thinking' in imagery and metaphor quite as strong as any we find in twentieth-century criticism. The difference again is that the premise is not narrowed into a set formalism. An example is his discussion of the 'metaphysical poets' of the seventeenth century, the first real critique of them in literary criticism. He was not concerned with constructing a platform. He was merely writing the *Life of Cowley* as the first of the fifty-two *Lives of the Poets* that were to serve as biographical prefaces to the collection that the London booksellers had planned. Yet at once, in seeking to place Cowley, Johnson expands what was to be a brief biography by reaching back to the group of poets, largely forgotten in Johnson's time, of which Cowley could be described as one of the last examples. Taking over Dryden's term, Johnson describes them as the 'metaphysical' poets, and tries to find a basis for evaluating them. Behind all the qualifications that Johnson's honesty suggests to him, as he brings these writers forward into notice, is his statement that, in order to write as they did, 'it was at least necessary to read and *think*'; and for Johnson this was a forceful attraction. Moreover, Johnson's interest in these poets is original and completely independent. 'The greatest part of mankind,' as he said, 'have no other reason for their opinions than that they are in fashion'; and the 'metaphysical' style was far from the

fashionable mode. Yet, in speaking of Pope's ability to condense thought, he could add, as Boswell said, 'There is more
sense in a line of Cowley, than in a page (or a sentence, or
ten lines, — I am not quite certain of the very phrase) of
Pope.' [43] So, in the *Dictionary*, he has used over a thousand
citations from the 'metaphysical poets'; [44] and much of Johnson's quotation, as we have noted, came from memory. Our
point is the 'energy' of mind — to use his own term — that is
never still in Johnson; and the energy shows itself both in
the attraction to 'metaphysical' poetry and also in the criteria
that immediately supplement this attraction. In the writing
of the 'metaphysical' poets, as he says, 'nature and art are
ransacked for illustrations': 'their learning *instructs,* and their
subtlety surprises.' These strong verbs are significant; and in
going on to say that, in order to write thus, 'it was at least
necessary to read and think,' Johnson adds that no one could
be a 'metaphysical poet . . . by descriptions *copied* from descriptions . . . by *traditional* imagery and *hereditary similes*
. . . the *mind is exercised* either by *recollection or inquiry*
. . . upon every subject [Cowley] *thought for himself,*
and . . . something *at once remote and applicable* rushed
into his mind.' Even in the obviously extreme metaphysical
verse of Cleveland — from whom Johnson had put a hundred
and twenty-five citations into the *Dictionary* — he could find
it notable that 'in a very few lines so many *remote ideas* could
be brought together.' [45]

Although he opposed laboring the ramifications of an idea
or image throughout a poem, Johnson's analytic sense of them
was so strong as to be almost a compulsion. As it appears in
the *Life of Gray*, especially, it disturbed romantic critics who
seem to have construed it as another instance of neo-classic
cavilling. But Johnson's reaction cuts across the nineteenth-
century dividing-lines between 'neo-classic' and 'pre-romantic.'
He has the same reaction to the sedate Augustan model of

decorum, Joseph Addison — 'he thinks justly; but he thinks *faintly*' — and Johnson at once begins to pry open the couplet of Addison:

> I bridle in my struggling Muse with pain,
> That longs to launch into a nobler [bolder] strain.

> To *bridle a goddess* is no very delicate idea; but why must she be *bridled?* because she *longs to launch;* an act which was never hindered by a *bridle:* and whither will she launch? into a *nobler strain.* She is in the first line a *horse,* in the second a *boat;* and the care of the poet is to keep his *horse* or his *boat* from *singing.*[46]

Far from being 'prosaic,' as nineteenth-century writers charged, Johnson's desire is only for an analytic potentiality of image or metaphor that will bear the test of 'intellect.' Acuteness and ingenuity can both be overdone in both literature and criticism. He speaks of writers who use either the 'microscope' or 'telescope of criticism.' The first concentrate on a tiny compass immediately before them, and the 'dissonance of a syllable . . . the slightest defect in construction . . . swell before their eyes into enormities'; while the latter, in searching the distant, overlook the obvious, and 'discover in every passage some *secret meaning,* some artful allegory, or some occult imitation, which no other reader ever suspected.' [47] Throughout his writing, Johnson implicitly assumes that analytic or abstract ingenuity, apart from human feelings and general aspirations, is never the sole aim of poetry. Yet the 'hunger of mind' that we have noticed in him is always seeking that 'amplitude' and 'variety' without which the fusion of experience and of poetry is faint. The Augustan ideal of 'correctness' in language had worked against the wealth of disparate detail. 'Comparisons' — metaphors and similes — began to turn into what Johnson called mere 'exemplifications.' This is his criticism of Addison's celebrated simile in the *Cam-*

paign, where the Duke of Marlborough is compared to an angel that 'rides' successfully through a storm. 'A simile may be compared to lines converging at a point, and is more excellent as the lines approach from greater distance; an exemplification may be considered as two parallel lines, which run on together without approximation, never far separated, and never joined.' So 'when Apollo running after Daphne is likened to a grayhound chasing a hare, there is nothing gained; the ideas of pursuit and flight are too plain to be made plainer.' [48]

Johnson himself considered the *Life of Cowley* the best of the *Lives of the Poets* because of the discussion of the metaphysical poets. We can thus infer that here, at least, in the *Life of Cowley,* is something for which he was not apologetic. Though its issues are relatively minor compared with those in the *Preface to Shakespeare,* it certainly reveals the capacity to make place for a thing, to provide it with both a critical basis and a shelter, and at the same time to note its limitations. He starts with the neo-classic idea of 'wit' in mind: the joining together of ideas and images is to be valued as it points to what is 'natural' and generally true. But this conception of 'wit' can easily move into stereotype and wash out variety. This is suggested by Pope's definition of 'wit,' which Johnson attacks: 'What oft was thought, but ne'er so well express'd.' It is both 'foolish and false,' as he said on another occasion. Here his point is that it reduces *'strength of thought'* to mere 'happiness of language.' A 'more noble and more adequate conception' of wit than Pope's is that which is 'at once natural and *new.*' The 'natural' — whether in the form of 'familiarity' or the 'grandeur of generality' — is not the strong point of the poets he is discussing. The 'search for novelty' tends to dominate their interest. Accordingly, Johnson conservatively goes back to an old critical distinction between 'wit' as a term to describe a poem, or the end-product of what is written, and 'wit' as a psychological activity, as a species of 'invention,' which 'abstracted from its effects upon the hearer, may be more rigorously and philosophically considered as a kind of *discordia concors* . . ." And here he proceeds to the famous premise on which the poetic criticism of the 1920's built, in its discussion of the 'metaphysical' poets, and with which it quarreled as it added further qualifications and refinements, although usually within the same general premise. Johnson's own qualifications involve other premises, the 'familiar' or the 'pathetic' (what moves the 'passions' of the readers with obvious directness) and the largeness of 'generality' in which the imagery of poetry would not (as he felt was the case in much 'metaphysical' poetry) drain attention off through ingenuity and complexity of allusion in such a way as to transfer the attention to the allusion itself.

But 'men are seldom satisfied with praise introduced or followed by any mention of defect.' Because Johnson's misgivings arose from a different source — different, at least, from the interest in psychological range and complexity that had interested him in the metaphysical poets in the first place — they were thought to be irrelevant by apologists for 'metaphysical' verse thirty years ago; and they were construed as the 'classical' attack on metaphysical poetry by an opposite camp. What we have, of course, is both a classical defense and attack. Or rather we have a discussion of a mode of writing poetry that resurrects and justifies, with little help from precedent or fashion, while at the same time it employs other standards and recalls other needs.

9

Johnson's practical use of tradition thus refuses to allow special or fixed concepts of tradition to serve as ends in themselves. Instead it becomes the critic or evaluator of traditions in the light of further ends. If only because form cannot be considered apart from the changing details of human experience, any attempt to 'circumscribe' poetry in terms of form alone — whether traditional or not — is one more example of the fallacy of imagination that criticism, as Johnson said, detects in the works it discusses but overlooks in itself. If tradition is to be used, it is function, rather than special forms, that is to take precedence. Of course even so broad an interpretation of the function of literature as to 'instruct by pleasing' is always becoming barnacled over by set criteria, where 'that will always seem best to every man which he himself produces,' and which can become especially important for 'the critic, whose business is only to propose, without the care of execution.' But without scrapping the ideal to 'instruct by pleasing,' it is always possible to enlarge our conception of what can 'instruct' and to become less static and fastidious in reminding ourselves of the range of what can 'please.'

In a very real sense the intelligent use of tradition involves the ability to free oneself from the control of what we imagine it to be, and from the use of it through those slogans by which, as Johnson said, 'some discourage others and some themselves.' As Harry Levin points out, Mr. Tradition in Bunyan's *Holy War*, is placed in a position of trust for the defense of the city, *Man's-Soul*. But the moment Mr. Tradition is captured, he quickly goes over to the side of the enemy, the devil.[49] What is wanted, if tradition is to be invoked, is not the letter but the spirit that gave rise to the letter in the first place, or was able to turn it to new advantage. In this respect, Johnson may be described as the opposite of Mr. Tradition, particularly since he so rarely invokes tradition. If tradition enters, it is not as an excuse but rather as something which is being indirectly protected or continued because of the concern for other things. As the example of Burke shows, it is only by recurring to larger and more persistent issues than they themselves comprise that technicalities are either pre-

217

served or introduced in a stable way. Left naked by themselves, or pushed up as the sole issue, for either conservation or for change, they then become the focus for automatic attack as well as automatic support; and can be tossed out just as arbitrarily as they were advocated.

Indeed the closest parallel to Johnson's critical thought in his own era is not to be found among the minor critics of his own day but in the capacious political thought of his friend, Edmund Burke. If we follow Sainte-Beuve's healthful suggestion, to estimate our over-ready and routine bracketing of writers by trying to judge what they would think of *us* and of what we ourselves are saying, we may be confident that both Johnson and Burke would have welcomed the comparison. In Burke's thinking, the maxim 'Reform in order to preserve,' has its counterpart in the corollary, preserve in order to reform — preserve what is best in order to give root to the desired change and enable the change to be something more than a purely negative reaction. It is the conservative Burke who refuses to 'draw up an indictment of a whole people.' There is always the acceptance of concrete fact and the willingness to work within it. But to proceed through and by means of a thing is not the same as to take it for a static and eternal norm. It is significant that the energies of the greatest conservative in English or American politics were — with one notable exception — devoted to altering the *status quo.*

So the criticism of Johnson proceeds through the tradition of neo-classic theory that had grown up since the Renaissance; but he accepts it as a pivot on which to revolve rather than a frame to limit the horizon. The most obvious instance is his expansion of neo-classic values in such a way that they not merely make place for Shakespeare, but give him 'new honours' of the highest order, and thus bestow back on themselves renewed dignity and opportunity. The inventive and fertile variety of Shakespeare, in other words, is not used as an argument to junk the classical ideal of decorum, of what is 'fitting' or 'appropriate,' only because this ideal had been used as a platform to justify stereotypes. Instead the ideal of decorum is made kinetic and more ample. So, in the criticism of Milton, the Augustan ideal of 'correctness' is enlarged and limbered rather than discarded. Unity of theme and structure is valued less by what is excluded than by the massiveness of what is being unified, and by the variety and range of images and allusions. Johnson's response to *Lycidas* is merely one of his few quaint misfires: the poem struck his stock antipathy to anything that savored of the pastoral tradition, and his remarks were foolishly haggled over during the nineteenth century. Also he felt that Milton's blank-verse style had been drastically over-used in imitations for three-quarters of a century. But what is really significant is the way in which the body of Johnson's critique of Milton's own works evolves through the formal analysis of *Paradise Lost,* gradually illustrating the active strength of Milton's 'mighty genius,' and pushing aside minor considerations in favor of the 'vigour and amplitude of *mind*' that Johnson prized so highly. In everything, Milton was a *'thinker for himself';* and 'the thoughts . . . are such as could only be produced by *an imagination in the highest degree active and fervid,* to which materials were supplied by incessant study and unlimited curiosity. The heat of Milton's mind might be said to *sublimate* his learning.' [50] In Johnson's attempt to provide the first critical basis for evaluating the metaphysical poets, we have an analogous example of a habit of thinking at once independent and conservative. The independence is obvious. The conservatism is that there is no need to cast out something else in return; that if a premise compels one to do this, then a reconsideration of the premise is in order; and that, in the reconsideration, the premise need not be thrown over so much as enlarged and limbered.

Johnson's use of neo-classic ideals when he turns to the great writing of the period before the Restoration is thus a *revision* of neo-classic theory in the original sense of the word, not of mere change but rather of a re-looking, a second vision. So, too, in any reservations he had about the literature of his own day. He was not really very happy about it, as Eliot notes. Whitehead rightly states that, far from being a conventional landmark for his own age, Johnson is in more significant ways 'still in essence of the seventeenth century.' Yet one of the first functions of the critic, as Johnson implies, is to be able to understand and live with the literature of his own era; not to be eager to do so would be a fearful indictment of one's own curiosity. Also, there is his strenuous dislike of whatever could intimidate creative effort or freedom of any sort, and his antagonism to any attempt to use the past in order to club or enervate the present. Accordingly, the *Lives of the Poets* still serve as the best condensed preface to English poetry from the time of Dryden through the middle eighteenth century. The principles enlivened and applied there are one of the glories of English neo-classicism. But if they justify English neo-classicism, and help to prevent it from slipping too easily into one more category of the 'vanity of human wishes,' it is because the misgivings and qualifications Johnson states are drawn from neo-classicism itself — or, to apply Aristotle's distinction, they are drawn from neo-classicism as it 'should be' if it were carried out ideally. Johnson's effect on the neo-classic tradition is thus to replenish and expand it to a state where, without losing identity, it can merge into traditions that are still larger; and the net result is that it can still be conserved as valuable. We are close to the function of tradition that T. S. Eliot has described. For any new work to copy or to conform automatically, as Eliot says, is not in the last analysis for it 'to conform at all': the tradition is kept alive only when the new is able to push ahead, thus altering our total picture of what the tradition is — of where it can go, of what it can become — as our conception of a road is extended by knowing what further turns and destinations are possible.

Even if we restrict Johnson's achievement merely to the history of criticism, we can say that in his work, as in that of no other critic, neo-classic theory becomes awake and self-corrective. This is no mean tribute. But it is still confined and parochial. Such abbreviations of historical (or of analytic) abstraction as 'neo-classic' somehow trivialize the achievement. Historical bracketing, like any other, rarely bestows sweep or dignity on what is already large and creative. Its generosity is toward the minor who would be otherwise forgotten. Perhaps in all systems it is the minor that receives new importance, while the major becomes reduced and flattened; and what is lost in the reduction, as Whitehead says, is the human sense of relevance in its full concreteness.

10

In Johnson, the fairness and strength with which he moves through the accumulated weight of literary traditions call into action the same unfearing courage and insight with which he faces most of the other forms of anxiety that complicate life. His criticism, in other words, draws on the power of context. It also persuades because he himself anticipates objections and reservations by sharing them so sympathetically. Hence the relief and catharsis that his phrasing often gives. What lurks in most of us, as uneasiness or even dormant fear, is plucked out and aereated into vigorous impatience before it conscientiously begins to inform and qualify itself.

We have spoken, for example, of Johnson's similarity to Burke. Both the end-product of his criticism and also the final stages of his thinking that produce it are indeed similar. But he has far less tender reverence for the past. If anything, his first inclination is to react against it, and his second to pause and reconsider his reaction. There is a humanly reassuring, almost instinctive impulse to kick out at once against anything that will intimidate or tower over man's independence. Most of the traditional rules of art that pressed upon the academic mind of his own era — so similar psychologically to the Alexandrianism that intimidates us in our own era — are *'blind reverence acting upon fancy.'* The opening part of the *Preface to Shakespeare* is an eloquent statement of the intelligent use of the history of taste, and of the practical help this use can give us in finding out what persists most strongly in touching and satisfying human nature. But the *Preface* begins altogether typically: 'That *praises are without reason* lavished on the dead . . .' This splendid appeal to tradition is alive because it is already bristling with a latent, restless individualism that is able to clarify and persuade itself by its own fair-mindedness and by reaching out to more general considerations. Behind it is his repeated antagonism to all the easy, run-of-the-mill talk about the 'decline of the arts' — about the automatic decline of anything which would suggest that man is no longer a 'free agent' — and that dislike of any regressive cult of the past which made him say repeatedly that he never wanted to hear of the 'Punic War' again as long as he lived, and that led him to 'withdraw his attention' and think of 'Tom Thumb' rather than talk with Charles James Fox about Cataline's conspiracy. 'We are as strong as they, and a great deal wiser,' he said as soon as Lord Monboddo started to eulogize the vigor of his ancestors; and any reader of Boswell can multiply the citations. Yet, in his heart, Johnson knew there were no Shakespeares: 'in almost every country,' as he permits Imlac to say, the earlier writers excel in 'strength and invention,' have wider sweep, and are closer to nature, whereas later on we move into more special corners, and cultivate various forms of refinement. Johnson himself cites a remark of Joseph Warton which deserves, he was afraid, 'great attention': that 'In no polished nation, after criticism has been much studied, and the rules of writing established, has any very extraordinary book ever appeared.' [51] This is not a fear of the critical spirit — a fear of what Wordsworth calls that 'false secondary power by which we multiply distinctions' — but a reminder that one of the first results of anxiety is that we narrow our sights. Again, 'the burden of government,' as he says 'is increased upon princes by the virtues of their immediate predecessors. . . . He that succeeds a celebrated writer, has the same difficulties.' [52] The psychological effect on ourselves is undeniable. Even the belief that weather affects our invention — to go back to one of his favorite shibboleths — while it 'has possession of the head . . . *produces the inability which it supposes. Our powers owe much of their energy to our hopes.'*

We are back at once to the social or academic gatherings where, 'condemned to vigilance and *caution,*' the faculties become 'frozen.' Like the wits brought together to display themselves — 'Nothing is more hopeless than a scheme of merriment' — or like the poor man Johnson describes who shows up at the dinner-party, sleepless and exhausted, because he knows the company will be passively awaiting his brilliant talk, we discover that 'invention is not wholly at the command of its possessor'; and that it needs a context of hope and active participation by others if it is to go forward. So, in Johnson's reaction to rules and critical regulation, he swings back to the reassurance that 'excess,' of almost any kind, however awkward, is preferable to 'deficiency.' For it is easier 'to take away superfluities than to supply defects.' Since 'timidity is a disease of the mind more obstinate and fatal,' he that passes 'the middle point' is *'a fairer object of hope'* than he who makes his bid by 'falling short.' Repeatedly he comes back to the need to *'encourage* those who endeavour to *enlarge* the power of art,' or of any other study — since experiments so 'often succeed beyond expectation; and when they fail, may sometimes benefit' by their example.[53] The conscience that weighs the achievements and example of the past must still make room for that 'hope' which is the basis of present and future invention. So, discussing the explorations of Drake, he had once said that

> there are some men, of narrow views and *grovelling* conceptions, who, without the instigation of personal malice, treat . . . every endeavour to depart from the beaten track as the rash effort of a warm imagination . . . Such have been the *most formidable enemies* of the great benefactors to mankind . . .[54]

The conservatism desired is therefore one that conserves ends. So comprehensive an aim continues to replenish or suggest new means while protecting others from slap-dash dismissal. The word 'conservative' is, of course, a liability. This is not merely because we can use it as a shelter for conserving anything, even if, like Bunyan's Mr. Tradition, we go over to the attacking forces of the devil. Most other terms face the same misuse. The real liability is that it can always be interpreted by others in the light of the particular conditions or restrictions they themselves least want to see conserved, and then be fought automatically. Other banners, in the theory of government or art, usually refer to some sort of aim or manner — liberalism, realism, symbolism, and the like; even classicism suggests a particular area of works, however debatable the line between suburbs and country. Significantly, the only catchword more colorless than 'conservatism' — the term 'romanticism' — has rarely been espoused by direct advocates; few writers during the last century and a half would care to be called 'romantic.' (Goethe claimed he had popularized the dichotomy of 'classic' and 'romantic' before the

Schlegels took it up; but he did so in order to show that he himself was 'classic.') In abstract discussion, it seems no paradox at all that conservatism can include the conserving of liberalism. But that we forget it as soon as we are faced with some particular context is shown in the haste to classify — in the 'bustle' Johnson pictures as 'getting on horseback in a ship' — which not only characterizes the daily, domestic experience of man but, as Johnson stresses, continues on into academic dispute.

11

'The Sabbath was made for man, not man for the Sabbath.' The failure to remember this injunction is one of the principal reasons why man is always stumbling into a state where, as Johnson says, 'his faculties can serve only for his torment.' If 'torment' is too strong a word for the present context, we may substitute his other phrase, 'secret discontent.' The assurance Johnson gives is that the Biblical injunction works in actual practice. So the variety of his methods of approaching literature could continue to invigorate each other because the aim was never to subserve or conserve a method but rather to fill out curiosity about the subject — a subject that is potentially 'inexhaustible' in the changing modes of life, thinking, and feeling it reflects. In Johnson there is not the slightest trace of the cant about 'serving scholarship' or 'serving criticism.' On the contrary, there is the reminder of the futile animosities, useless fears, the shortening of sight and growing 'secret discontent' that come from making a graven image of method as of any fixed 'scheme' of life. When knowledge becomes comprehended in 'exact methods,' as Bacon said, 'it may perchance be further polished,' but seldom grows 'to a further stature.' Also, 'after the distribution of particular arts and sciences, men have abandoned universality.' Yet no large

225

discovery 'can be made upon a flat or level; neither is it possible to discover the more remote and deeper parts of any science, if you stand but upon the level of the same science.' [55] That Johnson himself could so easily turn from the *Dictionary* — which is more than a word-list partly because, as he said, he thought it could be used to illustrate 'a kind of intellectual history' — to formal analysis of literary conventions and style, or to biography, is not particularly surprising when we recall the range of his other writing. In fact, the diversity seems relatively minor in comparison with the variety of his other interests. Even Johnson's close knowledge of the manual trades is more than a picturesque embellishment to a range that covered the western literature known at the time, history, law, theology, and science. For we are dealing not with personal hobbies but an energy of mind that explores concrete activity in any form, while its ultimate satisfaction, as Mrs. Thrale said, was in 'metaphysical reasoning.' Johnson is almost the last great example of the humanist ideal of the polymath — of the man who could move with equal dispatch in every field of learning. The significance is that there is an interest that can take precedence over method and even create it.

The '*common* interest of learning,' as Johnson said, demands that we 'cease from intestine hostilities,' most of which are the unnecessary product of 'envy and competition.' [56] The common interest of learning is not apart from the common interest of man. We do not deny this abstractly. But few abstractions, as Johnson says, really lie in the forefront of our imagination and concern: a need or desire has to draw them and keep them there. Largeness of sincerity is necessary. The criticism of literature, like literature itself, is fruitful and inventive to the degree that it sprouts from such a need or interest, extending or refining it without losing the sense of what originally gave rise to it. The point, therefore, is not brute coverage, but the continual 'renovation' of interest and the process of thinking that create and use the coverage. Johnson's uncanny memory is much less significant, as we have noted, than his impressive testimony that 'novelty' and 'attention' are the parents of it. So with other capacities of mind, from which memory is not an insulated compartment. His immediate reaction, as Mrs. Thrale said, was to *relate* every fact' to others. 'His superiority over other learned men,' as Boswell wrote near the close of the *Life of Johnson,*

> consisted chiefly in what may be called the art of think-
> ing, the *art of using his mind;* a certain continual power
> of seizing the useful substance of all that he knew . . .
> So that knowledge, which we often see to be no better
> than lumber in men of dull understanding, was, in him,
> true, evident, and actual wisdom.[57]

In a sense, Johnson's entire career as a critic — so emotionally fretful, so harassed by indolence and an inner resistance to writing, and yet so varied and inventive compared with that of lesser critics — could be quite soberly and accurately described as a restless search for novelty not only of subject but approach, with a complete awareness of what alone will provide an 'inexhaustible stock of materials' to the moral conscience as well as the intellect and imagination of men. The recurring remarks about 'vivifying the moment,' 'filling the day,' relieving the 'vacuities' of life, come back to mind as Boswell describes finding him roaming about his library, picking up books, devouring them for a few moments, and then throwing them impatiently on the floor and plucking out others. There is something altogether typical about the picture. So, too, is Bishop Percy's story of Johnson snatching at the folio of old romances, reading them avidly in Percy's summer-house and then confessing that he had gone through so many in the past.

The relief is to find a critic whose thinking habitually

stretches out to touch the highest uses of literature, and who
at the same time can afford to say that 'The only end of writing is to enable the readers better to enjoy life, or better to
endure it.' 'Life,' as he said to Mrs. Thrale, 'is a pill which
none of us can bear to swallow without gilding.' In the case
of Johnson we feel that such a critic is the last in the world to
'dehumanize the arts,' in Ortega y Gasset's phrase. We can also
imagine how much Johnson's behavior — particularly his unpredictable play of fancy and sense of human comedy — could
disturb the noted scholar, William Warburton. We are not
sorry to hear it — not because we value so little what Warburton stands for, but only because we value other things still
more. Warburton might not always make place for Johnson
although Johnson could always make place for Warburton.
Again, few writers have defended the dignity of scholarship
with more understanding, and with more uncanny ability to
anticipate and forestall objections. Yet Johnson, though subsuming what scholarship can offer, is also above it, as the
human spirit itself is above the machinery it creates; and in
his own personal life, as Fanny Burney said, he always preferred the company and conversation of intelligent 'men of the
world' to that of professional scholars. The confidence that
Johnson describes as deliverance from the pain of self-reproach
is also in learning once again that the impulse and need for
novelty that stirs within us is not the enemy of insight and
achievement but rather the necessary momentum and incentive
for it. Characteristically, on the occasion when he spoke most
favorably of himself, he thought not in terms of sheer coverage,
but rather of time, process, and the ability to 'renovate' interest: 'I value myself upon *this*, that there is *nothing of the old
man* in my conversation'; and he went on, in the account we
have already cited, to mention the remark of Mrs. Thrale's
mother that, if he lived in the country where they talked solely
of runts, he himself 'would *learn* to talk of *runts*.'

12

Johnson, as Sir Walter Raleigh said, is 'great by his reserves
. . . his books are mere outworks' whereas so many other
writers — and Raleigh cites Rousseau as an example — ten-
derly husband their gifts, economically tamp their insights into
one or a few books, and leave a drained specimen and 'mere
husk' of a man for the reader who later tries to approach him.[58]
Whatever Johnson does or says, there is always an abundance
left. It is salutary to remind ourselves what this abundance
is. Especially in a world where so much is to be 'endured,' an
intelligent being 'who thinks rationally *must* think morally' —
must think, above all else, in terms of what can be 'put to use,'
what can minister to the largest and most compelling needs.
To go back to Mrs. Thrale's statement that Johnson 'related
every fact': we have repeatedly noted what every fact is immediately related to by Johnson. It is the destiny and possible
freedom of man.

The drama of Johnson's criticism lies in the easy exertion of
power with which he wades forward to the obvious, and
pushes aside the 'competitions and anxieties' that are always
surrounding literature, and drawing off attention. Like all good
drama, Johnson's sure-footed push to the obvious brings a
catharsis or relief. For it carries always the vivid and ample
sense that, like government, religion, morality, or anything else
closely connected with human life, the use of literature can
work in any way, trivial, malignant, or noble. It can serve as
one more way of feeding our vanity. By 'diligent cultivation of
the powers of dislike,' we can wear out our energies in creating
an 'artificial fastidiousness,' only to end in the irritable neutrality Johnson so happily describes as '*elegance refined into impatience.*' Or special interests, developed by building on insights
they would now discourage, may bully our allegiances in schol-

arship or criticism until the 'truth to be investigated is so near to inexistence' or unimportance that its bulk has to be 'enlarged by rage and exclamation.' Faced with all this, it is small wonder that most of us lapse into another form of the 'superiority of inattention,' view literary criticism as something we can very easily live without, and are ready, as Imlac predicted Rasselas himself would feel when he faced the world, to 'quit hope to be free from fear.' Again, much of the occupation of reading is animated with the desire — to use Bacon's phrase — to 'confute or contradict,' and we then busy ourselves, as Johnson added, in such time as we have, to create issues that 'engross' the mind 'but do not improve it.' In Johnson all this is plucked up, quickly taken through every ramification it sprouts into, given its fair due, even defended, and then put into its place so that it need no longer intimidate us. And it is effectively reduced to size not because there is a cheap and petulant dismissal of criticism, but because so much more is being brought to bear as a supplement.

'He may be said,' as Sir Joshua Reynolds wrote, 'to have informed my mind, and to have brushed from it a great deal of rubbish.' [59] The result, far from being destructive, is cleansing and encouraging. In our hearts we suspect that the literature of the world, taken as a whole, provides the greatest and most complete rendering or duplicate of humanity's experience. In fact, it is limited only to the extent that words themselves — and all possible combinations of words — are limited. The limit is a real one, of course. But otherwise this rich prism, this intensified record, is as diverse and fluid as human experience itself. We therefore want to believe that it can somehow be 'turned to use' rather than snow us under.

We also want the healthful assurance and actual, concrete display that to pick one's way through the large, chaotic body of man's literature, evaluating and getting anything out of it, involves first of all the use of the same qualities of mind needed to extract any point or meaning from life itself. This indeed — as the Greeks saw — is the great justification of the humanities. This is what gives them their dignity, their consistent relevance. Most of us believe this at bottom, or would like to if we only dared. To the extent that we depart from this, our talk or writing about the arts and our use of philosophy or history, may perhaps grow more refined, accurate, and difficult. But we also suspect that it may become more trivial. For the accuracy will not always be an accuracy about what is most important. Difficulty by itself is no value at all except to a mind revengeful toward itself or toward others; it is to be endured only when it is inevitable. Refinement is desirable; but much depends on what is left and what has been removed. As the chalk-like bread of today illustrates, certain kinds of refinement can lack both flavor and nourishment. In writing a prologue for David Garrick to deliver at a festival for Shakespeare, Johnson, speaking of the drama that followed Shakespeare, described it as 'crush'd by rules,' and added that it was *weaken'd as refin'd* until from one writer to another 'the *frigid caution* crept.' The fears, inevitable or unnecessary, that produce 'vigilance and caution' are swept up by Johnson and assimilated within a larger concept in which 'Delicacy,' is seen as the opposite of 'impossibility to be pleased.'

No affirmation of the human function of literature, equally strenuous, has so successfully resisted doctrinaire simplicity as that of Johnson. For none has been so chronically incapable of denying fact. This includes the disturbing fact that we can so easily simplify even the noblest of ends into slogan, flatten their deep vertical relevance into platitude, or fix upon exclusive procedures to attain them. Nor has any such affirmation of the value and use of literature involved so intimate a sharing, so pressing and compassionate a sense, of the full variety of human needs and motives, and of the ease with which we can all forget that variety, and betray our own interest, as we become ensnared in the 'stratagems of self-defense.'

Characteristically, at the outset of his *Reflections on the Present State of Literature*, he writes that 'Whatever may be the cause of happiness, may be likewise *made* the cause of misery.' If humane letters were considered solely in terms of the sheer delight or happiness they produce, any intelligent man, as Johnson adds, might well 'doubt in what degree of estimation they should be held; but when they are referred to *necessity* the controversy is at an end; it soon appears that though they may sometimes incommode us, yet human life could scarcely rise, without them, above the common existence of animal life.' We know, as he states elsewhere, that, for every civilization, there was a time before it existed; and how, he asks, could it have ever developed without 'precept and ad-monition'? — unimportant as any single work may seem when viewed naked and alone. Literature, taken in its totality, is a kind of 'intellectual light.' It may certainly 'enable us to see what we do not like; but who would wish to escape by con-demning himself to perpetual darkness?' [60] The statement was written after the *Dictionary*, after the great essays on human experience, the hack-work on so many subjects, and not long before the *Preface to Shakespeare*, which, from circumstances so appalling as to seem a caricature of what human frailty is forced to face, had risen through the accumulated weight of past criticism to the large, renovating premise that the 'mind can only repose upon the stability of truth.'

'The *heart*,' as Coleridge later wrote, 'should have *fed* upon the *truth*, as insects on a leaf, till it be tinged with the colour, and show its food in every . . . minutest fibre.' On the other hand the 'truth,' as 'helpless man' soon learns, is far from simple or immediately satisfying as it filters in, while the 'heart,' in its panic or calculated defenses, is far from being automatically receptive. Splendor of the heart is at most a slow and, in man's tragically short life, a partial attainment; nor can it proceed apart from example. This indeed is the first premise and probably the final justification of the humanities: that the actual process of concrete example, in its particular and struggling context, takes precedence over abstractions. Accordingly it does not minimize Johnson's criticism or indeed his writing on human experience itself to say that his ultimate greatness lies in the example they provide. There is 'no substitute,' as Whitehead said, 'for the direct perception of the concrete achievement of a thing in its actuality. We want concrete fact with a high light thrown on what is *relevant to its preciousness.*' A part of this human relevance is that it proceeds from what is familiar to us and uses it. 'His soul was not different from that of another person, but . . . greater.' The final 'preciousness' comes in realizing that the concrete achievement is possible. Trust — and from trust the open receptiveness that permits us to grow and learn from one another — is instilled by the union of familiarity and triumph, however precarious and hard-won. In Johnson the triumph is not added to the familiarity: it rises through the familiarity and by means of it.

NOTES

In order to keep notes to a minimum, they have been provided only for longer or more significant quotations or for particularly disputable points. Where the source is already stated in the text (as, for example, a particular issue of the *Rambler*) it is not repeated in the notes. Commentary is cited only when it is specifically referred to in the text, or when the writer has been unusually indebted to it in a particular section. Citation of commentary would otherwise stretch to a length completely out of keeping with a book of this sort. Nor is it necessary since the publication of James L. Clifford's admirable bibliography, *Johnsonian Studies* (1951). Italics, especially in longer quotations from Johnson or from contemporaneous accounts of him, are generally my own.

References to the *Lives of the Poets* are to the edition of Birkbeck Hill (Oxford, 1905); those to the *Preface to Shakespeare* are to Sir Walter Raleigh's *Johnson on Shakespeare* (Oxford, 1908; impr. of 1931). Otherwise quotations from Johnson's works are taken from the edition of Oxford, 1825, unless otherwise noted. Since the periodical essays are short, however, and the chapters of *Rasselas* very short, they are referred to simply by number. Quotations from the *Prayers and Meditations*, which are taken from Birkbeck Hill's *Johnsonian Miscellanies* (Oxford, 1897), are not footnoted since they can be easily located, in any edition, by the date in each citation.

The edition of Boswell's *Life of Johnson* is that of Birkbeck Hill (rev. L. F. Powell, Oxford, 1934–50); the *Tour to the Hebrides* is cited as published from the original ms., ed. Pottle and Bennett (New York, 1936). Quotations from Fanny Burney's diary are from the readily available selection of the Johnsonian parts by Chauncey B. Tinker, *Dr. Johnson and Fanny Burney* (New York, 1911). Where works such as Mrs. Piozzi's *Anecdotes* have been reprinted in the widely used and richly annotated *Johnsonian Miscellanies* of Birkbeck Hill, it has seemed best to cite this edition of them. In the notes, the *Johnsonian Miscellanies* are referred to by the initials, *J.M.* Where numerals alone appear, the work is that cited in the immediately previous note.

I

1. Piozzi, *Anecdotes, J.M.*, I, 153–4.
2. The account given is the more detailed one of the Rev. Richard Warner, *J.M.*, II, 426–7. Cf. Boswell's *Life of Johnson*, IV, 373.
3. Aleyn Reade, *Johnsonian Gleanings* (1909–52), III, 180; V, 1.
4. Boswell thought Johnson returned to Oxford and remained until 1731. Reade has established the earlier date (*Johnsonian Gleanings*, V, 25–6, 45–63).
5. Piozzi, *Anecdotes, J.M.*, I, 234–5; cf. I, 423. Boswell, *Life*, I, 64n.
6. *Rambler*, No. 85.
7. See generally Donald and Mary Hyde, *Dr. Johnson's Second Wife* (priv. pr., 1953), esp. pp. 1–4.
8. Loc. cit.
9. Boswell, *Life*, IV, 408–9.
10. I, 71, 146–7.
11. II, 138–9; Arthur Murphy, *Essay on the Life and Genius of Samuel Johnson, J.M.*, I, 378–9.
12. Percy, *Anecdotes and Remarks*, and Hawkins, *Life of Johnson, J.M.*, II, 213–14, 94–5. Cf. Boswell, *Life*, I, 182–9.
13. *Rambler*, Nos. 2, 6, 13, 74, 99, 103, 127, 196.
14. C. B. Tinker, *Dr. Johnson and Fanny Burney*, p. 65.
15. Boswell, *Life*, I, 247.
16. *Rambler*, No. 127.
17. Katharine Balderston, 'Johnson's Vile Melancholy,' *Age of Johnson: Essays Presented to Chauncey B. Tinker* (1949), pp. 5–6.
18. Boswell, *Life*, I, 483; Piozzi, *Anecdotes, J.M.*, I, 199–200, 234–5; *Thraliana* (ed. K. Balderston, 1942), pp. 384–5.
19. *Preface to Shakespeare*, Raleigh, p. 11.
20. Piozzi, *Anecdotes, J.M.*, I, 335.
21. George Steevens, *Anecdotes, J.M.*, II, 325.
22. *Tour to the Hebrides*, pp. 208–9, 175; Piozzi, *Anecdotes, J.M.*, I, 212; Boswell, *Life*, III, 337.
23. Frances Reynolds, *Recollections, J.M.*, II, 273.
24. Piozzi, *Anecdotes, J.M.*, I, 213–14.
25. Boswell, *Life*, IV, 431; Piozzi, *Anecdotes, J.M.*, I, 328–9; *Tour to the Hebrides*, p. 50.
26. Frances Reynolds, *Recollections*; H. D. Best, *Personal and Literary Memorials*; and Piozzi, *Anecdotes, J.M.*, II, 277–8, 391; I, 150, 287–8.
27. Piozzi, *Anecdotes, J.M.*, I, 204–5.
28. Rev. Percival Stockdale, *Anecdotes, J.M.*, II, 333.
29. Frances Reynolds, *Recollections, J.M.*, II, 278.
30. *Tour to the Hebrides*, pp. 84, 314, 121.
31. P. 98n. Cf. Sir W. R. Brain, 'Dr. Johnson and the Kangaroo,' *Essays and Studies for the English Association* (1951), pp. 112–17.
32. Boswell, *Life*, IV, 228–30.
33. *Essay on the Life and Genius of Samuel Johnson, J.M.*, II, 439.
34. Boswell, *Life*, IV, 364, 379, 253–4, 339, 379.

NOTES

35. John Hoole, *Narrative,* and Hawkins, *Life, J.M.,* II, 160, 134.
36. Boswell, *Life,* IV, 420–21.

II

1. *Rasselas,* chs. 30–32.
2. *Rambler,* No. 41.
3. *Anecdotes, J.M.,* I, 251.
4. *Rambler,* No. 41.
5. No. 6.
6. *Idler,* No. 44.
7. *Rambler,* Nos. 45, 115.
8. *Biographia Literaria* (ed. Shawcross, 1907), I, 167.
9. *Rasselas,* ch. 22.
10. *Rambler,* No. 6.
11. No. 45.
12. *Tour to the Hebrides,* pp. 256–7.
13. *Rambler,* Nos. 170, 131.
14. No. 202; Boswell, *Life,* II, 79.
15. *Rambler,* Nos. 202, 58, 48, 131.
16. No. 73.
17. *Idler,* No. 73.
18. *Anecdotes, J.M.,* I, 263, 329–30; Boswell, *Life,* III, 459.
19. *Idler,* No. 58.
20. *Rambler,* No. 17.
21. *Tour to the Hebrides,* p. 226.
22. Cf. *Rambler,* Nos. 82–3, 103, 177.
23. No. 2.
24. Loc. cit.
25. No. 150.
26. *Anecdotes, J.M.,* I, 202.
27. *Rambler,* No. 54.
28. *Rasselas,* ch. 22.
29. *Rambler,* No. 134.
30. Nos. 19, 159.
31. No. 101.
32. *Idler,* No. 58.

III

1. Edward Hitschmann, 'Samuel Johnson's Character, a Psychoanalytic Interpretation,' *Psychoanalytic Review,* XXXII (1945), 207–18.
2. *Rambler,* No. 115.
3. *Anecdotes, J.M.,* I, 199.
4. *Rambler,* No. 93.
5. No. 29.
6. Boswell, *Life,* II, 165.
7. *Rambler,* No. 79.
8. No. 76.

237

9. No. 176; cf. No. 19 and *Idler, No.* 27.
10. *Rambler,* No. 28.
11. No. 76.
12. No. 74.
13. *Adventurer,* No. 50.
14. *Rambler,* No. 13.
15. No. 76.
16. No. 183.
17. No. 160; cf. No. 206.
18. Nos. 16, 183, 206–7; *Idler,* No. 34; *Rambler,* No. 205; *Adventurer,* No. 131.
19. *Rasselas,* ch. 9.
20. *Rambler,* No. 32.
21. No. 76.
22. No. 196.
23. Nos. 31, 40; *Adventurer,* No. 45.
24. *Idler,* No. 23.
25. No. 32; cf. No. 50 and *Rambler,* No. 180.
26. *Rasselas,* ch. 16.
27. Boswell, *Life,* III, 344–5; W. B. C. Watkins, *Perilous Balance* (1939), pp. 36–7.
28. *Rambler,* Nos. 188, 72.
29. Boswell, *Life,* II, 362.
30. *Rambler,* No. 72; cf. No. 75.
31. Piozzi, *Anecdotes,* and Hawkins, *Life, J.M.,* I, 269, 287; II, 98–9.
32. Boswell, *Life,* II, 261–2.
33. Piozzi, *Anecdotes, J.M.,* I, 260.
34. Hazlitt, 'Conversations with Northcote,' *Works* (ed. Howe, 1930–4), XI, 265.
35. *Dr. Johnson and Fanny Burney,* p. 61; Watkins, p. 69. In this section generally I am indebted to Mr. Watkins' perceptive discussion of Johnson's humor.
36. *Tour to the Hebrides,* pp. 211–12.
37. 'Swift,' *Lives of the Poets,* III, 61.

IV

1. *Idler,* No. 69.
2. *Rambler,* No. 25.
3. Boswell, *Life,* II, 440.
4. *Rambler,* No. 89.
5. Nos. 2, 146; cf. No. 21.
6. Nos. 2, 49.
7. No. 49.
8. No. 60.
9. *Idler,* No. 24.
10. *Rasselas,* ch. 11.
11. *Life of Johnson,* I, 339.
12. Raleigh, p. 11.

13. *Rambler*, No. 4.
14. *Life of Johnson*, IV, 122–3.
15. *Rambler*, No. 7.
16. No. 5.
17. *Anecdotes*, p. 199.
18. See above, ch. I, n.17.
19. Sir W. R. Brain, 'A Post Mortem on Dr. Johnson,' *London Hospital Gazette*, XXXVII (1934), 225–30, 288–9. Any discussion of Johnson's personal melancholy can especially profit from the sensitive and balanced article by H. W. Liebert, 'Reflections on Samuel Johnson: Two Recent Books and where They Lead,' *Journal of English and Germanic Philology*, XLVII (1948), 80–88.
20. Hitschmann, 'Samuel Johnson's Character,' cited above, ch. III, n.1.
21. R. M. Ladell, 'The Neurosis of Dr. Samuel Johnson,' *British Journal of Medical Psychology*, IX (1929), 321–2.
22. Katharine Balderston (cited above, ch. I, n.17), pp. 4–14. See also notes in her admirable edition of *Thraliana* (1942), pp. 203, 205, 384, 386, 415, 423, 625, 728.
23. Cf. 'shackles of prescription' (No. 135); 'Ten years longer,' said the nephew waiting for his wealthy aunt to die, and 'giving the future full power over my mind,' 'I *dragged* the *shackles of expectation*' (No. 73); 'daily *dragged* by habit . . . burst the *shackles of habitual vice*' (No. 155); in sorrow, 'the faculties are *chained* to a single object' (No. 47); 'They whose souls are *chained down* by coffers' (No. 203); writing is an unpleasant task to which 'the mind is *dragged* by necessity or resolution' (*Adventurer*, No. 138). Echoing the *Book of Common Prayer*, Johnson prays to be 'loosed from the *chain* of my sins' (*Prayers and Med.*, Sept. 18, 1765). He tells Boswell not to 'accustom yourself to *enchain* your volatility by vows' (*Life*, II, 21), and sympathetically describes his friend Collins as in 'that depression of mind that *enchains* the faculties without destroying them' (*Lives*, III, 338).
24. Unpublished ms., from Boswell's *Journal*, Easter Day, April 20, 1783, under the heading of 'Extraordinary Johnsoniana Tacenda' (Isham Catalogue No. 88), Yale University Library. For permission to read and use this interview, I am indebted to the kindness of the McGraw-Hill Book Company and the Editorial Committee of the Yale Editions of the Private Papers of James Boswell.
25. *Rambler*, No. 14.
26. Boswell, *Life*, IV, 397.
27. *Rambler*, ch. 46.
28. Piozzi, *Anecdotes*, pp. 301–2.
29. Boswell, *Life*, IV, 300 n.1, 299; Murphy, *J.M.*, I, 439; *Life*, III, 295–6.
30. *Rambler*, No. 87; Boswell, *Life*, II, 440.
31. IV, 53.
32. Bertrand H. Bronson, 'Johnson Agonistes,' *Johnson and Boswell: Three Essays* (1944), esp. pp. 392–7.
33. Boswell, *Life*, II, 476–7; III, 200–204; V, 77n.
34. IV, 293–4, 376.

35. 'Edmund Smith,' *Lives*, II, 20–21.
36. In his admirable *Prose Style of Samuel Johnson* (New Haven, 1941), esp. chs. 3 and 7; and *Philosophic Words* (New Haven, 1948).
37. 'Pope,' *Lives*, III, 217, 222; *Preface to Shakespeare*, Raleigh, pp. 14, 9.

V

1. *Idler*, No. 36.
2. *Rambler*, No. 176.
3. 'Life of Sir Thomas Browne,' *Works*, VI, 486.
4. *Rambler*, No. 23.
5. *Preface to Shakespeare*, Raleigh, pp. 9–10. Cf. *Rambler*, No. 121.
6. Nos. 158, 184; 'Pope,' *Lives*, III, 251.
7. *Adventurer*, No. 107. Cf. generally W. R. Keast's excellent article, 'The Theoretical Foundations of Johnson's Criticism,' *Critics and Criticism* (ed. R. S. Crane, Chicago, 1952), pp. 389–407.
8. *Rambler*, No. 99.
9. No. 156.
10. 'Dryden,' *Lives*, I, 454; *Preface to Shakespeare*, Raleigh, p. 33; 'Prior,' *Lives*, II, 206.
11. *Idler*, No. 84.
12. 'Dryden,' *Lives*, I, 425.
13. *Rambler*, No. 125.
14. 'Milton,' *Lives*, I, 183, 181, 194, 188, 178; Boswell, *Life*, I, 500.
15. Boswell, *Life*, II, 91; 'Milton,' *Lives*, I, 194 (cf. *Idler*, No. 40); *Rambler*, No. 121.
16. 'Hammond,' *Lives*, II, 315; 'Prior,' II, 207; 'Waller,' I, 295; 'Thomson,' IV, 289.
17. Boswell, *Life*, I, 421.
18. IV, 236.
19. Piozzi, *Anecdotes*, J.M., I, 186.
20. 'Cowley,' *Lives*, I, 58.
21. 'Thomson,' III, 298; 'Congreve,' II, 216, 228.
22. 'Dedication to Mrs. Lennox's *Shakespeare Illustrated*,' *Works*, V, 432.
23. *Gespräche mit Goethe*, January 29, 1826.
24. *Rambler*, No. 129.
25. *Preface to Shakespeare*, Raleigh, pp. 14–15.
26. *Rambler*, No. 36.
27. 'Shenstone,' *Lives*, III, 355.
28. *Adventurer*, No. 95; cf. *Rambler*, Nos. 124, 129.
29. 'Butler,' *Lives*, I, 213–14; 'Pope,' III, 114.
30. W. J. Bate, *From Classic to Romantic* (1946), ch. 3. This discussion is cited as an opportune means of disowning it. J. H. Hagstrum, *Samuel Johnson's Literary Criticism* (1952), ch. 1, offers a corrective by stressing the English empirical tradition that follows Locke.
31. 'Rowe,' *Lives*, II, 76.
32. *Rambler*, No. 156.
33. 'Milton,' *Lives*, I, 176; 'Addison,' II, 135.

34. *Preface to Shakespeare*, Raleigh, pp. 26–9.
35. *Rambler*, No. 66.
36. 'West,' *Lives*, III, 332.
37. 'Pope,' III, 242, 99.
38. 'Thomson,' III, 299–300; cf. 'Pope,' III, 225.
39. *Preface to Shakespeare*, Raleigh, pp. 12, 23.
40. *Tour to the Hebrides*, p. 54.
41. 'Gay,' *Lives*, II, 283.
42. 'Collins,' III, 341; 'Somerville,' II, 320; Boswell, *Life*, III, 159.
43. *Tour to the Hebrides*, p. 348.
44. David Perkins, 'Johnson on Wit and Metaphysical Poetry,' *Journal of English Literary History*, XX (1953), 210. In discussing the subject generally, I am indebted to the fine studies of Perkins; of W. R. Keast, 'Johnson's Criticism of the Metaphysical Poets,' *Ibid.*, XVII (1950), 59–70; and of W. B. C. Watkins, in *Johnson and English Poetry Before 1660* (1936), pp. 79–82, and in *Review of English Studies*, XII (1946), 131–4.
45. 'Cowley,' *Lives*, I, 20–22, 56, 27.
46. 'Addison,' II, 128.
47. *Rambler*, No. 176.
48. 'Addison,' *Lives*, II, 129–30; 'Pope,' III, 230.
49. 'The Tradition of Tradition,' *Hopkins Review*, IV (1951), 7–8.
50. 'Milton,' *Lives*, I, 194, 177.
51. *Rasselas*, ch. 10; review of Warton, *Works*, VI, 433–4; cf. *Adventurer*, No. 137.
52. *Rambler*, No. 86.
53. *Rambler*, Nos. 25, 129; *Adventurer*, No. 99.
54. 'Sir Francis Drake,' *Works*, VI, 338–9.
55. *Advancement of Learning, Philosophical Works* (ed. J. M. Robertson, 1905), p. 59.
56. *Rambler*, Nos. 145, 83.
57. Piozzi, *Anecdotes, J.M.*, I, 225; Boswell, *Life*, IV, 427–8.
58. *Six Essays on Johnson* (1910; impr. of 1927), p. 34.
59. *J.M.*, II, 227.
60. Reprinted in *Works* (1825) as 'A Project for the Employment of Authours,' V, 355–6.

INDEX

243

INDEX

Romances, Johnson's reading of, 5,
123, 227
Rousseau, J. J., 229
Rowe, Nicholas, 199
Rules of art, 179, 195–209, 211,
222–5, 231
Rymer, Thomas, 195

Sainte-Beuve, C. A., ix, 56, 218
Salusbury, Mrs. Hester Maria, 47
Sanderson, Bishop, 87
Santayana, George, 122, 155
Savage, Richard, 14, 15; Johnson's
life of, 14
Schlegel, A. W. and F. von, 225
Scotland, 48, 53–4, 78
Scott, Sir Walter, 18
Scruples, Johnson's struggles with,
158–9
Self-consciousness, crippling effect
of when excessive, 87–9; effect
on literary invention, 222–5
Self-defense, stratagems of, 92–122,
passim
Self-delusion, 84, 95–128, passim;
140
Seward, Anna, 161
Shaftesbury, Lord, 69
Shakespeare, William, 62, 133, 181,
190–91, 231; Johnson's criti-
cism and edition of, 25, 33,
37, 40–41, 48, 175, 194–5,
200–203, 210–11, 218, 222
Shaler, Nathaniel, 31
Sherburn, George, ix
Sheridan, Thomas, 45
Sidney, Sir Philip, 90
Simile, see Metaphor
Slander, see Gossip
Slavery, Johnson's antagonism to, 46
Smith, Adam, 42; on Johnson's
range of learning, 15; on John-
son's Preface to Shakespeare,
41
Somerville, William, 211
Spenser, Edmund, 207–8
Spinoza, Benedict de, 146
Steele, Sir Richard, 29
Stoicism, 135

Strahan, Rev. George, 168
Style, Johnson's, 170–76
Sublime, 188
Swift, Jonathan, 70, 78, 87, 94,
112, 117, 126–7, 144, 146
Swinfen, Dr. Samuel, 11, 153

Taxation no Tyranny, 48, 167
Taylor, John, 12, 47
Temple, Sir William, 60
Thomson, James, 189, 192, 209
Thoreau, Henry, 165
Thrale, Henry, 8, 49, 51, 57, 58
Thrale (Piozzi), Mrs. Hester
Lynch, Johnson's first meeting
with, 38–9; remarriage, 58;
119–20; quoted, 4, 29, 33–5,
38, 47, 49–51, 64, 79, 85, 86,
94, 115–16, 127, 147, 151,
158–60, 163, 168, 185, 190–
91, 227, 229; mentioned, 42–
4, 46, 47, 49, 74, 75, 112, 150,
228
Tillotson, Geoffrey, ix
Tinker, Chauncey B., 43
Tolstoy, Leo, 155–6
Tory party, Johnson's support of,
36, 51, 165–7
Tour to the Hebrides, 46, 48, 49,
54, 82, 125
Tradition, Johnson's use of and at-
titude toward in literature,
216–25
Tragi-comedy, see Mingled drama
Travel, Johnson on, 71–2, 78–81
Trinity College, Dublin, 36
Truth, attaining stability and free-
dom through, 129–30, 142–7
Tyers, Thomas, vii, 42, 147

Unities, Johnson on, 202–3

Vanity, 99–128, passim; 132, 138–
9; effect on literary criticism,
177–8, 229–31
Vanity of Human Wishes, The, 18–
22, 30–31, 81–2, 92–3, 95,
119

247

'WHAT IS NEAREST US,' said Johnson, 'touches us most.' Johnson is the most humane of the world's great humanists. To whatever he discussed—from the most general problems of human life and experience to the practical criticism of literature—he gave a brilliant, independent interpretation, and at the same time brought it home to the common interests and needs we all feel.

This is the life story of his mind, telling how, against almost insurmountable odds, he rose through struggle into greatness. Johnson's physical ills, his battle with poverty, his wit and brilliance in conversation are well known. But more important is his great writing on human nature—the humor and powerful grandeur of the moral and psychological insights wrung from his own wide-ranging experience. The personal side of Johnson's heroic struggle is always brought to bear in this fresh reconsideration of his achievement. There are the scenes of the young Johnson at Oxford, fighting against idleness and